THE ABRAHAM MAN

THE ABRAHAM MAN

MADNESS, MALINGERING

AND THE

DEVELOPMENT OF MEDICAL TESTIMONY

R. GREGORY LANDE

Algora Publishing
New York

Library of Congress Cataloging-in-Publication Data —

Lande, R. Gregory.
  The Abraham man : madness, malingering, and the development of medical testimony
/ R. Gregory Lande.
    p. ; cm.
  Includes bibliographical references and index.
    ISBN 978-0-87586-936-0 (soft cover : alk. paper)—ISBN 978-0-87586-937-7 (hard
cover : alk. paper)—ISBN 978-0-87586-938-4 (ebook)
    I. Title.
    [DNLM: 1. Expert Testimony—United States. 2. Forensic Psychiatry—history—
United States. 3. Deception—United States. 4. History, 19th Century—United States. 5.
Malingering—history—United States. 6. Mental Disorders—diagnosis—United States.
W 740]

  614'.15—dc23
                          2012031370

Front cover: Scene of Bethlehem Hospital from William Hogarth's *A Rake's Progress*.

Printed in the United States

To my family: My mother, Anne, who modeled compassion, my father, Maurice, who taught objectivity, my wife, Brenda, who tirelessly supports our relationship, and the radiant light of my life, my son, Galen.

TABLE OF CONTENTS

The Abraham Man vanished about one hundred years ago. Before that time, the Abraham Man was a well-recognized term describing ne'er-do-wells plying a special sort of fraud. These practitioners were skilled actors in all manner of deceptions, simulating mental and medical maladies in exchange for various benefits. Mental illness and seizures were two mysterious conditions that evoked mixtures of pity and fear, both exploited by the Abraham Man. Even though the Abraham Man is no longer a commonly used term, his multi-century presence left an historical presence behind. By tiptoeing through time, a modern history sleuth can detect the faint clues of the Abraham Man from the earliest use of the term in the fifteenth century through the end of the nineteenth century.

Malingering propelled the growth and development of forensic psychiatry. By constantly challenging the skills of the physician, the malingerer paradoxically increased the sophistication of medical inquiry. The evolution of efforts to unmask the malingerer developed slowly alongside with scientific advances in medicine, against the back drop of changing nineteenth century mores, and through some of America's most famous trials.

In the nineteenth century, a surge in litigation forged ties between medicine and the law, beginning with contested wills and then enveloping all aspects of civil and criminal law. The Civil War brought the practice of soldier shamming to the front and center. Unprecedented numbers of soldiers did their best to duck and dodge the hardships of war. Military surgeons responded to the escalation of malingering with a variety of interventions, some clever and some crude.

When the battlefields finally fell silent, several Army doctors translated their war experiences into further study of emotional disorders. Some combat-hardened physicians eventually became leading experts in the fledgling field of the management of insanity. At the same time, vast institutions otherwise known as America's insane asylums started dotting the landscape, ushering in a new era in the treatment of the mentally ill. These mammoth facilities housed legions of mentally ill individuals. Insane asylums also acted like magnets attracting hordes of Abraham Men.

Nineteenth century American medical practice occupied a tense intersection with religion, pseudoscience, and developing scientific precepts. At virtually every evolutionary step along the path of scientific thought lurked the Abraham Man. The relentlessly adaptive malingerer exploited every new discovery. The Abraham Man challenged important historical figures like Mesmer, Franklin, Rush, Gall, and Brigham. Fraud came in all forms, sometimes even foisted by deceiving doctors. In most cases, the duplicitous behavior was practiced by skilled practitioners intent on avoiding an unpleasantry or gaining some advantage.

The explosive growth of civil and criminal litigation after the Civil War brought lawyers, doctors, and the Abraham Man together. In the beginning, most of the contests involved disputes over large estates. These early cases paved the way for more complex trials involving matters of insanity, mental competency, and an endless array of exculpatory mental maladies. The Abraham Man positively flourished.

Around this time, the practice of medical legal medicine began to take shape. Lawyers increasingly sought poised physicians able to contend with court room drama. Asylum doctors, given their daily contact with the mentally ill, seemed the natural choice. Another group not affiliated with the large institutions challenged the asylum doctors' hegemony. In fairly short order these disparate camps coalesced around two dynamic doctors.

William Hammond was a polarizing man, a strong-willed and gifted physician with a penchant for fighting. Many of Hammond's Civil War experiences are well known but his life after an ignominious court-martial is not. In many respects, his life after the military was even more fascinating and influential. It was during this time that Hammond turned his attention to the study of mental and nervous disorders. The courtrooms of America were the perfect stage for Hammond to seek the limelight, engage in an adversarial process, and contribute to the growth of forensic psychiatry. Hammond recognized the imperative need to ferret out the ever present Abraham Man, as evidenced by extensive tracts devoted to the subject of malingering throughout his extensive medical legal writings.

Hammond met his match in John P. Gray, a bombastic asylum superintendent. Gray is less well known than Hammond, but during the nineteenth century many physicians considered this man America's foremost authority on mental illness. The criminal cases of Ann Barry, Elizabeth Heggie, and Daniel McFarland offer both detailed glimpses of life in the nineteenth century and Gray's medical legal approach. Gray authored far fewer articles than Hammond but his treatises on insanity provide revealing insights.

It seemed inevitable that Hammond and Gray would butt heads. Most of these visceral disputes erupted in legal cases with Hammond and Gray always staking out opposing opinions. The sensational case of David Montgomery captured America's attention as the dueling expert witnesses waged war. Both doctors recognized and reacted to the Abraham Man in different ways.

Hammond and Gray attracted loyal followings. This supporting cast of physicians extended the reach of the embryonic field of forensic psychiatry. Their stories are told through medical legal cases in which they participated. Charles Nichols, for example, evaluated one of Lincoln's conspirators in a less-known page of history. The indomitable Isaac Ray wrote extensive tracts about medical jurisprudence including lengthy sections on malingering. Another figure rarely mentioned now days is John Ordronaux. As a prolific writer and tentative expert witness, he cast considerable influence over the early development of forensic psychiatry. One of his specialties was uncovering the Abraham Man. Edward Spizka orbited about Hammond, at the same time displaying his own brilliance. Spizka would later stake out a lonely but entirely credible position in the Guiteau trial.

The earliest sustained professional relationship between the law and medicine involved disgruntled heirs. Contested wills offered an opportunity to study the contortions and confabulations of medical expert witnesses opining on the mental state of a testator. The skills learned in these adversarial encounters shaped the future roles of expert witnesses. Specific cases illustrate common legal arguments employed, such as the mental state of the testator.

The Vanderbilt will case showcased an embarrassing moment in the growth and development of forensic psychiatry. During his life Commodore Vanderbilt was a prototypical industrialist, focused on building an empire and collecting a vast fortune along the way. Upon his death, a completely different picture of the magnate was painted by aggrieved family members. Dozens of professed experts bent and twisted the testator's life into an insane pretzel.

The ever increasing participation of doctors in criminal trials was a significant step in the growth of medical legal practice and a boon to the Abraham Man, who played major roles.

At this point the dueling doctors, Hammond and Gray, discussed in detail in subsequent chapters, take center stage. Hammond encountered examples of malingering while in the Army and even more in his subsequent civilian life. In a similar fashion, various legal cases highlight Gray's relationship with the Abraham Man. In each case discussed, be it Joseph Waltz or Michel Trimbur, the criminals' stories are just as fascinating as the doctors' efforts at detecting the Abraham Man. The selected cases clearly illustrate the criminal manifestations of the Abraham Man, discuss long forgotten crimes, and reveal the opinions influential doctors reached after examining the defendants.

The expanding presence of the insanity expert in America's courtrooms generated increasing controversy. To a skeptical public, it seemed that insanity experts could twist any deviant behavior into a new form of insanity. This troublesome trend in the growth and development of forensic psychiatry became evident in the trials of Charles Huntingdon, Elizabeth Beatty, and Mary Harris. Monomania entered the medical legal lexicon with a vengeance, as did its family members dipsomania, kleptomania, and pyromania. The elastic definition of insanity invited all sorts of mischief, chiefly perpetrated by the Abraham Man.

The public disillusionment with insanity experts, driven by an inability or unwillingness to accept the possibility of malingering, was peaking when the crime of the century shocked America. The assassination of President Garfield brought all the actors on stage for one final play. Charles Guiteau exhibited a multifaceted personality but the nature of the crime guaranteed he would have few sympathizers. A detailed behavioral portrait of Guiteau paints a man with a disorganized life in search of greatness. The courtroom "theatrics," and the parade of doctors arrayed against Guiteau, marked a turning point in the assessment of malingering. Blinded by the magnitude of the crime and bowing to the winds of public opinion, prominent doctors interpreted Guiteau's every word and action as counterfeit. Once again Hammond and Gray, along with their surrogates, squared off in the main event of the nineteenth century. The Abraham Man lurked and laughed in the shadows.

Chapter 1: Introduction to the Abraham Man

The Abraham Man was not a noble character. In fact, the label was first derisively affixed to drifters and beggars in England who simulated insanity. The Abraham Man was an actor, a virtuoso tugging at the audiences' heartstrings by feigning an illness or injury. A good player evoked considerable compassion, and most importantly, charity. The actor's reward was food, money, or shelter. The fraudulent practice became widespread, creating as much cynicism as philanthropy.

By the late nineteenth century a common definition of the Abraham Man appeared in medical dictionaries.[1] According to the official lexicon, Abraham Man was "A name given three centuries ago, to one who, for purposes of imposition, personated a 'Tom of Bedlam' or vagrant lunatic ... who feigns sickness or infirmity of any kind."

Bedlam was the colloquial name for the Hospital of St. Mary of Bethlehem, a facility for the mentally ill. The Hospital's ceaseless commotion and cacophony eventually came to be equated with Bedlam. In spite of the pandemonium, many individuals fabricated all sorts of ailments in an effort to trade a life of poverty for the relative sanctuary of Bedlam. A main section at the Hospital of St. Mary of Bethlehem was aptly referred to as the Abraham ward.

Tom of Bedlam, otherwise known as the Abraham Man, was popularized by a song that spanned three centuries. The lyrics told a woeful tale

---

1 Richard J. Dunglison, MD, *A Dictionary of Medical Science* (Philadelphia: Henry C. Lea, 1873), 5.

of insanity. A seventeenth century authority on the ballad suggested that Tom of Bedlam's origin could be traced to Shakespeare's King Lear.[2]

The earliest use of the term Abraham Man can be traced to an obscure book of 1561 titled *Fraternity of Vagabonds*. According to this ancient text, "An Abraham Man is he that walketh bare-armed and bare-legged, and feigneth himself mad, and carryeth a pack of wool, or a stick with bacon on it, or suchlike toy, and nameth himself Poor Tom."[3] For his efforts, the Abraham Man joined similar actors at the Hospital of St. Mary of Bethlehem. Even with the chaos of Bedlam, these artful dodgers enjoyed a better existence than wandering the rural back roads of England, starving and homeless. Tom of Bedlam survived through cunning and guile. When discharged from the hospital, Tom complained bitterly about the poor treatment and once again tugged at the gullible purse strings of anyone willing to listen. So began a revolving door with Tom faking a mental disorder, the caretakers at Bedlam endeavoring to unmask the fraud, and a public alternately expressing compassion or contempt.

The Abraham Man was a resilient figure. In feudal times, the Abraham Man apparently kindled equal amounts of pity and scorn. In fact, the earliest poems about Tom of Bedlam portray a character that is both romantic and wretched. Tom could be admired for his skillful acting, which apparently deceived the institutional gatekeepers charged with guarding admission to charitable hospitals. Viewed in this way, Tom the poverty-stricken beggar temporarily defeated an unjust social system. Of course the tragedy resumes when Tom is discharged from the hospital and finds his lot in life unchanged.

Over time, the equilibrium slowly changed and the Abraham Man was seen as less heroic and more pathetic. A number of factors contributed to the drop in social support. The sheer numbers surely taxed the patience, and pocketbooks, of average citizens. The steady growth of industrial mechanization changed the social structure, placing a premium on timeliness, attention to detail, and hard work. The Abraham Man was lazy and shiftless, the antipathy of an emerging work ethic. Religious views which demonized all sorts of immorality cast a broad net and trapped the mentally ill along with the Abraham Man. Taken together, these were powerful influences which marginalized the Abraham Man.

---

2   Roger Bourke, 'The moon's my constant mistress': Robert Graves and the Elizabethans 1999. http://www.robertgraves.org/issues/18/9573_article_75.pdf.

3   Kim Mi-Su, *Men on the road: Beggars and vagrants in early modern drama* (Dissertation, Literature, Texas A & M, 2004).

The term was still used during America's Civil War but would fade away afterwards. Perhaps the insurmountable obstacle that led to the demise of the Abraham Man can be traced to the increasing sophistication of medical practice. As knowledge of both physical and mental diseases increased, it became more difficult to fabricate genuine disability. As a consequence, the Abraham Man adapted, in the process losing his name but not his beguiling methods.

In the middle part of the nineteenth century, the legal profession began aggressively courting doctors. The forces driving the relationship were necessity and greed. Doctors supplied important testimony in criminal and civil trials. In criminal trials, for example, doctors could explain the cause of death. In civil trials, doctors might testify in a malpractice case or a contested will. In both examples, a medical witness bolstered the attorney's arguments by providing scientific credibility. The doctor's reputation might sway the jury, a particularly common practice during insanity trials. A skeptical juror, suspecting the criminal defendant was a malingerer rather than someone suffering from insanity, might be soothed by an impressive medical witness. As an expert in mental illness, the doctor could confidently, or so many claimed, discriminate between real and feigned illness.

Greed also fueled the marriage of convenience between doctors and lawyers. In the early part of the nineteenth century, the legal profession in America was entering a new phase dominated, at least in part, by an emerging pecuniary appetite. First evidence of this trend materialized with a progressive interest in, and litigation of, wills. Like a treasure map, it seemed that a person's last will and testament simply pointed towards great riches waiting to be plundered. Increasingly, the sanctity of a person's final wishes came under attack by disappointed relatives and other interested parties. Attorneys helped manage the disappointment, particularly with sizeable estates. In many ways, the litigation of contested wills represented the first serious and ongoing collaboration between medicine and the law. The relations forged by the two professions while sparring over a testator's mental state set the stage for future legal ventures, including the imperative importance of neutralizing the Abraham Man.

For a variety of reasons, the litigation of wills became commonplace. As America grew in prosperity, more individuals managed to accumulate sizeable riches. A proliferation of attorneys made their services available. A more subtle but significant factor involved the will's actual construction. Individuals typically composed their will in the waning days of life.

Beset with physical and not well-understood mental infirmities, the testator was left open to a variety of legal challenges. Over time, arguments challenging testamentary capacity increasingly relied on medical explanations. Physicians offered opinions equating all sorts of illnesses with mental incapacity. Some of these opinions stretched the limits of science and seemed dangerously close to advocacy. For every physician supporting a claimant's position, another physician testified just as stridently in opposition. Physicians bickered in the courtroomby casting doubts on each other's medical skills, experience, and ability to detect fraudulent symptoms. Contested wills of the rich and famous attracted the best legal minds and the most respected physicians.

In the years before the Civil War such cases rarely occurred, but because those few cases involved large estates, they attracted a good deal of attention. Such cases increased after the Civil War to the point of epidemic. "There is one class of persons that has a fixed and never failing test of dementia – and that is disappointed heirs. To an expectant legatee no better proof could be adduced of a testator's absolute, incurable madness than the one fact that he has left his money elsewhere."[4] The epidemic was spread by attorneys who eagerly sought expert medical witnesses. Medical testimony was increasing stretched beyond its scientific limits, and while influential in the short term, it suffered grievously in later years.

Attorneys understood that to be valid, a will only required a few simple steps. The author of the will, otherwise known as the testator (if a man) or testatrix (if a woman), must understand the general purpose of making a will, in other words that it represents a process by which to legally transfer wealth to survivors. Authors of wills must have a general idea of what they possess, sufficient to detail its distribution to the heirs. In addition, they must accurately identify members of the immediate family or, in the language of the law, the "natural objects of their bounty."[5] They must have the ability to resist undue pressure and freely and voluntary dispose of their wealth. Guiding every step of the will-making process is the author's sound mind and memory. Impartial witnesses attest to the author's sound mind. An exception to the legal rigmarole was the nuncupative will.

---

4 "Testamentary insanity," *New York Times*, Jan. 13, 1873.
5 Isaac Redfield, *The jurisprudence of insanity; The effect of extrinsic evidence; The creation and construction of trusts, so far as applicable to wills* (Boston: Little, Brown and Company, 1864), 130.

A nuncupative will is a verbal statement made in the presence of a witness. The oral declaration was the dying person's last wish and in olden times, before pen and paper were so widely available, this was a common way to leave a legacy. But a nuncupative will invited mischief. In time, most legislatures restricted the use of oral wills. During the Civil War era, paper, pens and lawyers were in abundant supply, drastically reducing the need for nuncupative wills, with the notable exception that the law recognized an oral will for "any soldier in actual military service, or any mariner or common seaman being at sea."[6] The exception seemed reasonable, since "The imminent dangers, the diseases and sudden death which constantly beset soldiers and sailors; the utter inability oftentimes to find the time or the means to make a deliberate or written testamentary disposition of their effects, seem at all times to..." make an oral will a useful expedient.[7]

American military law in the nineteenth century addressed the disposition of personal property through Articles of War 125, 126 and 127. The law authorized officers to itemize, secure, and ship the deceased service member's property. Military law recognized nuncupative wills but also maintained that oral declarations did not absolve obedience to the aforementioned Articles. Nuncupative wills required only one witness who could faithfully recite the dying person's last wish.[8]

Many attorneys fondly recalled the challenge of a contested will. Lieutenant General Jubal Early, the irascible Confederate general, had practiced law in Mississippi in the 1840s and steadily built a reputation as an aggressive attorney. When writing his memoirs, Jubal Early fondly reached back to his early adult life to resurrect his greatest legal triumph. "My practice had become very considerable, and at the close of my professional career, I believe I was regarded as among the best lawyers in my section of the State. My most important contest at the bar and my greatest triumph was in a contested will case in Lowndes County, Mississippi, in the autumn of 1852, in which a very large amount of property was involved. I went to Mississippi to attend to this case specially, and I contended single-handed and successfully with three of the ablest lawyers of

6 John Proffatt, *The curiosities of wills* (San Francisco: Sumner Whiney and Company, 1877), 43.

7 Ibid.

8 William Winthrop, *Military law* (Washington, DC: W. H. Morrison, 1886), 1091-97.

that State."[9] Many physicians also believed that contested wills provided the ultimate demonstration of their medical-legal skills. Isaac Ray, one of America's preeminent nineteenth century jurists, noted that "to the medical jurist, no class of cases can be more interesting than that of wills involving questions of mental condition." What led Ray to that conclusion? Part of the reason was a change in social sentiment regarding who were the natural heirs. "The power to make a will giving a different posthumous course and disposition of property, is of such long and universal allowance, that it is now almost as strong as it were a natural right."[10]

Obviously, the Abraham Man had no role in authoring deceptive wills. In these medical legal cases, fraudulent practices surfaced among the litigants. The claimants would accuse the deceased of all manner of idiosyncratic behaviors, aided and abetted by attorneys who handpicked willing medical witnesses. From the slenderest threads, the attorney would spin a law suit hoping to unravel the testator's will.

During the Civil War doctors turned their collective attention away from wills and focused on the subsequent battlefield misery and mayhem. As doctors quickly discovered, the rigors of military service soon ground away patriotic fervor. Some men sought a quick exit, and the Abraham Man flourished in this environment. The Abraham Man was still a viable concept succinctly labeling the shirker, dodger, coward, and faker, but all romantic elements were stripped from the Civil War Abraham Man. The practice was apparently widespread as documented in the diaries, official records, and courts-martial of the era. Civil War surgeons employed a variety of "treatments" specifically designed to counter the pernicious influence of malingering. Feigning epilepsy was a favorite among the shammers and doctors often employed special tactics to detect the fakers. Medical journals and Army manuals spread the knowledge. "In real epilepsy, so complete is insensibility that neither the loudest sounds, nor the most penetrating and irritating odors, like ammonia and burning sulfur, nor tickling the soles of the feet, nor even cauterizing the surface, can provoke any sensation."[11] Military commanders, surgeons, and

---

9 Jubal Early, *Jubal Early: Autobiographical sketch and narrative of the War Between the States* (Philadelphia: J. B. Lippincott Company, 1912), xxiv.

10 Isaac Ray, "The Angell will case," *American Journal of Insanity* 20 no. 2 (1863): 145-186.

11 John Ordronaux, *Hints on health in Armies and manual of instructions for military surgeons on the examination of recruits and discharge of soldiers* (New York: D. Van Nostrand, 1863), 58.

civilian authorities understood the importance of defeating the Abraham Man. Left unchecked, the personnel losses from feigned illness potentially threatened the war effort. Soldiers replicated virtually every disease and sometimes resorted to more drastic measures including painful self-inflicted injuries.

Shrewd, shamming soldiers challenged the medical surgeons' skills. In response, physicians steadily improved their diagnostic abilities, becoming more aware of, and adept at, identifying fraudulent symptoms. In the beginning the efforts at detecting the artful dodger were crude and occasionally cruel. In fact, the Abraham Man forced physicians to steadily adopt more evidence-based decision-making grounded in scientific principles.

After the war, a new era in medical-legal collaboration engaged the talents of some of America's finest physicians. There was a dramatic increase in the number of wills contested. Sensational criminal trials splashed across the front pages of influential newspapers and captivated the public's attention. Many of the physicians who provided expert medical testimony bolstered their diagnostic formulations with impressive scientific explanations. Nonetheless, the Abraham Man embarrassed many inexperienced medical witnesses who overlooked his crafty simulations.

In the several decades following the South's surrender at Appomattox, two fiercely determined groups waged a bitter battle in America's courtrooms, each seeking anointment by professional colleagues and the public as the undisputed expert on mental illness. Both groups diligently avoided traps set by the Abraham Man and in the process advanced the nascent field of medical legal jurisprudence.

The two groups were composed of physicians who in future years would be considered neurologists and psychiatrists; they grew increasingly hostile towards each other as they wrestled with the definition and description of insanity, especially as it applied to criminal responsibility. Through the prodding and probing of attorneys, the expert witness revealed the etiology of insanity and how it either incriminated or exculpated a criminal defendant.

The first cohort of medical experts gained their experience in the insane asylums. Before the advent of these institutions, during the colonial years, the mentally ill were mostly considered a nuisance.[12] Those who were hale, hearty, and inoffensive could roam about freely. This group probably endured periodic taunting, abuse, or assault.[13] Jails were used to protect citizens from the unpredictable behavior of those who might be hostile. No special provisions separated the insane from common criminals and the two mingled together. The criminal class often made sport of the insane. Families with resources spared their kin the danger and indignity of a public jail in exchange for a securely locked room on the relative's estate.

With the passage of time, the indigent, harmless insane in early America evoked slightly more pity than derision, a trend that slowly led to their placement in almshouses. These human warehouses, supported by public good will, provided a degree of safety. Occasional scandals involving deplorable living conditions, amplified by the willing newspapers, injured the reputation of almshouses and eroded public confidence in them.

Roughly seventy-five years after the American Revolution, a wave of optimism swept across the country, blowing aside the pessimism surrounding care for the insane. The forces that set this trend in motion included a faith in medical science, social enlightenment, and an extended period of peace in America during the interlude between the War of 1812 and the outbreak of national hostilities in 1860. Social issues percolated to the top of political interest, among them a new found compassion for the mentally ill.

Spearheading the crusade for change was Dorothea Dix.[14] Dix was an outspoken advocate for institutional care. Her epiphany came about after observing firsthand the scenes of depravity resulting from the comingling of the mentally ill with felonious wrong doers. Although she was not universally successful, Dix can be credited with launching the asylum movement.

Over time, asylums came to resemble sprawling fortresses gobbling up vast acreages of land. Asylum architecture, ostensibly designed to promote a healthy environment, assumed forbidding characteristics blending medieval facades with the security of a prison. These bastions

---

12   Albert Deutsch, *The mentally ill in America* (New York: Columbia University Press, 1945), 24-54.

13   Charles Folsom, *Diseases of the mind in the treatment of insanity* (Boston: A. Williams and Co., Publishers, 1877), 3-8.

14   Francis Tiffany, *Life of Dorothea Lynde Dix* (Boston: Houghton Mifflin Company: 1890), 74.

of benevolence sheltered the mentally ill and, at the same time, sent a powerful security message to the public. Asylum superintendents were "king of the castle," an appropriate analogy given the great power these men amassed over time. The superintendents exerted their influence in medicine, law, and politics. Naturally, these elite physician managers banded together, increasing their stature and their stranglehold on care for the mentally ill.

The first broad based and public attacks on the asylum superintendents' hegemony unfolded in the courtroom. In the beginning, there were a few relatively unnoticed criminal insanity cases. The attacks, mounted by determined foes of the asylum superintendents, continued and culminated in a string of highly publicized insanity cases. Verbal volleys between the two increasingly antagonistic camps of medical experts exploded.

The lack of precision defining mental illness, and the all too common capricious and concocted medical diagnoses, eroded public support. Medical excuses flourished, distorting the connection between crime and punishment. Jurors in such cases often heard the testimony of many medical witnesses, as if sheer numbers would tilt the scales of justice. Eventually, the public's fatigue with the endless medical excuses seemed to reach a peak with moral insanity.

Moral insanity was a controversial species of madness which supposedly perverted a person's temper, habits, and decorum. Victims exhibited all manner of depravities and immoralities, such as kleptomania, dipsomania, and pyromania. The key feature uniting the disparate behaviors under the moral insanity banner was an irresistible urge to engage in the immoral acts. It was just a matter of time before some doctors started equating habitual drunkenness with insanity. This turn of events alarmed other doctors as well as large segments of the public. "Nothing is more painful in the history of our criminal jurisprudencé nor a greater hindrance to its equitable administration than the growing tendency to apologize for every sin according to its magnitude ... Every vice, every crime is disease, nothing short..."[15]

An elastic definition of insanity favored malingering. The Abraham Man reveled in this environment, cleverly confusing eminent expert medical witnesses. Naturally, the doctors responded by adopting more

---

15   John Ordronaux, "Is habitual drunkenness a disease?" *American Journal of Insanity* 30, no. 4 (1874): 430-443.

sophisticated tests to unmask the fraud in a game of cat and mouse. There was an ethical challenge confronting practitioners of medical jurisprudence as they sought to draw a line to distinguish the promotion of a blatant legal advocacy from the available scientific evidence, and testify accordingly. Contested wills represented the first battlefield where attorneys and doctors struggled and the mixture of madness, malingering, malfeasance, and money shaped the future of forensic psychiatry.

CHAPTER 2: MARCH OF SCIENCE

The Abraham Man was born at a time when religion and superstition dominated society. Science, which favors facts over faith, was gaining traction and beginning to challenge cherished concepts. The scientific method enshrined skepticism, demanding reliable and replicable evidence as a prerequisite to belief. Over time the credibility of science grew at the expense of purely belief based systems. In response to the threat, some groups hardened their dogma while others embraced the adversary.

The infancy of the Abraham Man was passed during the Middle Ages, when Heinrich Kramer and Jacob Sprenger were toiling over the pages of the *Malleus Maleficarum*. Otherwise known as the "hammer of witches," the *Malleus Maleficarum* was the inquisitor's handbook. The Catholic Church denounced the fifteenth-century work but the despotic treatise found a receptive audience in a world possessed by a belief in witches. The *Malleus Maleficarum* set forth an ecclesiastical argument documenting the existence of demonic influences on earth. Women were vessels containing satanic influence and the *Malleus Maleficarum* set forth the process to eliminate the devil's work. Torture was recommended since witches were insensible to pain and only the most violent means could extract a confession of collusion with the devil. The *Malleus Maleficarum* remained an important work for the next three hundred years.[16]

Witch mania spread to America in the 17th century. One of the prime movers was Cotton Mather, a Puritan minister, preacher of the faith in

---

16 Howard Williams, *The superstitions of witchcraft* (London: Longman, Greene, Longman, Roberts & Greene: 1865), 101-8.

Boston, distinguished alumnus of Harvard and published author. Mather wasted no time in diagnosing the satanic scourge infecting Boston. In 1688, the Goodwin family children developed spasmodic fits. Mather got wind of it, and after a period of investigation, settled his suspicion on a female domestic. In due course, the woman was branded a heretic for communing with the devil and executed. Mather published an authoritative ecclesiastical account of the case which surely fanned the flames, spreading witch hysteria across New England. The first embers from Mather's fiery rhetoric landed in Salem, Massachusetts. A minister's family in Salem, burning with pious conviction, started the local conflagration. Bridget Bishop was hanged in June of 1692. Many others would share her fate. Cotton Mather's role as an erudite cleric resonated well with the powers of government. Mather, government officials, and members of the judiciary worked hand in glove to stamp out Satan. Ten people died as witches during the summer months of 1692. The flimsiest allegations served to impeach all manner of people, the down and out along with the well to do. Alarmed citizens fought back and stemmed the tide. Mather was undeterred, and from his righteous pulpit took every opportunity to reignite the witch craze. Until his death in 1728, Mather remained faithful to his lifelong creed, "I have indeed set myself to countermine the whole PLOT of the Devil, against New-England ..."[17]

At roughly the same time Cotton Mather was battling Beelzebub, Franz Anton Mesmer challenged Johann Joseph Gassner. The former advocated the new science while the latter tenaciously clung to established religious traditions. Gassner was a Catholic priest from Austria, skilled in exorcism. The priest's abilities were legendary and attracted a large following. Gassner could cast out the devil, the typical explanation for fits and convulsions, through prayer and command.[18] In spite of support from the local citizenry, Gassner's reputation soon dulled, in no small part due to the unrelenting criticism of Franz Anton Mesmer.

Mesmer was born in 1740, received his medical degree in Vienna, Austria, in 1765, and then wrote an influential tract, "On the influence of the planets upon the human body." Over the next decade Mesmer perfected a new approach, one that promised a medical cure for all sorts of human ailments. Mesmer's newfangled treatment, referred to as animal magne-

---

17 Cotton Mather, *The wonders of the invisible world* (London: John Russell Smith, 1862), III-XII, 4.
18 Robert Lawrence, *Primitive psycho-therapy and quackery* (Boston: Houghton Mifflin and Company, 1910), 149.

tism, offered a bridge, however rickety, between the traditions of religion and the emergence of science.[19]

Proponents of animal magnetism carefully followed Mesmer's postulates. The basic theory held that every living organism had vital fluids responsive to the influence of celestial bodies. Much as the moon created oceanic tidal forces, so did the moon and stars create an ebb and flow in the vital animal fluids. The human body also had inherent magnetic properties which, once again, came under the influence of planetary forces. Animal magnetism referred to the magnetic connection between earthly and heavenly bodies.[20]

To the practitioner of animal magnetism, disease was the result of some disturbance in the flow of the vital fluids. Ordinary magnets, even the toys of children, could influence the flow of the vital fluids. Magnets were rather quickly discarded in favor of a new concept. According to Mesmer, some individuals possessed certain characteristics such as charm, charisma, and a coy seductiveness which totally captivated the vast majority of people lacking that powerful influence. These traits were an expression of magnetism. "Man has the faculty of exercising on his fellow man a salutary influence by directing on them at his own will the principle which animates us and causes us to live." The practitioner's strong will power, not magnets, became the agent of therapeutic change.[21]

As it happened, Mesmer's real repulsion from magnets grew out of a heated disputed with another practitioner of animal magnetism. The rival claimed that Mesmer hijacked his ideas and particularly the use of magnets. In a pique of anger, Mesmer orchestrated the same magnetic effects by simply pressing his fingers to the sufferer's afflicted body. From that point on, controversy followed the animal magnetist. In Vienna, Mesmer widely circulated his extraordinary achievement in restoring the sight of a famed diva. Unfortunately for Mesmer, the woman vigorously denied the claim. Mesmer fled to Paris, hoping to revive his tattered reputation. He found a receptive audience in France and soon counted some of the most famous people as patients or newly converted practitioners.[22]

---

19   Baron Du Potet, "Account of mesmerism," *London Medical Gazette* 1 (1838): 291.

20   Alphonse Teste, *A practical manual of animal magnetism* (London: Hippolyte Baillierre, 1843), 1-5.

21   Ibid.

22   A Surgeon, *Animal magnetism: Its history to the present time* (London: G. B. Dyer, 1841), 11-15.

The crush of interest in Mesmer's clinical practice spawned the invention of the *baquet*. The baquet was a curious contraption to accommodate the crowds. It was a large wooden tub around which thirty people were neatly arranged. Inside the baquet Mesmer placed a thin layer of iron filings on top of which lay an array of glass bottles. Metal rods connected the interior of the baquet to the participants seated along the edge of the tub. To increase the dramatic presentation, the room featuring the baquet was darkened with thick curtains. Mesmer, the great impresario, strode about the room variously touching participant's afflicted areas, transfixing the sufferer with his magnetic gaze, or focusing energy with a metal rod.[23]

Much like the Abraham Man, a whiff of fraud came from Mesmer. Some members of the public suspected the man of borrowing the status of the scientific method to foist an elaborate charade. With Mesmer's fame came implacable foes. The French Government assembled a committee from the Academy of Sciences to study animal magnetism. The year was 1784; America was victorious in her struggle with England; France was a close ally, and Benjamin Franklin a respected diplomat. It seemed a likely choice to include America's Renaissance man in the scientific inquiry of Mesmer's techniques.

Even before his appointment to the scientific commission, Franklin harbored deep skepticism regarding Mesmer's clinical practice. In a letter to a friend, Franklin commented, "As to the animal magnetism, so much talked of, I must doubt its existence till I can see or feel some effect of it ... I cannot but fear that the expectation of great advantage from this new method of treating diseases will prove a delusion ..."[24]

The scientific committee gathered evidence through firsthand observation of Mesmer with a variety of victims. After several weeks, the commission retired and reported their results in a short missive titled, *Exposé of experiments made at the examination of animal magnetism*. Mesmer was surely disappointed. The authors collectively concluded, "We said the effects attributed to magnetism and to a fluid which is not manifested take place only when the imagination is roused and perhaps excited. The imagination, then, seems to be the principle." The report precipitated Mesmer's final fall from grace and ignominious death in 1815.[25]

---

23 Edward Hale, *Franklin in France* (Boston: Roberts Brothers, 1888), 294-8.
24 Ibid.
25 Ibid.

His method, mesmerism, underwent a metamorphosis and emerged as hypnosis. In the reincarnated state, hypnosis could not completely jettison the doubt and ridicule which plagued mesmerism. Hypnosis also suffered the carnival effect, being a staple feature as an amusing side show. A few medical doctors championed hypnosis as an effective anesthetic. In that capacity, hypnosis competed with ether, chloroform, and nitrous oxide. Most mid-nineteenth century surgeons opted for a chemical anesthesia. Sometimes a physician could demonstrate the value of hypnosis by inducing a deep trance which permitted a pain-free operation.

Most hypnotists agreed that an essential ingredient for a successful trance rested on the poise and confidence exuded by the practitioner. Hypnotists attempted to demystify the practice through scholarly publications which added the aura of scientific credibility. Instruction manuals provided step by step guidance. These books instructed the would-be hypnotist to "bring the crown of the patient's head to the end of the bed, and seat yourself so as to be able to bring your face into contact with his, and extend your hands to the pit of his stomach, when it is wished; make the room dark, enjoin quiet, and then shutting your patient's eyes ..." begin a series of slow repetitive hand motions across the person's body. During the procedure, which could last upwards of an hour, the rhythmic breathing of the hypnotist on the patient's face helped induce a quiet but alert repose.[26]

Mesmer had started an example of an avant-garde movement fusing emerging scientific principles with philosophic ideas, religion, and a dash of entertainment. Practitioners promised or promoted all sorts of commercial cure-alls. Benjamin Franklin, however, was not amused. His insatiable appetite for knowledge extended to science and medicine. In fact, among Franklin's nearly endless list of accomplishments is his role in cofounding America's first hospital in Philadelphia.[27]

Franklin's most famous scientific contributions involved electricity. His curious mind naturally linked his experiments with electricity with potential medical applications. In one experiment, Franklin had individuals with a paralyzed limb sit on an "electric stool." Through the use of a Leyden jar, Franklin would deliver a strong jolt of electricity to the affected limb. In most cases some degree of improvement occurred, ranging from an improved sensory experience to full movement. Unfortunately,

---

26   James Esdaile, *Hypnosis in medicine and surgery* (New York: Julian Press, 1850), 27-35, 144.

27   Theodore Diller, *Franklin's contributions to medicine* (Brooklyn, NY: Albert T. Huntington, 1912), 21.

the beneficial effects lasted only a few days. Franklin wondered whether the gains resulted from electricity or simply from "the hope of success ..."[28]

Benjamin Franklin joined a number of like-minded individuals such as Benjamin Rush in promoting a more scientifically-based approach to medical care. Religion, medicine and philosophy coexisted, often competing, at this point in history. It seemed inevitable that some conflict would arise, in a world still smoldering from witches burned at the stake. Along with Franklin, Benjamin Rush was a sort of transitional figure forcefully attempting to move society along a more enlightened path.

Benjamin Rush was born in 1745, spent his early childhood in Maryland, and later studied medicine in Edinburgh, Scotland. In due course, the University of Pennsylvania appointed him as the Chair of Medicine. Rush signed the Declaration of Independence, and with the outbreak of hostilities, lent his considerable talents as a physician to the war effort. Among the principal tools the famous physician frequently used were bleeding and purging, the latter accomplished through the liberal application of calomel. Rush unabashedly shared his vision of medical practice, a blend of philosophy, religion and, science, in a series of books. As the father of modern psychiatry, Rush set forth his views on emotional disorders in a classic work entitled *Medical Inquiries and Observations upon the Diseases of the Mind.*[29]

America was thirty-seven years old when Benjamin Rush authored *Medical Inquiries and Observations upon the Diseases of the Mind.* Rush prayed for wisdom from the Almighty as he embarked on his ambitious task. He began by subdividing the functions of the mind as "understanding, memory, imagination, passions, the principle of faith, will, the moral faculty, conscience, and the sense of Deity.[30] A person's intellect, or the mind's role in understanding and perceiving, was the highest human function and the one most often subject to damage. An impaired intellect distorted the person's thinking and resulted in odd behavior.

As an enlightened doctor not subject to the social paranoia of his day, Rush believed that madness resulted from physical disease. In building his argument, Rush reviewed the common physical diseases believed to be responsible for insanity. Many physicians thought that disease of the

---

28 Benjamin Franklin, *Memoirs of Benjamin Franklin* (New York: Derby and Jackson, 1859), 324.

29 Daniel Hack Tuke, *The insane in the United States and Canada* (London: H. Wolfe, 1885), 3-6.

30 Benjamin Rush, *Medical inquiries and observations upon the diseases of the mind* (Birmingham, AL: Gryphon Editions, 1988), 174-213.

spleen produced mental disturbances, especially hypochondriasis. Others fervently blamed gastrointestinal problems for spasms of anger, fear, and madness. This opinion was a slightly modernized version of Hippocrates' assignment of madness to disordered bile. Rush disagreed with his colleagues who insisted insanity arose from disease in the nervous system, or solely in the mind. Instead, the visionary healer saw vascular disease in the brain as the source of madness. Rush reached the connection through careful observation and thoughtful deliberation. According to his observations the most replicable symptoms of insanity involved headache, flushed face, fever, insomnia, and an oscillating heart rate. An elevated heart rate was almost considered a pathognomonic of insanity. Rush cited an experiment where a colleague restored sanity to a madman by lowering his pulse. Adding further weight to the vascular disease theory were numerous instances of insanity following fever epidemics and autopsies among the insane revealing brain inflammation.[31]

The cause of insanity extended to brain injuries, some through trauma and some from imprudent habits. Among the latter group, Rush included malnutrition, alcoholism, onanism, extraordinary pain, back-breaking labors, and exposure to extreme weather, grief, excessive study, and terror. Madness seemed to strike during the most productive years of adult life, sparing the young child and elderly alike. According to Rush, women suffered insanity more often than men, principally because of their reproductive life cycle. The mentally stimulating effect of a rich lifestyle exposed the wealthiest members of society to a disproportionate share of insanity. Individuals who in the normal course of their avocation excessively employed their passions, such as writers and actors, also weakened the mind sufficient to admit madness. The decay of a society, marked by chaos, confusion, and moral crisis, created a fertile environment for mental derangements.[32]

Rush's detailed observations and publications provided an unintended consequence: the education of the Abraham Man. Malingerers had every incentive to perfect their game, as it could help them avoid military conscription, win special favors in jail, and garner unwarranted compassion. It was worth careful study.

Rush provided a useful nosology listing hypochondriasis, mania, and various derangements of the passions as the leading types of emotional disorders. Hypochondriasis was a commonly recognized mental state

31 Ibid.
32 Ibid.

noted for an exclusive and unshakeable false belief in some catastrophic physical ailment. Some hypochondriacs had other singular and similarly unmovable ideas involving possession by a plant, animal or spirits. Naturally, such thinking led to changes in mood, which fluctuated widely, often without any particularly obvious provocation. The treatment of hypochondriasis followed the common etiologies. Since Rush believed most emotional disorders arose from vascular distension, it logically followed that bloodletting would relive the congestion and return the pulse to a normal state. Failing that, the physician might suggest calomel or similar cathartics to cleanse the intestinal tract. Emetics would empty the stomach, paving the way for a diet rich in protein and good wine. Mercury increased salivation, through which various toxins left the body. The application of blistering agents to the skin mobilized the circulatory system. Less drastic prescriptions included exercise, bathing, and travel.[33]

Mania was a broad category which included the many different manifestations of madness. Rush recognized that optimum treatment required the person's removal from their family and placement in a facility capable of safely controlling the violent behavioral outbursts. The physician's demeanor — stern, controlling, and authoritarian, was an indispensable ingredient in the proper management of mania. If the person remained aggressively out of control, Rush advocated various mechanical devices guaranteed to restrain the strongest madman. A cure for mania rested on the same causal factors underlying hypochondriasis. As a consequence, Rush advocated bloodletting, as much as 40 ounces or to the point of fainting. Rush also liberally prescribed purging agents, blisters, and emetics. The rest of the treatment focused on decreasing mental stimuli by keeping the person's room dark, providing a diet rich in vegetables, and the use of frequent cold showers.[34]

Benjamin Rush was an avid reader and author. Through careful observation, long hours of study, and endless discussions with the preeminent thinkers of his day, Rush broadened the therapeutic approach to disease by including dietary, climactic, and moral nostrums. His ideas influenced generations of physicians. He died in 1813 at the age of sixty-eight.

The writings of Benjamin Rush loomed large in the study of the mentally ill. Although his use of bloodletting found fewer advocates in succeeding years, his diagnostic classification and biological etiologies

---

33 Ibid.
34 Ibid.

paved the way for new discoveries. But in spite of Rush's enlightened nineteenth century views, the treatment of the mentally ill remained mostly outside the province of medicine.

That changed in succeeding years and a more organized medical approach to mental illness developed. Franz Joseph Gall, a German physician, complemented the scientific studies of Benjamin Rush by advocating a structural connection between mental functions and the brain. Gall, born in 1757, promoted a novel but controversial theory explaining the workings of the mind. As a young student, Gall was a quick learner but he envied classmates who could effortlessly memorize lengthy assignments. Gall closely scrutinized his competitors and came to the conclusion that students skilled in recollection also had large eyes. It seemed as if the larger eyes funneled more information to the brain. From this observation, Gall broadened his inquiry and soon made other discoveries. Some people, for example, never get lost. Those fortunate few could innately blaze a path and then retrace their steps. Gall noticed that such individuals had two small facial appurtenances. Persons with a dominant character, decisive and authoritarian in nature, also displayed predictable skull protuberances. The casual connection between character and skull anatomy led Gall to conjecture that the origin of this relationship resided in the brain. Gall tested his theory by visiting insane asylums and prisons, carefully studying the inmates' aberrant behaviors, and concluded with greater conviction that the mental faculties reside in the human brain and make their presence known anatomically. Taking his research to the next logical step, the curious doctor eagerly performed autopsies and reported a topographical correlation between the brain and the skull. John Spurzheim, Gall's first and most ardent medical advocate, refined and spread the emerging science of phrenology to England and America.[35]

Phrenology was revolutionary in the sense of taking tentative steps placing personality traits within the brain. Other scientists and philosophers considered the heart, liver, or spleen as the anatomical repository of human characteristics. None of these free thinkers dared define the human spirit, the spring from which flowed universal morality, as anatomical. Morality remained a purely metaphysical construct nurtured by faith. Even though the earliest practitioners of phrenology eschewed any effort to structurally locate morality in the brain, their nascent scientific

---

35   Frederick Bridges, *Phrenology made practical* (London: George Philip and Son, 1861), 10-11.

endeavors nonetheless started treading on religion's turf. The result was predictable and phrenology suffered considerable criticism.

Phrenology asserted two basic propositions, claiming that the brain was the source of human intellect and that it discharged that function through a variety of specialized brain organs. Gall identified twenty-seven such organs which he referred to as faculties. The twenty-seven faculties included such attributes as friendship, cunning, pride, religion, sarcasm, memory for words, firmness, benevolence, and vanity. Each faculty had a home on the brain's surface and influenced the skull's growth and development. It fell to the skilled phrenologist to make a careful study of the subject's cranium.[36]

Phrenology drew its share of admirers and critics. The list of believers included prominent physicians along with the literati and intelligentsia. The critics were a vocal group who ridiculed phrenology and essentially equated the "science" with astrology, only looking at the bumps on the head as opposed to stars in the heavens. The critics never fully silenced the ardent advocates, who happily published erudite tracts on the principles and practices of phrenology in books and medically-oriented journals. The tug of war between the two camps obscured a bigger picture. The practice of phrenology decidedly advanced a more scientific exploration of human behavior.

Phrenology fascinated the public and authors responded with popular interpretations of the subject. A Civil War era reader could learn, and no doubt apply, the rudimentary principles of phrenology. Students quickly discovered that phrenology involved far more than a simple reading of the skull's topology. A person's head size gave irrefutable evidence of intellect. Any man with a head circumference less than nineteen inches would be severely incapacitated and most likely unemployable. Add a mere three inches and now the man could join the ranks of the professional elite. The shape of the head also held important clues. Narrow heads indicated lassitude while wide heads suggested an abundance of emotional energy. Phrenologists equated congenital skull defects with a corresponding brain dysfunction, often used to explain insanity. Mental aberrations could also come about from a disturbance in the animal organs located at the base of the brain. The animal organs comprised the most basic human instincts, so named because animals shared the same behaviors. Phrenologists recognized at least ten animal organs such as

---

36 Pierre Flourens, *Phrenology examined* (Philadelphia: Hogan and Thompson, 1846), 48.

social connectedness, interest in children, reproduction, attentiveness, and persistence.[37]

Practitioners of phrenology faced a mountain of criticism. Anatomists scoffed at the notion of "organs" but the faithful countered by criticizing their tormentors' utter lack of sophistication in identifying the brain's functions. A sort of standoff left the two camps convinced of each other's folly. Nonetheless, phrenology gained adherents, both professional and lay, from the common sense side of the new field. A person's facial features, after all, did seem to correlate with behavior. Authors made liberal use of such observations to colorfully illustrate personality characteristics. Criminals also relished the possibilities. Phrenology certainly suggested a constitutional role in personality development and seemed tailor-made for a legal defense. Decades before the American Civil War, medical jurists predicted a day when a criminal proceeding would be interrupted to secure the services of a phrenologist.[38]

Phrenologists thought crime arose from an abnormally accentuated animal organ in the brain. Some decried society's punishment, believing that criminals were victims of heredity. Phrenologists advocated education instead of punishment, reserving incarceration for the most dangerous and recalcitrant offenders. Even then, criminals would be housed not in a prison but in a hospital for purposes of treatment.[39]

On the eve of the Civil War, phrenology remained an active area of medical study but still hobbled by controversy. Many physicians studied phrenology, with some claiming extraordinary skill in its everyday application. One physician, citing his own personal experience, chided his non-believing brethren. This physician recalled strolling through a large jail and casually noting the inmates' features. On several occasions he made a more in depth analysis, oft times claiming that the moral propensities evident in the inmate's skull firmly suggested innocence. The medical doctor turned phrenologist regretted the incarceration of such obviously non-criminal people, implying that a just society should better discriminate between the moral and immoral residents of jails and prisons.[40]

---

37   Cornelius Donovan, *A handbook of phrenology* (London: Longmans, Green, Reader, and Dyer, 1870), 18.
38   Thomas Wakley, "The responsibility of criminals," *The Lancet* 2, (1842): 252.
39   Hewett Watson, *Statistics of phrenology* (London: Longman Publishers, 1836), 66.
40   James George Davey, "Phrenology," *Social Science Review* 2, (1864): 81-3.

Phrenologists extended their study to diseases of the mind. One of the earliest publications on the subject admiringly concluded that mental dysfunction was indeed often accompanied by changes in brain structure, as noted in autopsies and reflected on the victim's skull. In cases where no obvious connection existed, the early medical phrenologists reasoned that insanity was essentially a disorder involving the brain's function, a condition not always represented by anatomical changes. Naturally, medical doctors sought diagnostic clarity but treatment was even more important. Phrenologists often detected pain, swelling, or, heat emanating from various locations on an insane person's skull. These symptoms were assumed to arise from inflamed or congested brain tissue directly underlying the affected portion of the head. Through the use of leeches or cold compresses, some doctors claimed a restoration of sanity after relieving the congestion or swelling. Another advantage claimed by phrenology involved a more accurate assessment of prognosis. Phrenologists could distinguish, based on structural characteristics of the head, those individuals with more pronounced and incurable forms of insanity.[41]

Phrenologists and physicians in general believed that injuries to the head, with resulting structural malformations, could directly cause insanity. Case reports surfaced in medical journals describing the debilitating mental disorders arising from head wounds. In one example, a sailor fell from a lofty yard arm, striking his head on the descent. The fall went unremarked for ten years, during which time the sailor's behavior steadily deteriorated into an aggressive form of insanity. Eventually, the sailor wound up in an insane asylum where some improvement occurred in his mood but his violent rages remained unchecked. An astute physician who carefully performed a phrenology evaluation noted tenderness and a shallow concavity along one side of the sailor's skull. After some deliberation, the physician removed the dented portion of the skull. The sailor experienced a rapid improvement and suffered no further violent behavioral paroxysms.[42]

Proponents of phrenology published their findings in leading medical journals. In time, the profession's respectability attracted the attention of criminal lawyers. Phrenologists skillfully examined a criminal's head and then offered learned opinions that swayed juries. In a circular fash-

---

41 David Noble, "Noble on the brain," *American Journal of Insanity* 3, no. 3 (1847): 262-72.

42 C. Lockhart Robertson, "Remarks on insanity," *American Journal of Insanity* 3, no. 3 (1847): 273-7.

ion, the phrenologist's testimony enhanced their credibility, which in turn led to more requests. As the allure of fame and fortune grew, so did the testimonial musings of phrenologists who saw all manner of human deviancy in the lumps and bumps on a prisoner's skull. Clever malingerers could exploit the liberal trend by connecting insanity with a long forgotten head injury.

As the medical community debated the scientific basis of insanity, firmly held religious concepts of morality and offbeat belief systems such as spiritualism shackled the progressive thinkers. It was difficult, or nearly impossible, to advance a unified scientific theory of mental illness without paying due homage to man's spiritual nature. The nineteenth century physician sometimes resolved the dilemma through philosophy, oft times quoting the work of René Descartes. Descartes lived two centuries earlier, but the great philosopher's persuasive arguments enshrining thinking over perceiving, the value of critical inquiry, and locating the metaphysical mind in the pineal gland remained as critical touchstones when discussing sanity. Descartes' concept of dualism conveniently separated the physical and mental side of man. According to this view, the essence of humanity was man's unique ability to think. The conscious, analytic part of man resided in a distinctly separate, immaterial area referred to as the mind. The physical side of man, his body, was the non-thinking animal component which, when combined with the mind, formed two separate entities which effected each other through the brain's pineal gland. The spiritual side of man would naturally reside in the mind.[43]

By the mid-nineteenth century insanity evoked a wide range of responses. Although a palpable scientific movement towards understanding mental illness was underway, it was a nascent effort competing against moral explanations and societal fear. As a consequence, the mentally ill person could just as easily end up in jail, wander the countryside, become a target of ridicule, find his way to an almshouse, or receive treatment in an insane asylum. Over time, increasing numbers of the insane found refuge and treatment in the asylum.

The ascendancy of the asylum movement can broadly be traced to several factors. The large institutions offered reassuring reminders to a skittish public that the unpredictable and dangerous madmen were safely locked away. The same facilities also offered the hope of a therapeutic

---

43 Oswald Kulpe, *Introduction to philosophy* (New York: Macmillan and Company, 1897), 134-6.

haven for the mentally ill and possibly a restoration to normal behavior. Interested physicians, and lay advocates for better treatment, fueled an optimistic movement promising recovery through skillful, scientific treatment.

In 1860, fifty asylums delivered care to 24,000 individuals diagnosed with insanity. Nearly half, twenty-one in total, were built in the decade preceding 1860. A number of factors limited asylum growth before that period, including the cost, lack of faith in successful treatments, and moral opposition. The first institution recognizing the need for treating the mentally ill was the Pennsylvania Hospital in Philadelphia, which admitted eighteen patients in 1752. Twenty-one years later, in 1773, the Williamsburg Hospital in Virginia became America's first facility devoted entirely to the treatment of insanity. Four years later two asylums opened, one in Baltimore, Maryland, and the other in Bloomingdale, New York. Another twenty years passed before another asylum opened. From 1817 until 1850, twenty-four asylums were built in various locations.[44]

In 1840, lurid tales of abuse in asylums across the ocean in England cast a baleful spotlight on these institutions. Virtually all patients were restrained with hand cuffs or strait jackets. Containment took priority over curability. The social backlash forced the asylums to adopt more humane practices. Paradoxically, once the asylums cleaned up these abuses, a renaissance of hope propelled their dramatic growth. In America, the 1850s witnessed the construction of twenty-one new institutions. Perhaps in an effort to counter lingering concerns about the treatment of the insane, many asylums reported fairly impressive rates of cure. The Utica Asylum in New York state reported that ninety-five percent of individuals admitted within three months of their first attack of insanity would be cured in six months. Delay adversely impacted a favorable outcome and accounted for many of the chronically insane who never fully recovered. The Asylum's message was simple enough, urging family members to bring their loved ones for treatment at the earliest sign of insanity. Asylums also appealed to the public and legislators by emphasizing their thriftiness. The average cure, requiring a six month stay, cost only fourteen dollars.[45]

The average physician during the Civil War era had little scientific knowledge about insanity. Medical schools did not teach the subject and physicians shunned the mysterious disorder unless forced to confront it.

---

44 E. T. Wilkins, *Insanity and insane asylums* (Sacramento, CA: TA Springer, State Printers, 1871), 189-222.

45 Ibid.

Occasionally, a person accused of a crime would raise insanity as a legal defense. Lawyers no doubt relished the prospect of skewering any unwary physician who dared enter the court room.

Many of the Civil War concepts about insanity reached back to the writings of Benjamin Rush. Even then, the average person understood that insanity plagued certain family trees. Of course, applying that general principle to a specific family in the doctor's office was a more difficult task.[46] The exact mechanism accounting for familial transmission was incompletely understand but skillful observations, recorded in family records and discussed in medical journals, certainly lent credibility to the idea that hereditary factors affected insanity. A physician might be able to predict that insanity seemed to follow gender lines, such that if a patient's mother had insanity, there was a risk it would show up in the patient's female child. If the case of insanity was more distant in the family history, then the certainty of transmission declined. Insanity could skip generations, acting like a wild card. When a prospective mother had a prior history of insanity, the physician might advise against the marriage, given the high probability of insanity reoccurring with pregnancy or shortly after delivery.[47]

Habitual drunkenness was considered to be another leading cause of insanity. Alcohol's role seemed indisputable, and this linkage was touted by the growing temperance movement. One chaplain with two and a half decades of experience at the Michigan Asylum in Kalamazoo, having seen the devastation wrought by excessive use of alcohol, set out to review the admission characteristics at other asylums. He learned that a Massachusetts asylum cited alcohol abuse as the cause of insanity in nineteen percent of admissions. The chaplain estimated that fully one third of all cases of insanity were directly or indirectly caused by alcohol. He strongly supported a broad based educational reform movement advocating temperance.[48]

In addition, advocates of abstinence held that a person with an inherited predisposition to alcohol abuse could avoid triggering a possible inherited predisposition to insanity through a temperate life, as all too often though, insanity revealed itself after a prolonged period of mental excitement brought about through the over indulgent use of hard liquors.

---

46 Fielding Blandford, *The treatment, medical and legal, of insane patients*, 4th Ed. (London: Oliver and Boyd, Tweeddale Court, 1894), 141-62.

47 Ibid.

48 Daniel Putnam, *Twenty-five years with the insane* (Detroit: John McFarlane, 1885), 106-9.

Many doctors could fortify the connection between alcohol use and insanity through careful observation. And then there was *delirium tremens*, which could terminate a bout of heavy drinking with a combination of violent muscle spasms, mental confusion, and fever. Some people who survived it were plagued ever after with insanity, a fate perhaps worse than death.

American society in the nineteenth century vigorously debated the pros and cons of alcohol. Alcohol was a well-accepted medicinal agent with applications ranging from elixirs to anesthetics, but alcohol was also seen as a cause of moral depravity ranging from poverty to psychopathy, which created alarm among some doctors, preachers, attorneys, and members of the lay citizenry.

By one account, the temperance movement began in the small community of Moreau, New York, where every social event, family get-together, and worksite overflowed with alcohol. From dawn to dusk, it seemed that every man in Moreau was habitually drunk. The movement's first cheerleader was Billy J. Clark, a physician, who grew increasingly convinced that the town's domestic violence, workplace accidents, ill health, and financial ruin all stemmed from excessive drink. Impressed with Benjamin Rush's stern warnings against the excess use of alcohol, he voiced his concern to the local minister. The pastor and physician joined forces and started a local crusade. A total of forty-three likeminded Moreau citizens banded together and formed America's first temperance society in 1808.

The Moreau Temperance Society adopted a set of bylaws according to which each member took a pledge to abstain from all intoxicating beverages, pay a fine if caught violating the prime directive, and report any offenders to the group's leaders. Naturally this curious complement of teetotalers attracted widespread ridicule, derision, and hostility. But in spite of the community scorn, this tiny seedling grew stronger with each passing year. By 1826, two larger groups, the American Temperance Union in Boston and the New York Temperance Society carried the message to ever more receptive audiences. A decade later, in Saratoga Springs, New York, the American Temperance Union held a convention during which the assembled delegates passed a resolution urging a national ban on the use and sale of all intoxicating beverages.[49]

---

49 Lebbeus Armstrong, *The temperance reformation*, 2nd Ed. (New York: Fowlers and Wells Publishers, 1853), 18-34.

This clarion call reached the ears of Neal Dow. Dow, who later commanded a Maine regiment during the Civil War, became a zealous and forceful temperance reformer. With a carefully crafted and flawlessly executed strategy, the young reformer joined a small group of like-minded teetotalers traveling the length and breadth of Maine. Dow preferred the force of law over moral persuasion, and politicians in Maine obviously agreed as they passed the first prohibition act in America in 1851. The State of Maine ordered that "No person shall be allowed at any time, to manufacture or sell, by himself, his clerk, servant or agent, directly or indirectly, any spirituous intoxicating liquors, or any mixed liquors ..." The law allowed for certain exceptions, such as the medicinal use of alcohol.[50]

Against the gathering forces clamoring for government control, another group arose, less vocal but more thoughtful, to decry prohibition. For many people of the mid to late nineteenth century, legislative and judicial intervention seemed a reasonable exercise of state and federal governments. Politicians trumpeted the populist message that the evils of alcohol could be eliminated from society using the tools of law, giving way to a world free of crime and full of domestic bliss. The message resonated with some voters since the problems associated with alcohol abuse permeated all aspects of social life and defied simple interventions. The government seemed omnipotent, and that fantasy was stoked by beguiling, power-hungry politicians. Other citizens, however, understood the blunt force nature of government action, which often lacks any precision and smashes both its target and many innocent bystanders. This group bitterly complained that a maze of rules, regulations, and laws directed towards prohibition simply usurped individual responsibility. As one writer at the time observed, legal restraint was a poor substitute for moral self-control. "Observe that man walking down the street. He passes a liquor store, and now he passes a street which leads to brothels. Why? Is it the fear of the law which restrains him? When you, my reader, walk through a city, and pass a thousand temptations, are you restrained by the law? Is it the fear of the constable, or is it your conviction that vicious indulgences are harmful, with the consciousness that society is observing you?[51] Of course the reader was not concerned about his own pious nature but fretted about a neighbor's or stranger's deviant behavior. Clever politicians exploited this fear and drafted all sorts of

---

50   Charles T. White, *Lincoln and prohibition* (New York: Abingdon Press, 1921), 165.

51   Dio Lewis, *Prohibition a failure* (Boston: James R Osgood and Company, 1875), 16.

legislative bromides designed to protect the upstanding citizenry from the debaucheries of the immoral class.

For the most part, habitual drinking was viewed as a moral failure. Responsible citizens controlled their drinking. Even so, some doctors proposed various medical explanations for alcoholism. These theories were never very popular, since they tended to excuse the drinkers' personal responsibility, but of course, the Abraham Man cheered their efforts. It was extraordinarily easy to claim to be a helpless inebriate and possibly escape the consequences of a criminal act.

The medicinal use of alcohol was the exception to the moral rule. Civil War doctors relied on alcohol as an anesthetic, tonic, and general cure-all. At the outbreak of the War Between the States, much was known about human anatomy but less about disease etiology. The former permitted extensive surgical operations but the latter meant untold numbers died from both unsanitary medical procedures and unhealthy camp conditions. The crowding, poor hygiene, limited exercise, fatigue, and mostly unpalatable diets weakened the soldiers' natural resistance to disease, setting the stage for rampant contagion. A number of infectious diseases such as typhoid fever, measles, smallpox, and malaria decimated the ranks of fighting men. Diarrhea and dysentery immobilized many more. In many of these cases, the doctor prescribed a tonic, heavily laced with alcohol, to invigorate a sick soldier.[52]

Malaria plagued many Civil War soldiers but its causation remained mysterious. It seemed to be associated with a moist climate, and one theory blamed it on decaying plant material that emitted toxic vapors. Physicians of the era would have scoffed at the notion that tiny creatures carried by a mosquito caused the dreaded disease.[53]

Great stock was placed in alcohol's stimulant properties and doctors liberally ordered its use, especially brandy, although in a pinch whiskey, wine, or anything fermented would be pressed into duty. Alcohol found its way into seemingly endless concoctions hawked as patent medicines, elixirs, or simple battlefield preparations. Among the latter, many Civil War physicians favored various milk combinations, such as milk-whey made by mixing wine and milk, for conditions such as typhoid fever, malaria, dysentery, and chronic diarrhea.[54]

---

52 Charles Johnson, *Muskets and medicine* (Philadelphia: F. A. Davis Company, 1917), 157-66.

53 Joseph Janvier Woodward, *Outlines of the chief camp diseases of the United States Armies* (Philadelphia: J. B. Lippincott and Company, 1863), 30.

54 Ibid., 132, 135, 231, and 254.

Vying for popularity with alcohol was opium. Infectious diseases, intestinal disorders, and just about anything associated with an ache or pain would be treated with a prescription containing opium, alcohol, or both. Many physicians considered opium and its many formulations as a soothing palliative, almost a panacea, given its broad applications. Physicians liberally treated the wounds and diseases of the Civil War soldier with all manner of opium preparations. The intractable nature of many conditions such as diarrhea and unrelenting pain fostered the chronic administration of narcotics. Opium was so effective in so many medical situations that it came to be abused by some practitioners and caused dependency in some patients.

According to the medical thinking of the era, the chronic use of opium and morphine produced no discernible difficulties among most people. On the other hand, a sizeable minority of individuals developed an opium neurosis. According to the enlightened view, an opium neurosis was the direct consequence of the narcotic perpetually bathing the brain and actually altering its physiology and morphology. As a consequence, the opium neurotic assumed the wasted, fatigued and debilitated aspect characteristic of "opium takers." Opium takers usually hid their addiction, going to great lengths to furtively maintain their habit. After the War ended, some physicians noted that "Many veterans of the late war have become opium maniacs for the relief of their pains and sufferings, and this is often concealed where it might possibly peril the procuring of a pension."[55]

Medical practitioners generally agreed that opium neurosis resulted from hereditary factors and constitutional deficiencies. Alcoholism and opium abuse went hand in hand and a careful study of a family tree would identify numerous instances of a generational transmission. A parent, for example, might display flagrant alcoholism but a daughter might avoid that fate, only to fall victim to an opium neurosis.

In the rare case where an opium taker received treatment, doctors resorted to a fairly well defined strategy to wean the person off the toxic compound. The first decision confronting the physician involved the speed at which to taper off the use of opium. In some cases the physician ordered a rapid reduction in the opium while in other cases a more leisurely approach was adopted. The physician carefully monitored the development of the expected withdrawal symptoms, such as melancho-

---

55 American Association for the Study and Cure of Inebriety, *The disease of inebriety from alcohol, opium, and other narcotic drugs* (New York: E. B. Treat Publisher, 1893), 323.

lia, agitation, suicidal tendencies, and alcohol abuse. Opium takers probably received the best care in an institution devoted to their specific care, where ridged rules and close observation reduced temptations. Institutional care also offered proper nutrition, rest, medicinal baths, and various pharmacologic restoratives. One of the most common, and vexing, symptoms plaguing the opium taker's recovery was insomnia. A variety of soporific medications, including bromides and cannabis, provided welcome relief.[56]

Physicians of the nineteenth century often combined the roles of doctor and pharmacist. When it came to the *materia medica*, the doctor often used a mixture of potent botanicals. A wide variety of plant extracts found their way into both solid and liquid forms for all sorts of medical ailments. The doctor commonly prepared these various mixtures, often as pills formed in a device similar to but smaller than a bullet mold. After the ingredients were combined and pressed together in the mold, the pills were extracted.

Patients sometimes preferred powders over pills. Powders were susceptible to moisture, limiting their shelf life, but were convenient in that a foul-tasting medicine could be disguised with a more palatable beverage. Certain powders, such as Dover's, enjoyed widespread use. Dover's powder was a mixture of ipecac, opium, and potash. It was used to cause sweating to ward off the chills of an advancing fever. Physicians routinely prescribed the opium-containing powder for victims of most infections, dysentery, and rheumatism. Other solid preparations commonly used included plasters, ointments, and suppositories.[57]

Blistering agents were a common fixture of medical practice, prescribed on the notion that an irritant applied topically somehow affected underlying structures and organs. A particularly effective blistering agent relied on the crushed remains of the cantharis beetle. Liquid medicines, such as tinctures, evacuants, tonics, and elixirs, also relied on plant extracts. Common ingredients once again included the old standbys, alcohol and opium. Laudanum was the best of both worlds in combining morphine with alcohol to produce a popular tincture. Even surgical disinfectants often managed to combine whiskey with ingredients such as coal tar. As might be imagined, many of these preparations found considerable favor with physicians and patients alike.

---

56   Ibid.
57   Michael Flannery, *Civil War pharmacy* (Binghamton, NY: Haworth Press, Inc., 2004), 34-40.

Medicines and surgery were the mainstays of nineteenth century medical practice. Slightly more adventurous physicians used a variety of other scientific treatments, particularly those involving electricity. Benjamin Franklin probably believed that his rudimentary experiments in the healing power of electricity would evolve towards a credible medical treatment.[58] Progress was slow, perhaps delayed by a fear of electricity along with more practical concerns involving the invention of a reliable means of generating and storing the energy. Eventually, inventors built small, dependable batteries that stored electricity and soon thereafter little machines amused crowds with their capacity to crack the air with miniature lightning.

As scientists learned more about the mysterious force, it soon became clear that two different types of electricity existed. Batteries generated a constant current, which physicians referred to as galvanism. By contrast, faradism requires a mechanical contrivance, which sometimes was operated in concert with a battery to generate pulses of electricity, resulting in an alternating current. It was only a matter of time before doctors started using both types of electricity.

Skilled operators of electrical medicine drew distinctions between the continuous and alternating currents. Galvanism, or the application of continuous current, was a favorite for diseases of the central nervous system. Physicians believed that a vital energy coursed through the nervous system and any number of organic lesions could disrupt the flow. A steady dose of continuous current overcame the obstructions commonly believed to be the root cause of paralysis. The use of alternating currents, or faradism, worked best with peripheral nerves and muscle diseases. In most cases, the electricity was applied closest to the points of the presumed the internal nerve damage.

The Abraham Man almost met his match with electricity. Practitioners of electrical medicine touted the idea that "Shamming certain diseases for the purpose of extortion, or for exciting compassion or interest, and avoiding the necessity of work, is much more frequent than is generally supposed."[59] Imagine the malingerer, pretending some loss of function in a limb, heartened by a physician's diagnosis of possible paralysis, and then facing an unknown, mysterious contraption that delivers a powerful jolt. The shirker's yelp of pain, and the electrically-induced

---

58 Julius Althaus, *Notes on the use of galvanism and faradism* (London: Longmans and Company, 1876), 2-36.

59 Ibid.

involuntarily muscle contraction, both gave evidence of the shammer's deceit.

Another disorder which bedeviled doctors while excusing its sufferers from exertion was hysterical paralysis. Hysterical paralysis most commonly affected young women, yet despite its functional, nonphysical etiology, it rarely brought the same moral opprobrium as malingering. This was a difficult condition to treat and even ardent advocates of electrical therapies rarely reported success with galvanism or faradism.[60]

It only seemed logical that electrical therapists would turn their apparatuses towards healing a disturbed mind. Physicians theorized that some mental disorders developed after cerebral congestion robbed the brain of necessary nutrients. It seemed axiomatic that the lethargy, insomnia, and dysphoria associated with a malignant melancholia were a direct result of the brain's impaired physiology. The doctor would apply electrodes to the base of the neck, hoping the electricity would relieve the cerebral congestion. If successful, the faradism would ostensibly improve cerebral blood flow, increase the supply of nutrients to the brain, and resolve the morbid despondency. In a similar fashion, some doctors believed that the incipient, silent phase of insanity, when a person's behavior steadily grew more worrisome, could be traced to an irritable nervous system. Electricity could calm the nerves and possibly forestall a descent into madness.[61]

Perhaps the physicians operating on the battlefields and in the hospitals of the Civil War had a distant awareness of electrical therapy but such contrivances could not relieve a soldier's pain and suffering from combat injuries. Military doctors used general anesthetics such as chloroform; they treated pain with narcotics; and they only heard distant whispers of sterile surgery. It was not until 1867 that Joseph Lister, the pioneer of sterile surgical technique, published his ground-breaking discoveries.[62]

Doctors, overwhelmed by physical casualties, could hardly be faulted for ignoring a soldiers' sentiments. Study of the mind remained embryonic but, perhaps propelled by certain maladies of the Civil War, attracted the attention of a small number of studious doctors. Among the curiosities of the mind that fascinated some doctors was a little discussed condition called nostalgia.

---

60 Ibid.
61 Ibid.
62 Joseph Lister, "On the antiseptic principle in the practice of surgery," *The London Lancet* 12, (1867): 741-5.

Nostalgia was a quirky disorder which variously infuriated and infatuated Civil War surgeons. Amidst the gore of battlefield wounds a silent sufferer, sporting no visible wounds, wasted away, sometimes culminating in an inglorious death. Nostalgia was a disorder of the mind, a morbid form of homesickness which nearly every soldier, in its milder forms, could identify with. Busy surgeons scoffed at the concept and turned their attention to the daily carnage, but a few doctors were amazed that nostalgia could rob people of the will to live. Surely some scammers made a lame effort to copy the disease in an effort to steal compassion, but what separated the malingerers and lesser forms of homesickness was the depth of despair. The victim of nostalgia withdrew from all social intercourse, assumed a listless lassitude, and forsook all nourishment in a downward spiral towards death. A few decades after the War ended, a keen observer poetically described nostalgia.

> "Oh Strange, O Most Mysterious disease
> That layest hold upon the heart of man —
> La Grippe of soul from Isles of Discontent
> For whose attacks there remedy is none..."[63]

Nostalgia, a malignant form of melancholia, was indeed difficult to treat. The difficulty arose from its very simple cure: a ticket home, which if liberally applied would have spread through every army camp with a virulence unrivaled by the worst infectious disease. Most doctors ignored nostalgia. However, in some respects the efforts of the few who looked into it represented the first serious sustained study of the emotional consequences of war.

Another emotional disorder of the mid-nineteenth century was hysteria, which occurred mostly in women. Sage surgeons of the period attempted to steer a wide berth around it, while at the same time recognizing that the disorder could complicate diagnosis and treatment. The more astute surgeons understood hysteria to be a mental disorder chiefly characterized by emotional dysregulation. Literary authors accentuated dramatic emotional swings as the hallmark of hysteria, but a more accurate medical description focused on the hysteric's incredible capacity to simulate physical diseases. In that respect, hysteria overlapped with malingering, making detection of the Abraham Man even more difficult.

The hysterical patient, most often a young woman, would present with a physical malady. Maybe she complained of a painful limb and,

---

63   Wheeler Rand and John Rand, *Random rhymes medical and miscellaneous* (Boston: Otis Clapp and Son, 1897), 47.

when touched ever so lightly, would scream in agony. If the same patient was briefly distracted, and heavy pressure applied to the affected limb, the hysteric would betray herself by emitting no sign of discomfort. Through such artifice, the clever medical diagnostician separated the real from the fanciful. The same techniques crudely identified the Abraham Man. The central feature distinguishing hysteria, aside from gender, was motivation. The hysteric's sole motivation in posing as an invalid was to gain attention and keep doctors, family and friends firmly rotating in her orbit. The Abraham Man, on the other hand, had baser intentions, such as avoiding military duty. From this reason, the malingerer faced a harsher social response than the hysteric. Knowledgeable doctors likened hysteria to a sponge, capable of absorbing any symptom in the environment. As a consequence, wise practitioners never treated the hysterical symptoms as real, since that only reinforced the actor's presentation. Surgeons recommended patience, time, rest, and relaxation as conservative treatments which, while they might not provide recovery, certainly would not worsen the disorder.[64]

Students of hysteria often focused on the dramatic displays. The hysteric's behavior oscillated rapidly and often, with no discernible provocation. At one moment she might plumb the depths of despair ,followed an instant later by giddy, silly behavior. In a world still infused with substantial moral interpretations of behavior, many observers derisively dismissed hysteria as the product of a weak will, unable to restrain emotions. This immoderate, alternating expression of joy or dysphoria both captivated and repelled the audiences forced to witness the spectacle.

The hysteric's exaggerated presentation of physical and emotional symptoms always carried an aura of implausibility, challenging the compassion the actress desperately craved. Certain physical manifestations, such as *globus hystericus*, were essentially pathognomonic of hysteria. Globus hystericus was a tightening of the throat, with an accompanying fear of swallowing, which often heralded the onset of anorexia and seizures. Hysterical seizures often began with an imagined abdominal fullness which traveled to the throat and left the victim in a panic-stricken state. Breathing became labored and then in an explosive moment, the victim began violently thrashing about. The emotional seizure lasted for a protracted period, frightening onlookers but guarantying a rapt audience. An observant physician, well-schooled in the ways of hysteria,

---

64 Robert Druitt, *The principles and practice of modern surgery* (Philadelphia: Henry C. Lea, 1867), 41-3.

could differentiate hysterical seizures from epilepsy. The distinguishing features the doctor could count on included the lack of foaming at the mouth, tongue biting, and shallow but not extinguished breath sounds.[65]

The etiology of hysteria remained a mystery in the nineteenth century. Most physicians accepted it as a nervous disorder principally manifested by emotional dysregulation. Although hysteria was not unknown in men, this was by far the exception. Because of its predilection for women, and the nature of onset, hysteria seemed tied to the reproductive cycle. Attacks of hysteria commonly occurred during menstruation, pregnancy, and parturition. Since the etiology was uncertain, it might have logically followed that treatment was also tentative. Interestingly, many physicians of this era exercised a wise restraint in treating hysteria. Perhaps the unpredictable nature of the disorder combined with a whiff of deceit served notice on doctors to proceed with caution.

The wild, out-of-control antics so commonly associated with hysteria exhausted many patients, as well as the families, and many physicians sought to quell the disturbance with a potent sedative. This was a treacherous course since "any of the narcotics may in exceptional cases produce an opposite effect from that which was intended ... Even when the patient is easily narcotized it is doubtless true that the habit of taking such remedies as the bromide of potassium or the hydrate of chloral in increasing quantities, may finally work serious mischief." Despite this fairly widespread concern, the temptation to terminate purposeless flailing, fits of crying alternating with incongruous joy, and belligerence bordering on assault, resulted in the very liberal prescription of addicting medications. In fact, some critics suggested that nearly half of all female complaints, physical or emotional, could trace their origin to a dependence on opium. A more conservative management of hysteria emphasized restraint in the use of any medication, instead favoring rest, relaxation, mental diversions, and a change of environment. Some advocates claimed that hysterical seizures could be brought to an abrupt close by bathing the head in copious amounts of cold water.[66]

The hysteric, like the Abraham Man, sometimes invited a coarse response from physicians. As a malingerer's duplicitous efforts to avoid a task or extort a favor preyed on doctors' compassion, the hysterical patient also earned some resentment from doctors, mostly for wasting their

---

65 Austin Flint, *A treatise on the principles and practice of medicine* (Philadelphia: Henry C. Lea, 1868), 717-25.

66 Reuben Ludlum, *Lectures, clinical and didactic on the diseases of women* (Chicago: S. S. Halsey, 1872), 292-315.

valuable time with simulated sickness. With the hysteric it seemed all too obvious that the exaggerated behavior was meant solely to captivate and control onlookers. But hysterical behavior, in all of its varieties, fascinated a small group of physicians. This purely emotional disease could simulate any physical condition, even pregnancy. As doctors probing this mysterious malady gained a greater appreciation of mental processes, a small band of physicians began to undertake a serious study of insanity.

Around the time of the Civil War the study of psychological medicine was just gaining the attention of academically-oriented physicians. This was not a popular field of study owing to the dangerous, unpredictable nature of the mentally ill. In addition, the chronic, unrelenting nature of the disorder seemed to fit better with institutional care provided in almshouses, jails, or later in large hospitals. Medical schools rarely mentioned the subject. The one exception was the highly respected and frequently consulted *Manual of Psychological Medicine*,[67] which was issued in successive editions. When the Southern States forcefully left the Union with a history-making bombardment of Ft. Sumter, the *Manual of Psychological Medicine* was entering its second version.

In the mid-nineteenth century, various authors proposed diagnostic classifications of the mental disorders, but none garnered a widespread following. The broadest labels, insanity, mania, dementia, and melancholia, found a sort of universal acceptance but the nosology beyond this limited field was fractured. Mania seemed to break into the most pieces, almost as if the frenetic nature of the disorder infected the classification schemes. Physicians might speak of monomania, homicidal mania, suicidal mania, kleptomania, erotomania, pyromania, and dipsomania. Insanity might be delusional or emotional, partial or full. Naturally, the lay public was content to label the whole lot as mad or lunatic, only learning of the diagnostic intricacies when newspapers published detailed testimonies of physician witnesses deposed in a sensational legal matter.

Physicians seemed to agree even less when discussing the presumed etiology of lunacy. Clearly, the various types of insanity seemed to be partially or fully transmitted to succeeding generations, as documented in family histories. Head trauma, ranging from injuries at birth to the countless examples in later life, also correlated with insanity. The mysterious hysterical insanity occasioned curiosity as did the poorly understood concept of epileptic insanity. An astonishing array of toxic sub-

---

67 John Charles Bucknill and Daniel Hack Tuke, *A manual of psychological medicine* 4th Ed. (London: J & A Churchill, 1879), iii-iv.

stances, such as alcohol, opium, lead, and even marsh miasma, were seen to upset a person's delicate mental balance. Physicians also considered insanity a byproduct of modern civilization with its intricate, confusing demands which required constant mental activity. The constant stress was understood to create an unnatural mental overload resulting in a nervous breakdown, a condition almost unheard of in "less civilized" societies. Even the moon's potential influence on behavior, which might seem like the sort of notion a physician would deride, remained an open question. The relationship between the phases of the moon and madness was enshrined in the popular term of the day, "lunacy." Benjamin Rush studied the moon's influence on madness, and while he did not discard the entire idea, he modified the theory. Rush believed the light from the moon, or its absence, was a decisive factor affecting human emotions, and he offered as evidence the notion that darkness calmed and bright light energized the manic patient.

The mid-nineteenth century physician could broadly lump insanity under two causal factors, moral and physical. The moral causes of insanity included domestic strife, religious excitement, an emotionally traumatic event, overwhelming fear, and an excessive devotion to work. The physical causes of insanity included the usual culprits and vices such as an over-indulgence in liquor, excessive interest in sex, onanism, fever, starvation, sunstroke, head injury, pregnancy, lactation, and menstruation. Among all of the causes, careful studies concluded that nearly half of all newly diagnosed cases of insanity could be traced to overindulgence in alcohol.[68]

The census of 1870 reported "36,786 lunatics and 24,395 idiots in asylums across America, or 1 such person out of 622 across the country."[69] The same asylums reported an astonishing 72% cure rate in the first three months of the illness.[70] In reality, a cure simply meant that the insanity had subsided to the point that a person could be discharged. No doubt, the insanity smoldered on, only to reignite at some future point, possibly leading to another short stint at the local asylum.

At least intuitively, it would seem that the Great War that tore America apart should have led to a spike in the number of mentally ill. The stress of the conflict invaded every social and economic nook and cranny. However, the reported cases of insanity actually declined. An asylum su-

---

68 Ibid., 34-45.
69 Ibid., 116.
70 Ibid., 120.

perintendent, and contemporary commentator noted, "The breaking out of the war in 1861 was attended by a great and sudden increase for a few months of cases of mental disorder. It may also be noted as a remarkable fact, that while a great increase was noticeable at the commencement of the war, yet after the attention of the country was fully engrossed in its prosecution and in all the cares and duties consequent upon its continuance, mental disorders were less frequent ..."[71] It seems a strange conclusion, but the war had a salutary impact on mental activity, perhaps by trivializing the emotional vicissitudes experienced during the preceding years of peace and prosperity.

Among all the various mental disorders, for the public, insanity captured the essence of madness. The lunatic was unpredictable, often violent and disrespectful of social conventions. Society resorted to a mixture of compassion, cruelty, control, and connivance to isolate the insane. Despite all of these efforts, the lunatic still managed to run afoul of the law, causing mayhem and murder. In these situations the creaky wheels of justice struggled to cope. In obvious cases of delusional insanity, where the madness was palpable, a fairly quick resolution might land the criminal in an asylum. The asylum superintendent then assumed control of the case and would only allow release if he was satisfied the person was cured. This led, in practical application, to an indeterminate sentence for many insane individuals.

In many cases of criminal insanity, the outcome was less certain. The medical definition of insanity was vague and this afforded endless opportunities to enterprising attorneys. Concepts such as partial insanity were eagerly embraced, especially as professional witnesses at criminal trials offered increasingly expansive, and exculpatory, definitions of insanity. Perhaps no single classification generated as much controversy as moral insanity.

The definition of moral insanity can be traced to James Prichard.[72] Prichard was an English physician frustrated by the multiple, vague descriptions of mental illness. The physician sought to simplify the disparate diagnoses and classify mental disorders, but, probably unwittingly, he stoked controversy by including a new category of illness he termed "moral insanity." According to Prichard's characterization, moral insanity could, at times, be traced to a family history of insanity. In some unknown fashion, a mutated version of family insanity might afflict the off-

---

71 Ibid., 102.

72 James C. Prichard, *A treatise on insanity and other disorders affecting the mind* (Philadelphia: E. L. Carey and A. Hart, 1837), 20-9.

spring with a peculiar form of madness. Over time, the person's behavior became increasingly capricious, with every whim requiring instant gratification. The victim of moral insanity was like a butterfly aimlessly flitting from one outrageous act to another. To the observer, the behavior appeared tempestuous, often incited by the tiniest obstacle blocking indulgence. If the behavior continued unchecked, it typically culminated in the financial ruin of a family, incarceration, and even a violent death.

A surprising but key feature of moral insanity, according to Prichard, involved the preservation of the intellect but the crippling of the ethical faculties. If he asked the person why he or she had engaged in such egregious conduct, the interrogator would receive a thoughtful and superficially logical response. Delusions and hallucinations, the sine qua non of traditional lunacy, were not features of moral insanity. A high browed, contemporary description of the disorder noted, "He suffers from entire perversion of the moral principles, from the want of every good and honest sentiment."[73] Less flattering and simpler vocabulary actually did a better job portraying the concept. Once stripped of the medical label of moral insanity, the individual stood exposed as an impulsive, selfish, cruel, sadistic, reckless criminal who reveled in licentious conduct.

Moral insanity infected its victim slowly, beginning in early adulthood and insidiously eroding the social restraints which govern civil behavior. As the mind succumbed to immoral thoughts and behavior, an unrelenting irritability kept friends and family at bay. The chronic petulance was probably a byproduct of the endless obstacles and frustrations which prevented the immediate gratification of some depraved desire. As the disease took root, the irritability spawned paranoia, frequently aimed at a person's spouse. Insane jealously, characterized by an endless, suspicious preoccupation doubting a partner's fidelity, dominated all aspects of the morally insane person's life. A deep-seated dysphoria fanned the flames of paranoia with alternating themes of suicide and homicide. In many cases the assaultive impulse won the battle and resulted in the commission of a criminal act.

Physicians, and asylum superintendents in particular, passionately debated the existence of moral insanity. The opponents reckoned, as seems correct today, that the concept of moral insanity medicalized and thereby excused purely criminal behavior. Nowhere in the lexicon of moral insanity could anyone locate irrational thinking, bizarre ide-

---

73 John Charles Bucknill and Daniel Hack Tuke, *A manual of psychological medicine* 4th Ed. (London: J & A Churchill, 1879), 30, 102, 116-19, 244.

ations, delusions or hallucinations. In fact, the concept of moral insanity assumed these faculties were spared at the expense of the emotional, ethical portion of the mind. As a consequence, proponents of the concept argued that victims of moral insanity could not control their feelings, appetites, and desires. Opponents argued in turn that violation of commonly held moral precepts was a conscious choice, an abdication of religious teachings, and a dangerous blight on society. The vigorous dispute often landed in court. The notion of moral insanity could be ruthlessly employed to exonerate virtually any criminal act. In actual court room application, a strenuous defense using moral insanity essentially equated any and all criminal behavior with mental disease. Moral insanity was a flawed idea which, while seemingly compassionate, threatened to upend the judicial system.

James Prichard described an even more controversial variant of moral insanity manifested by a victim's fanatical faith.[74] Imagine the relief among family members when a previously immoral son suddenly made a righteous turn and became the paragon of piety. Unfortunately, the breathtaking transformation soon revealed a dark side. The same traits which previously dominated the person's behavior such as arrogance, irritability, and impulsiveness were now filtered through hyper-religious fervor. The slightest social provocation was an invitation to critically judge, condemn, and punish non-believers. Victims of this variant of moral insanity lacked charity and compassion, opting instead for a hard, relentless cruelty cloaked by a pseudo fascination with religion.

The progressive Doctor Prichard was among the avant-garde in challenging the favorable social commentary on the role of religion in America. He cited the damage of religious fervor by noting, "Strong emotions excited by vehement preaching, produce continually, in females and very sensitive persons, fits of hysteria, and in those who are predisposed to mania there can be no doubt that similar causes give rise to attacks of madness."[75]

A contemporary of his, and a vocal critic of hyper religiosity, was Amariah Brigham. Brigham authored a landmark treatise examining the deleterious impact of religion on physical and mental health. Amariah Brigham penned his controversial thoughts about three decades before the Civil War. In a country and a time when religious influence was the

74 James C. Prichard, *A treatise on insanity and other disorders affecting the mind* (Philadelphia: E. L. Carey and A. Hart, 1837), 20-9.
75 Amariah Brigham, *Observations on the influence of religion upon the health and physical welfare of mankind* (Boston: Marsh, Capen, and Lyon, 1835), 275-6.

bedrock of most communities, any criticism resonated only among the most progressive thinkers. Brigham pays due homage to the role of spirituality before attacking it. "The Religious Sentiment appears to be innate in man. It forms a part of his nature as truly as benevolence, or attachment; and like all our sentiments, it is stronger in some individuals than others ..."[76] Over the course of succeeding chapters, Brigham traces the evolutionary history of mysticism, religion, and science. He concludes that faith, the absence of critical judgment and the recognition of a higher power, is a universal human trait. The author notes a subtle transformation, marked by the growth and development of religious thought, as it adjusts and adapts to social change. Organized religion can point to repeated examples of reformation as faith-based systems struggle to remain a central force defining the essence of social morality. Over time, though, religion's grip on the moral levers of human behavior slipped, corresponding with a rise in secular control of society through law enforcement agencies.

Brigham drew a distinction between the ordinary, perhaps even devout, practice of religion and the zealot who succumbs in frenzy to hyper-religiosity. Leading physicians of the time advanced a theory that mental excitement of any sort increased brain activity. The brain required extra energy, in the form of increased blood flow, to accommodate the demands. A perpetual state of mental excitement saturated the brain, increasing the likelihood of seizures, strokes, and insanity as a consequence of this cerebral congestion. Brigham buttressed his theory that equated cerebral congestion with insanity through autopsies which apparently provided physical evidence of brain injury.

Dr. Brigham indicted religious excitation as a leading cause of insanity, writing, "In all ages, this has been one of the most fruitful sources of the disease."[77] A person predisposed to develop insanity, and precariously holding madness at bay, might succumb after attending a religious revival, obsessively entertaining and endlessly warding off impure thoughts, or through an intense spiritual rebirth. The roller coaster of emotions unleashed as the person soared with religious exhalation and then sank to the depths of despair rattled the shaky mental architecture to its core.

Having laid out a persuasive argument connecting mental illness with religious fervor, Brigham set forth a number of suggestions to blunt the damage. Brigham faintly condemned the clergy by applauding their good

---

76 Ibid., 2.
77 Ibid., 275.

intentions even as they harmed many people. As a tonic for the disease of religious fervor, Brigham suggested the clergy become acquainted with brain anatomy and physiology. By appealing to men of faith through science, the good doctor sought to temper the clergy's scintillating sermons, by explaining the delicate nature of man's brain.

In some respects Brigham's concerns were prescient. In the years after the Civil War, a religious and spiritual boom echoed across the country. Cult-like communities banded together in an effort to rewrite long-established social contracts. Impressionable young adults joined the groups hoping for a better life. The murder of President Garfield ignited the debate about religion and insanity. Charles Guiteau, the assassin, spent several years in a utopian group and later blamed the experience for warping his mind.

The mid-nineteenth century doctor stood on the brink of a scientific revolution shaping the diagnosis and treatment of insanity. Part of the change was reflected in doctors' increasing acceptance of insanity as a byproduct of a physical disorder. Even so, most physicians remained deeply religious and struggled to reconcile their moral views with their scientific theories. The omnipresent Abraham Man, more than a perpetual nuisance, actually propelled the march of science by exposing the doctors' diagnostic deficiencies and forcing the physicians to exercise greater skill in separating the real from the unreal. As they did so, bitter disputes arose and the principal protagonists battled for recognition, credibility, and the role as America's undisputed insanity experts.

CHAPTER 3: HAMMOND'S WAY

One of the greatest medical duals of the nineteenth century simmered uneasily during the Great American Conflict. The two principal future adversaries built solid professional reputations, one in the military and one in a large asylum. Their careers were dissimilar but the forces driving each man, ambition, power, and adulation, were similar. Their shared personality traits acted like a magnet, with the same poles facing each other, and led to a violent repulsion. At first, these two extraordinarily strong-willed men remained distant from each other but, in time, a number of factors brought them closer together. Perhaps the foremost factor was an intense desire to be in the spotlight, and the court rooms of America served their vanity well. Most physicians avoided attorneys like a plague, but a few ventured into the swampy waters, swirling with controversy and conflict. Our two protagonists mostly settled for the power to shape verdicts and distanced themselves from their money-grubbing colleagues, hoping to remove any pecuniary taint that might prejudice their medical legal opinions. In the post-Civil War years, the two men developed an increasingly bitter rivalry, from which modern psychiatry, neurology, and modern medical-legal practices were born.

John P. Gray and William A. Hammond were the principal protagonists; around them orbited a number of lesser but still influential physicians. Both men were well educated, experienced clinical administrators, and respected medical authors. Both were famously known as adversarial, fearless, dogmatic and with a bottomless self-confidence bordering on arrogance. Between the two, Hammond suffered the peaks and troughs of success and failure more publicly and acutely. His hot temper boiled over on many occasions, often scalding both the subject of his scorn and himself. Despite this seemingly self-defeating streak, Hammond's intellectual force and his moral fortitude ensured long-term success.

William Alexander Hammond was born in Annapolis, Maryland, in 1828. William earned a medical degree from the University of the City of New York, and shortly thereafter, he began his career as a frontier assistant surgeon in 1849. With his new wife, Hammond traveled west, taking several months before arriving at his new Army duty station in New Mexico. The US Army, particularly in the western regions, was fighting various Indian tribes. It was a desolate, mostly boring life. No doubt the unit's morale was fairly low, with tedium interrupted by the risk of leaving the relative safety of the fort to attack the Indians.

Hammond spent eleven years in the army, moving from post to post, from West Point to Ft. Riley, Kansas, and Ft. Mackinac, Michigan. Common ailments presenting at sick call would include infections, diarrhea, constipation, fever, cough, and congestion. Ill-defined symptoms such as rheumatism suggested malingering and challenged the doctor's diagnostic skills. After a time, the novelty of frontier medical practice wore off and was replaced by a dull, monotonous routine. Hammond countered his boredom with the study of human anatomy and physiology. He published an article, titled "The Nutritive Value and Physiological Effects of Albumin, Starch, and Gum, when singly and exclusively used as Foods," which received national recognition. Hammond was building a reputation as a respected medical authority.

Hammond left military service and joined the faculty at the University of Maryland in 1860. Despite the prestige of the position, little money accompanied the appointment, forcing the doctor to supplement a meager income with a small clinical practice. Meanwhile, social storm clouds were gathering. The citizens of Maryland counted many Southern sympathizers and with the Civil War just months away, Hammond found his decidedly pro-Union stance at odds with that of some colleagues. In any event, as a loyal Army veteran, and despite receiving no credit for his eleven previous years of service, he happily donned the medical officer's uniform once again.

Hammond was ordered into Western Maryland to set up hospitals in anticipation of casualties. A promotion to a position as Inspector of Union Hospitals followed the successful tour of duty in Maryland. This placed Hammond in a close working relationship with the Sanitary Commission. The Sanitary Commission assumed a central role in prodding the Union Army to adopt a wide range of policies to promote battlefield medical care. As the Army Medical Department struggled to organize the necessary war support, the Sanitary Commission urged the appointment of William Hammond as Surgeon General. This was a prestigious position and Hammond's quick advancement rankled many. His critics complained about Hammond's junior status and political inexperience. Secretary of War Stanton favored another candidate. The relationship between Stanton and Hammond began on a most unsettled basis and progressively deteriorated. Both were strong willed, but Stanton had the advantage in terms of authority and political chicanery.

Oblivious of the coming storm, Hammond set about, in his characteristic manner, to overhaul and up-end the creaking Army Medical Department. Among his chief accomplishments, the new Surgeon General methodically set in motion a revamped and more rigorous examining board for prospective military doctors. Medical training at the time was not standardized and many different paths, ranging from university education to apprenticeships, could qualify a person to become a clinical doctor. Medical education also splintered into philosophically distinct and competing theories, which created fertile ground for hucksters, frauds, and charlatans.

The new Surgeon General quickly expanded the supply list for hospitals, providing comfort items such as hospital clothing, bedding, and other medical supplies. In some respects this was Hammond's most important contribution. It certainly improved patient care.[78]

Another notable contribution, far reaching in its vision but pragmatic, was Hammond's insistence that field medical reports be more detailed, and slowly but surely the field medical reports included more details about wounds and illnesses. The Surgeon General's insistence paid off with the post-war publication of the "*Medical and Surgical History of the War of the Rebellion.*" The expanded field reports formed the basis for the factual tabulations in the book's comprehensive summary of the Civil War.[79]

---

78 The Surgeon Generals of the United States Army: XI. Brigadier General William Alexander Hammond, Surgeon General, of the United States Army, 1862-1864, *Association of Military Surgeons of the United States Meeting* 15, (1904):145-155.

79 Champe C. McCulloch, LTC, "The scientific and administrative achievement of the Medical Corps of the United States Army," *Scientific Monthly* 4, no. 1 (1917): 412-3.

Unlike most of his colleagues, Hammond was fascinated by mental problems. America in 1863 was mostly rural and the soldiers, who typically had strong family ties, often came from isolated locations. The needs of the war transported many soldiers long distances from their homes. Active campaigns focused the soldiers' attention on the battlefield, but armies in garrison, winter weather, and siege tactics all created long stretches of boredom. During these protracted lulls many soldiers naturally turned their thoughts towards home. For most this was a pleasant diversion, but a small number succumbed to a morbid preoccupation called nostalgia.

Hammond described nostalgia as an obsessive focus on home life which created depression, decreased appetite, digestive problems, fever, exhaustion, and even death. Nostalgia primarily affected the youngest soldiers. The disorder could run rampant in hospitals near the wounded soldier's home. For this reason alone, Hammond recommended hospitals be built near the battlefield.

Hypochondria was another emotional problem more commonly seen among men. This problem occurred when the soldier spent too much time worrying about his health. Doctors treated hypochondria and nostalgia by increasing mental and physical activity.[80]

Hammond deplored the excessive use of alcohol but its consumption in moderation was extolled. The typical Civil War doctor viewed alcohol as a beneficial stimulant which restored energy. Hammond believed accessory foods played a vital role in sustaining soldiers in the field. Accessory foods included condiments, alcohol, tea, coffee, and tobacco. Condiments made food more palatable and aided digestion. Vinegar was a common condiment included in the Union soldier's rations. Many doctors believed that all actions of the mind and body led to a corresponding reduction in the vital energies of the organs. Only by eating food could the process of tissue destruction be reversed and strength restored. Many accessory foods also slowed the process of degeneration.

Hammond's position as Surgeon General and the need for fast growth in the medical infrastructure provided the perfect opportunity to build special hospitals. The Surgeon General had an inexhaustible curiosity and the sheer magnitude of casualties flowing from the battlefield to the hospitals magnified all manner of maladies. Minor pathologies, previously exciting no interest because of their infrequency, generated a surge of concern. The Abraham Man, wearing a Jacob's coat knit together

---

80 Ibid., 129-31.

not with colors but multiple symptoms, sowed confusion, concern, and acrimony.

The emotional problems of war also surfaced for the first time in sufficient numbers to merit study. Battlefield nerve injuries, manifesting with diverse presentations, also captured attention. Malingering, neurologic disorders, and combat stress frequently intermingled creating a fairly indistinguishable mixture. Treatment or management depended on the extent to which the components could be separated. Surgeons in the field had precious little time to manage the muddle, instead opting for a medical version of Alexander's solution of the Gordian Knot by simply eliminating the problem through a medical evacuation. Some of these medical conundrums eventually made their way to Turner's Lane Hospital in Philadelphia. Turner's Lane Hospital was a 400-bed facility specializing in the treatment and study of nerve injuries.[81]

Pretty much throughout his tenure as the Army Surgeon General, Secretary of War Edwin Stanton and William Hammond engaged in a series of political battles.

Hammond, with his feisty style, clashed with his boss. A particularly frosty exchange occurred when the pair first met. Hammond found Stanton's comment insolent: "if you have the enterprise, the knowledge, the intelligence, and the brains to run the Medical Department, I will assist you." Hammond bluntly responded, "I am not accustomed to be spoken to in that manner by any person, and I beg you will address me in more respectful terms... During my service in the army, I have been thrown with gentlemen, who, no matter what our relative rank was, treated me with respect. Now that I have become Surgeon-General, I do not intend to exact anything less than I did when I was Assistant Surgeon, and I will not permit you to speak to me in such language as you have just used." Stanton's reply was brusque and to the point, "Then, sir, you can leave my office immediately."[82]

Stanton eventually succeeded in removing Hammond through a rather devious maneuver. Secretary Stanton ordered Hammond to begin a round of medical inspections in New Orleans, then swiftly installed a new Surgeon General. In the fall of that year, Hammond received a

---

81 Horace Magoun and Louise Marshall, *American neuroscience in the twentieth century: Confluence of the neural, behavioral, and communicative streams* (Lisse, Netherlands: Swets and Zeitlinger Publishers, 2003), 29-30.

82 Mary C. Gillett, *The Army medical department 1818-1865: Center of military history, United States Army, Washington, DC* (Washington, DC: U.S. Government Printing Office, 1987), 177, 201.

curt letter from E.D. Townsend, an Assistant Adjutant General, accusing him of making improper supply purchases, "after you were relieved from the charge of the bureau, and the Secretary regards it as a violation of your duty ..."[83] Hammond politely responded to the Secretary of War, acknowledged that portions of the accusation were true, but countered by noting the medical necessity of the supplies ordered. Towards the end of the same letter, Hammond challenged the Secretary's authority to remove him from office. As might be expected, he received no response.

A few days after returning to Washington, in mid-January 1864, the proud Surgeon General was arrested. Hammond confidently awaited his public trial, certain it could only vindicate his honorable military service.

The prosecutor, Judge Advocate Bingham, listed three charges under which he accused William A. Hammond of eleven total specifications of criminal misconduct. The first charge, "Disorders and neglect to the prejudice of good order and military discipline," contained eight of the specifications. Hammond was accused of illegally buying hospital blankets and extract of beef, both, according to the charge, of such poor quality as to render their use impossible. The second charge, with one specification, accused Hammond of "Conduct unbecoming an officer and a gentleman." The third charge, "Conduct to the prejudice of good order and military discipline," rehashed the alleged illegal purchase of the hospital blankets.

Bingham was a venomous prosecutor who pursued the charges against Hammond with a vigor best reserved for serious crimes. His fanatical conduct earned many rebukes from the trial judge, but it did little to dissuade the prosecutor. The jury, perhaps underwhelmed by the passionate prosecution and the insignificance of the charges, initially signaled their resolve to acquit. Alarmed by a possible public vindication, the trial judge ordered the jury to reconsider. Curiously, after an additional period of thoughtful deliberation, the jury found Hammond guilty on nine of the eleven specifications of criminal misconduct. The Surgeon General was relieved of all military duties and dismissed from the Army.[84]

Now deeply in debt and publicly humiliated, Hammond made his way to New York City, where with a renewed sense of purpose he launched a

---

83 Ibid.

84 The Surgeon Generals of the United States Army: XI. Brigadier General William Alexander Hammond, Surgeon General, of the United States Army, 1862-1864, *Association of Military Surgeons of the United States Meeting* 15, (1904):145-155.

fresh career in medicine and writing. In many respects this proved to be a far more successful, and certainly more lucrative, employment.

Although many of his Army colleagues abandoned him, Hammond was blessed with a coterie of loyal civilian friends. The small group banded together and loaned Hammond enough money to buy a house and start his medical practice. J.B. Lippincott, the publisher, also chipped in a tidy sum. Hammond took up the literary trade and published a number of esoteric articles in a popular magazine. Hammond had an appetite for sumptuous living and through hard work he quickly built a large and predictable income. His house in New York matched his personality, eclectic and extravagant. A large library contained thousands of books. His desk sported an eccentric trademark, a pile of cash always conspicuously on display. Hammond carefully crafted his reputation as a prominent social figure in the city and an academician, such as with his appointment as a professor of psychiatry and nervous diseases at the University of the City of New York, and by joining with a small group of like-minded physicians to form the American Neurological Association. The general public knew a different side of Hammond, as author of several works of fiction and plays. To his professional colleagues, Hammond presented a number of facets. He was first and foremost a skilled medical doctor driven by curiosity. This trait lent a certain unfocused aim to his medical work, in which he dabbled in neurology, psychology, medical-legal activities, spiritualism, health, and nutrition.

Hammond distinguished himself with the publication of *A Treatise on Diseases of the Nervous System*. This popular work was frequently updated and remained an authoritative reference of neurologic disorders. Subjects covered included diseases of the brain such as aphasia, meningitis, epilepsy, and hysteria. The large volume also discussed a wide range of peripheral nerve disorders. A section on toxic nerve conditions reviewed the influence of alcohol on the body. Hammond diagnosed nervous disorders through physical examination and detailed clinical histories. The author encouraged the use of medical devices. He advocated the use of galvanic and faradic electrical devices to aid the diagnosis of nerve disorders. The aesthesiometer was a mechanical tool first introduced into American Medical practice in 1861. Its purpose was to determine the presence, absence and degree of sensation present in the skin. Becquerel's Discs were a mechanical contrivance which could determine, with amazing accuracy, the temperature of the skin. A dynamometer measured the muscular strength of the hands. Duchenne's trocar was a forbidding little instrument which, looking like a metal syringe, would puncture a muscle and remove a small fiber for microscopic examination.[85]

It might seem odd that a man devoted to the scientific study of nerve disorders would drift into spiritualism. Hammond was a renaissance man, drawn by a keen intellect and a curious mind, to examine all manner of human endeavors. Spiritualism was a popular influence in the nineteenth century. Hammond dedicated his book *Spiritualism and Allied Causes and Conditions of Nervous Derangement* "to all, few though they be, who are free from superstition".[86] The dedication seems to imply that the text to follow will favorably review the subject. Hammond prudently approached spiritualism by openly declaring no hostility towards religion or science but the gray zone in between. In this region dwelt the ill-informed, the gullible, entertainers, charlatans, and quacks. Hammond divided spiritualists into two camps, occupied by frauds and emotionally disturbed individuals.

Spiritualism and Allied Causes and Conditions of Nervous Derangement is a lengthy book which forcibly attempts to debunk the deceit of spiritualism and link any remaining cases to various emotional disorders. Hammond cast the frauds aside but the emotionally disturbed individuals caught up in the web of spiritualism found a compassionate doctor ready and willing to treat their illness. The detailed dissection was a forerunner of Hammond's approach to unmasking the Abraham Man.

The former Surgeon General relished the prospect of unmasking a fraud. Hammond was a keen observer of human behavior and always on the alert for the Abraham Man. His years of military service, where malingering was an art form, honed his detective skills. His glee was scarcely contained when he wrote, "Upon one occasion, while a so-called 'trance medium' was ... in an assumed state of insensibility, I took the liberty of treading on her foot as it rested under the table... The foot was at once quickly withdrawn, there was an unmistakable contortion of the countenance and a very emphatic "Oh!" escaped from her lips."[87] Hammond interpreted the medium's response as evidence belying the unresponsiveness that accompanies a true trance state.

After dispensing with the Abraham Man, Hammond turned his attention to a real mental behavior that mimicked the medium's artificial

---

85   William A. Hammond, *A treatise on the diseases of the nervous system* (New York: Appleton and Company, 1891), 16-28.

86   William A. Hammond, *Spiritualism and allied causes and conditions of nervous derangement* (New York: G. P. Putnam's Sons, 1876), iii.

87   Ibid., 139.

trance. Somnambulism was a naturally occurring trance like state which intrigued physicians. Otherwise known as sleep-walking, physicians of the nineteenth century studied the curious condition. Hammond related incidents where distressed family members sought his guidance in curing somnambulism. With his trademark attention to detail he would engage the sleep walker in several tests, finally convincing himself that the victim was indeed engaging in what appeared to be purposeful behavior while totally oblivious to their environment. The dissociated mental state of the sleep walker was a true-life trance.

The trance like state of somnambulism existed in a muted form among normal people. Somnambulism was behavior devoid of consciousness. The sleep walker retained no memory of the incident. In a similar fashion, the former Surgeon General observed that many every day behaviors are performed automatically, with no conscious awareness. As Hammond noted, every person can recall an incident of walking a considerable distance, often involving a complicated route, and then arriving at their destination perplexed at the intervening loss of memory. Playing a piano and simultaneously talking, or reading a book in the presence of loud music, are further examples of automatic behavior. The future father of modern neurology believed that automatic behaviors were spinal cord reflexes. In somnambulism, the spinal cord controlled the person's movements while the conscious brain slept.

In some people somnambulism could be induced. Various procedures, some employed by clever mediums, produced a state of artificial somnambulism. Hammond accepted the concept of artificial somnambulism, having witnessed the power of the mind to completely control the pain of a surgical procedure without anesthesia. A number of prominent physicians, including Jean-Martin Charcot the famous French neurologist, dabbled extensively with artificial somnambulism. Charcot became proficient at inducing this altered state of consciousness, otherwise known as hypnosis, among his patients. Hammond believed that the trance state of some mediums came about as a result of self-hypnosis.

The study of artificial somnambulism led Charcot, Hammond, and later, Sigmund Freud, to study hysteria. Hysteria was the unconscious simulation of physical disease, such as blindness or paralysis. Hysterical paralysis shared certain traits with a hypnotically induced trance. In both cases, the person was totally insensible to pain. Hammond reasoned that hysteria was an emotional disorder. Again, recalling his military life, "many a soldier wounded in battle, has not discovered his injury till the heat of the contest was over."[88] Greatly excited emotions overwhelm the sense of pain. The hysteric, suffering some hidden emotional injury, responds by anaesthetizing or numbing, some body part.

Only scientific study sated Dr. Hammond's curiosity and skepticism. To illustrate the value of science over superstition, Hammond discussed a number of odd cases. He did this by exposing misguided, even if well intentioned, interventions that often resulted in bad outcomes. A curious class of cases, known as fasting girls, served this purpose. This particular condition caught the public's attention and dramatized the struggle between medicine, religion, and spiritualism.

Sarah Jacob was ten years old in 1867 and lived in a rural section of England. The little girl's story traveled around the word, informing and amazing readers, about the mystery of extreme fasting. Sarah suffered a series of seizures shortly after her tenth birthday. The seizures were of the *grand mal* type, throwing her entire body into alternating waves of spasm and apparent tranquility. The episodes lasted for a month, at the end of which the little girl was physically spent and exhausted. Aside from the fatigue, Sarah also lost her appetite. As the weeks and months rolled by, Sarah consumed ever smaller amounts of food, finally culminating in the complete abdication of all oral sustenance.

A local pastor frequently visited Sarah's home. As the fasting girl's food and fluid intake steadily dwindled, the pastor at first challenged the parent's claim that divine intervention was supporting Sarah. Eventually the pastor's incredulity faded under the weight of repeated observations. The girl never consumed food and the parents remained steadfast in their conviction of God's intervention. Surprisingly, the young child never displayed any ill effects from the supposed nutritional deprivation, instead actually glowing with good health. Visitors descended on Sarah's house as word of the wonder spread. After witnessing the blessed miracle of the fasting girl, many left gifts or money behind.

In 1869, nearly two years after Sarah started her fasting, the once skeptical pastor penned a short letter proclaiming his unreserved belief in the miracle. In that letter the pastor issued a direct challenge for physicians to disprove the miracle. The pastor probably expected, or at least hoped, that no one would challenge his pious pronouncement. Local community citizens were galvanized by the pastor's letter and sought to throw their weight behind his divine proclamation. A small group of citizens declared their intention to mount a close vigil in Sarah's room

---

88 Ibid., 219.

and prove the miracle of the fasting girl. After two weeks of round-the-clock scrutiny, the citizens emerged to tell their story, and through their collective observations, authenticated the young girl's sustenance-free life. Unfortunately, some in the community challenged the result, pointing out that the observers often left for extended periods of time or were intoxicated.

The fasting miracle, touted by many as proof of God's work on earth, and by a smaller group as a supernatural phenomenon, directly challenged conventional medical thinking. Proper nutrition was a fundamental pillar of emotional and physical well-being and, according to common medical sense, was required for life. A prominent physician accepted the challenge to medical authority and designed a means to settle the matter. The doctor arranged for several nurses to carefully monitor the young child. Nothing escaped the vigilant watch of the nurses. In a few days Sarah showed signs of increasing discomfort, such as restlessness, insomnia, agitation, and muttering. The nurses pleaded with the parents to arrest the decline and offer Sarah sustenance. Sarah's parents would not relent and the steady deterioration resulted in the girl's death in late December, 1869.

The previously pious public arose en masse, condemning both the parents and the nurses. The coroner declared that Sarah's death was due to starvation. Sarah's parents were charged with manslaughter and both convicted. The doctors, and the nurses who created the medical moat which culminated in the starvation, were exonerated.[89]

Hammond weighed in on the burgeoning interest in medical legal practice with his literary tour de force *A Treatise on Insanity in Its Medical Relations*. This monumental work was published in the later years of his professional career, and as such, was liberally sprinkled with rich clinical experiences. Hammond, still nursing grudges against his adversaries after years of contentious court room cases, took a broad swipe at the asylum superintendents in the book's preface, "There are many varieties of mental derangement of which asylum physicians never see the beginning; and there are others, not requiring the restraint of an institution of the kind, which they never see at all. The day has gone by when they were looked upon as the sole exponents of psychological medicine..."[90] Hammond challenged the superintendents' hegemony, defending his own clinical expertise by noting, "I cannot claim to have seen so many cases

89 Ibid. 270-85.

90 William A. Hammond, *A treatise on insanity in its medical relations* (New York: Appleton & Company, 1883), 270-88.

of insanity as the average superintendent of an asylum with its thousand inmates, I do claim that a single case thoroughly studied is worth more as a lesson than a hundred that are simply looked at, and often from afar off. The medical student who dissects one human body is likely to learn more of anatomy than the janitor who sees hundreds of corpses brought to the dissecting-room."[91]

A Treatise on Insanity in Its Medical Relations opened a door into the author's mind and helped explain his approach to forensic cases. Hammond clearly and unequivocally attributed neural activity as the source of man's thinking. The mind was a cognitive organ. He considered the soul a matter of faith and not science. Other physicians attempting to straddle the mind-soul, science-religion debate chose middle, muddled ground. Hammond believed that clear definitions and precise diagnostic classifications removed much of the ambiguity plaguing the field of psychology. Following that prescription, Hammond drew a distinction between medical and legal insanity. Medical insanity described any mental aberration arising from an unhealthy brain. This was a broad definition, which was clinically useful in diagnosing and treating the whole range of mental pathology. Legal insanity was narrow in scope and socially defined. Its purpose was to allow for the compassionate treatment of a small number of mentally ill people, who, after a judicial proceeding, were declared not morally responsible for their criminal behavior. Physicians, politicians, pastors, and the public endlessly fought a tug of war defining the boundary between medical and legal insanity.

Medical insanity encompassed every shade of mental illness between normal behavior and the flagrantly insane. Hammond's classification of mental disorders included several which, although unusual, were located closer to the normal pole of human behavior. Under no circumstance would Hammond have considered these mild mental maladies sufficiently disabling as to meet the test of legal insanity. Many esteemed physicians did not share Hammond's view on this point and many pitched court room battles were fought in an effort to exonerate criminal behavior which exhibited even the slightest hint of mental dysfunction. As might be expected, the Abraham Man preferred the more liberal interpretations.

The milder forms of mental illness were basically stable oddities. Persons afflicted with one of these disorders could manage their life with

91 Ibid.

little disruption. In some cases the disorder almost seemed to aid the ascent of some particularly talented individuals. For the most part, the person suffering from one of these minor disorders was well aware of their peculiarity. This insight, coupled with an intact but weakened will, limited the social damage.

Eccentricity was an example of a mild mental disorder. This condition inhabited the zone closest to normal behavior. In all respects, save one, eccentric individuals passed through life without notice. Hammond believed that eccentricity was inherited and changed little over the course of a person's life. Eccentric people typically magnified an otherwise normal activity, in the process drawing attention to their excesses. An oft cited example was a parsimonious merchant who counted every penny but had what appeared to be an uncontrollable yen to collect certain items. The eccentric merchant might collect coins, art, books, or similar items and travel the world in a quixotic quest to obtain every known example. In some cases, particularly among the super-rich, the acquisition of money was defined less as an accomplishment and more as a specimen of mental illness called eccentricity.

Idiosyncrasies were one notch further away from normality. Individuals afflicted with idiosyncratic behavior were like their eccentric counterparts, fully functional on a day-to-day basis. Their disorder was tightly confined and very specific. Hammond's definition of idiosyncrasies was the forerunner of phobias, and included irrational fears of such things as heights, animals, insects, thunderstorms, and blood. The Abraham Man could easily feign idiosyncratic behavior because they were so specific. Hammond recounted such a case, "I was consulted in the case of a lady who it was said had an idiosyncrasy that prevented her drinking water. Every time she took the smallest quantity of this liquid into her stomach it was at once rejected, with many evident signs of nausea and pain. The patient was strongly hysterical, and I soon made up my mind that either the case was one of simple hysterical vomiting, or that the alleged inability was assumed. The latter turned out to be the truth. I found that she drank in private all the water she wanted, and that what she drank publicly she threw up by tickling the fauces with her fingernail when no one was looking."[92]

A person's habitual conduct could also be categorized in terms of temperament. This represented a resurrection of ancient philosophy when Hammond reintroduced the sanguine, phlegmatic, choleric, and

---

92 Ibid.

nervous temperaments. Hammond urged his readers to carefully asses a person's temperament since this held important clues about their character. A sanguine individual was an extrovert, full of energy but short on consistency. Their disposition could culminate in mania. Hammond recommended they avoid alcohol and other stimulants. The phlegmatic character was the opposite of the sanguine. They were ponderous in nature, slow to react but possessed a great perseverance. Phlegmatic folks approached ideas and projects warily but once adopted they tenaciously sought success. Choleric persons were powerful, decisive, and prickly. They suffered fools poorly. Their lofty ideals, and impatience with achieving them, often led to a brooding melancholia. The nervous temperament habitually approached life with timidity. According to Hammond these asthenic individuals, weak and passive by nature, defined a large swath of male denizens of banks and other business offices. Hysteria and insanity was common among the nervous types.

Hammond often returned to one of his favorite subjects, sleep, in explaining both normal and abnormal mental functioning. The author believed that dreams were a universal human experience and seemed to offer unique insights into a person's psyche. Philosophers, scientists, mystics, and clerics tried to make sense of the senseless night time reveries. Hammond joined the ageless effort questioning the purpose of dreams and settled on a scientific answer. The underpinning of dreams, according to Hammond, was memories and sensations. The memory fodder feeding the dreams can range from recent matters to long forgotten trivial events. Sensations can also fuel dream work such as cramped, hot, noisy, or sunny accommodations. A distressing nocturnal cacophony, for example, could be reinvented in the dream as a pleasant symphony or a dangerous descent to Hades. During sleep, the imagination is unfettered by the will. As a consequence, the mind is free to construct, from memories and sensations, the most fantastic stories.

Clerics and clairvoyants celebrated the prophetic power of dreams. Hammond also recognized the prognostic importance of dreams but ascribed the connection to medical causes. Citing numerous historical and personal clinical experiences, Hammond sought to convince the reader that prodromal or prophetic dreams arose from real diseases. During sleep the mind is acutely sensitive to the slightest sensations, one of which might be a subsyndromal illness. A dreamer might focus on a sore throat, for example, followed in a few days by rip roaring tonsillitis. Physicians could consult various medical references which correlated content with the disease portended by the dream. Sometimes prodromal dreams had a morbid outcome. A particularly frightening dream, perhaps of a paranoid or murderous nature, might became fixed in the dreamer's mind. Instead of dissolving into oblivion upon awakening, the terrifying dream could unshakably grip the person's imagination. Morbid dreams of this sort often proceeded, or even acted as the exciting cause, of insanity.[93]

As simple as it might seem, the terminology of insanity eluded efforts to forge a widely accepted definition. Legions of attorneys and doctors proposed different ideas, tailored to meet the needs of clinical or legal use. The two professions typically collided with doctors interested in treatment and attorneys in moral responsibility. One area where both groups unwittingly acted in unison was the creation of ever more complex and obscure definitions. One physician's tongue twisting, mind numbing definition stated, "Insanity is either the inability of the individual to correctly register impressions and experiences in sufficient number to serve as rational guides to rational behavior in consonance with the individual's age, tune, and circumstances, or, such impressions and experiences being correctly accumulated in sufficient number, a failure to co-ordinate them, and thereon form logical conclusions, or any other gross mental incongruity with the individual's surroundings in the shape of subjective manifestations of cerebral disease or defect, excluding the phenomena of sleep, trance, somnambulism, the ordinary manifestations of the neuroses, such as epilepsy and hysteria, of febrile delirium, coma, acute intoxication, and the ordinary immediate results of nervous shock and injury." Hammond proposed his own definition of insanity which was characteristically short and simple, "A manifestation of disease of the brain, characterized by a general or partial derangement of one or more faculties of the mind, and in which, while consciousness is not abolished, mental freedom is weakened, perverted, or destroyed."[94]

Hammond reserves the last chapter in *A Treatise on Insanity in Its Medical Relations* to treatment. The majority of this section is reserved for a severe and sustained attack on asylums. The author acknowledged that during the early years of the asylum movement the institutions were a haven for compassionate care but a subsequent series of scandals alleging inhumane treatment had eroded the public's trust. Hammond advised the use of private asylums, and taking a thinly disguised swipe at asylum superintendents, explained that, "the private institutions, the superintendent of which, finding it to his interest to take care of those

---

93 Ibid.
94 Ibid.

committed to his charge, devotes his time and attention and skill to his patients, instead of giving all these to looking after farms and manipulating legislatures".[95]

Clearly Hammond espoused a virulent disdain for insane asylums. In fact, he could only recommend the forsaken, destitute, and dangerous insane for asylum care. It goes without saying that Hammond's views provoked a fiery response from the entrenched bureaucratic interests of the asylums superintendents. Hammond's tolerant treatment of insanity further inflamed the relationship, probably by drawing such stark distinctions. Although he recognized the need to use mechanical restraints, this was a last resort when all less restrictive efforts to protect the insane person failed. Hammond vigorously advocated the hygienic and medical treatment of insanity. Hygienic treatment consisted of mental and physical activities. Mental hygiene included reading, study, organized amusements, and recreational activities. Physical hygiene included cold showers, warm baths, and exercise. Physicians treating insanity could choose from a fairly large *materia medica*. Hammond freely prescribed bromides for insanity, opium for melancholia, chloral hydrate for insomnia, hyosciamus for mania, arsenic as a tonic, and electricity for emotional insanity. Mini bloodletting, through cupping and leeches, was useful for insomnia and agitation.[96]

The specter of the Abraham Man haunted William Hammond. The skeptical physician acted as if the Abraham Man was lurking, and laughing, beside every medical opinion. When spiritualism gained traction in the public's imagination, Hammond immediately detected the deceit inherent in the mystical practice and sought to debunk it. His interest in feigned diseases stretched back to his early years in the Army. Hammond readily acknowledged that military service propagated malingering as soldiers maliciously maneuvered to avoid dangerous duty. One particular example confronted the young Army Doctor while stationed near "a miserable little hamlet" in New Mexico. As Hammond recalled, a large group of Indians descended on the tiny town, rounded up a sizeable number of cattle and mules, and promptly retreated.

The commanding officer of Hammond's unit ordered his troops to retrieve the livestock. Claiming illness, the captain in charge refused the order and instead passed the mission off to a lieutenant. Upon receiving the news, the commanding officer asked Dr. Hammond to examine the

---

95 Ibid.
96 Ibid.

captain. Prompting the decision were previous examples of the same officer getting sick just prior to a deployment. Hammond dutifully obeyed his senior officer's instruction and immediately went to the captain's quarters. As Hammond entered the room, he noticed the officer lounging in a chair, reading a book. The army doctor began his examination and met passive resistance, but eventually learned that eye pain was the chief complaint. A careful examination of the eye showed nothing out of the ordinary. Suspecting the age-old nemesis, the Abraham Man, Hammond confronted the captain with his lack of physical findings. The pseudo patient responded, "If you can see a pain you must be possessed of powers far in advance of the rest of your profession." The insolent remark angered Hammond, but there was little he could do except report his concerns to the commanding officer. The commander repeated his demand that the captain lead his troops in pursuit of the Indians. The captain assembled his unit and left on the mission. About halfway to the destination, the captain returned, complaining of intractable eye pain. His commanding officer was incensed, and following a threat of punishment the captain resigned. Hammond later learned that the officer became a wagon master and frequently bragged about the deception practiced on the surgeon and commander.[97]

In some cases the Abraham Man feigned illness for a different reason. Prisoners and soldiers faked illness and injury to avoid unpleasant duties. Hammond encountered a young woman with a strange story that strained credulity. Initially, the young woman complained of sharp pains near her knees. When it first occurred, she examined the area around her knee and discovered a small metal pin. She then remembered a few weeks before accidently swallowing a needle while getting dressed. The same event happened again a short time later. For some inexplicable reason the woman then developed an insatiable urge to swallow pins. By the time she consulted Hammond, over two hundred and fifty pins had been swallowed, later migrating to the skin at various locations. Hammond was unconvinced but did find a number of pins, head out, protruding from her body. After a period of observation Hammond confronted the woman, promptly receiving a volley of indignation in return. Hammond soothed the woman, trying to reduce the sting of his accusation. She responded and admitted the whole affair was a fraud, solely instigated to curry sympathy among family members.[98]

97 William A. Hammond, "Feigned diseases," *The Sunday Inter Ocean* (Chicago, IL), March 25, 1888.
98 Ibid.

The most likely way to encounter the Abraham Man was through an accident. As the country grew in prosperity one way to achieve the American dream was through litigation. A substantial number of individuals riding the railroads, streetcars, and steamboats claimed a variety of injuries and sued the transportation companies. Hammond was convinced that many of these were bogus claims and to illustrate his point he discussed a typical case. A young man, claiming he fell upon exiting a street car, apparently injured his back and could not easily walk. To support his medical claim, the young man sought an expert opinion from Hammond. The doubtful doctor lightly touched the young man's back, eliciting a piercing cry of pain. Although the patient complained of an excruciating lower leg pain, he demonstrated good muscle tone and strength. With some encouragement, Hammond persuaded the patient to walk about the room, all the while carrying on a conversation with him. The patient was caught unawares by the diversion and his gait dramatically improved. With his quarry subdued, Hammond attacked. "After numerous protestations he confessed that he had been drilled by an attorney to simulate spinal injury with a view to defrauding the railway company."[99]

Another curious cloak sometimes worn by the Abraham Man was the false confession. Hammond believed that a strange mental anomaly compelled certain people, wholly innocent of a crime, to publicly proclaim their guilt. Newspapers would sensationalize some particularly gruesome crime, and the closet confessor would begin his journey with a puzzling preoccupation. The morbid compulsion led the individual to devour every tidbit of news and typically progressed towards independent sleuthing. Acting as a sort of private eye, the false confessor might visit the scene of the crime, interview relatives, and study the victim's life history. Naturally, this detective work drew attention to his behavior, eventually casting an aura of suspicion about him. The long arm of the law would arrest the man who then promptly confessed to the crime. The police exposed the fraud after a bit more investigation. Newspapers celebrated the initial arrest with front page coverage but later hid their embarrassment deep in the publication.[100]

Dr. Hammond put his doubting nature to profitable use as an expert witness. Some of the most celebrated criminal insanity trials of the mid

99 William A. Hammond, "Pretending to be crippled," *Atchison Daily Champion* (Kansas), May 13, 1888.
100 William A. Hammond, "Self-accusation of crime," *The Sunday Inter Ocean* (Chicago, IL), March 11, 1888.

to late nineteenth century witnessed his testimony. Hammond insisted on the primacy of science, not morality, when explaining immoral acts. He firmly believed that insanity arose from a diseased brain, and like many other diseases, had periods of waxing and waning. During quiescent periods the impairment associated with the mental illness could approximate normal behavior, even though the brain remained unhealthy. Passionate debate often erupted in the court room between experts proclaiming that insanity, in any form, robbed the person's capacity to willfully and maliciously commit a crime. The other side of the debate insisted with equal vigor that insanity fluctuated, at times more or less severe. During times of less intensity the insane person could control their behavior, making them culpable for criminal acts.

Many asylum superintendents believed that even mild forms of mental illness profoundly affected a person's blameworthiness. Many also subscribed to the theory that insanity, even if in apparent remission, left an indelible scar on the reasoning faculty and forever vacated culpability for criminal behavior. Hammond argued that insane persons could exercise considerable self-restraint. He noted that virtually all asylum superintendents ascribed to the notion that rewards and punishment effectively modified most insane person's aberrant behavior. For example, an asylum attendant might restrict an insane person's food after an episode of flinging their dinner across the room. When mealtime again rolled around the now subdued inmate meekly consumed their food without incident. Hammond was a prickly character who jealously guarded his reputation. In the years following his tenure as the Army Surgeon General, Hammond increasingly acted as an expert witness in some of the most famous insanity cases of the era. He took his share of hits from the asylum superintendents who deeply resented this interloper treading on their hegemony. The superintendents tenaciously defended their turf as the undisputed masters of insanity. Until Hammond, no one really seriously threatened their authority. Over time the relationship between Hammond, his supporters, and the superintendents grew increasingly personal and bitter. Hammond even filed a lawsuit against his principal antagonist claiming libel. The principle subject of Hammond's ire was Dr. John P. Gray.

Chapter 4: Dueling Doctors

John Perdue Gray cast a broad shadow. He was a big man, brash in manner and totally intolerant of challenge. The practice of medical jurisprudence fit nicely with his personality. Gray probably never doubted his role as a medical expert witness on insanity. Even though the adversarial process ensured a challenge, Gray could rely on his position as an asylum superintendent to gain a credibility advantage against supposedly less capable medical opponents. Gray's skill in the courtroom, his imposing stature, and lengthy resume ensured his popularity with many attorneys. When a difficult case arose, and if Gray could be enticed to work with a particular attorney, it seemed the case was won before the jury heard a single word. Gray carefully fostered his reputation. He seemed to prefer high profile cases which guaranteed fawning newspaper coverage. Failing that, some of the cases anonymously appeared in the American Journal of Insanity, a flagship publication with Gray at the editorial helm. A few years after the Civil War ended, Gray's involvement in the case of Mrs. Elizabeth Heggie appeared in the journal.[101]

Sometimes a crime so shocked the public sensibilities that it left no conclusion possible other than insanity or perhaps some sort of demonic depravity. In the years just after the Civil War, with medical hegemony in ascendancy, the sentiments generally favored insanity. The case of Elizabeth Heggie certainly assaulted the moral persuasions of most people. Roughly eight months before police arrested Mrs.

---

101 "Case of Mrs. Elizabeth Heggie," *American Journal of Insanity* 25, no. 1 (1868): 1-51.

Heggie, tragedy struck their home. One of Elizabeth's daughters died, which no doubt brought great sympathy to the parents. Perhaps some rumors circulated among friends and family assigning a malevolent cause to the death. In any event, when another of Elizabeth's daughters died under similar circumstances, a coroner's inquest convened to determine the true manner of death. After hearing the evidence, the coroner's jury concluded that Mrs. Heggie most likely poisoned her daughter. The case was promptly bound over for trial on a charge of murder.

Elizabeth was eighteen years old when she married James Heggie. She was probably pregnant thirteen times, as quickly as nature would allow, and gave birth to nine children. When the children were young, Elizabeth was a doting mother who affectionately showered attention on each one. Aside from the expected fatigue of managing an ever larger brood, Elizabeth was frequently sidelined with incapacitating headaches. The headaches could be traced to a childhood injury. As a very young child, around the age of four, she suffered a fall from a second story set of stairs. She was knocked out and the family feared for her life. From that point forward, seizures and recurrent headaches plagued the young girl's life. The head injury also changed her personality. Mrs. Heggie was a good housekeeper, comfortable with the monotonous routine and never ending chores. Her young children were a source of unending gratification but a curious change took place as the girls reached adulthood.

At this time a rivalry developed between the mother and her elder daughters. Mary was the oldest, followed by Charlotte. Both were approaching the age of majority and were no doubt eagerly looking forward to starting their own families. These girls were bright, beneficiaries of an education their mother lacked. As such, they brought new ideas into the Heggie household. Instead of embracing her daughters' budding independence, Elizabeth felt threatened. Both daughters unwittingly stoked the mother's sneaking suspicions and fear of being supplanted as the head housekeeper. To counter Mary and Charlotte, the mother launched a sustained guerilla campaign. Elizabeth endlessly derided her daughters, sniped unmercifully, nurtured petty grievances, and was cold-hearted. Occasionally, the mother would ratchet the volume up, screaming and even resorting to physical attacks. It was against this back drop the Mary mysteriously died. Eight months later Charlotte also passed away.

The parents left their brood and dashed off to New York. Upon their return, the ever vigilant mother scanned the house and spied something amiss. Elizabeth lingered over the table linen, examining the material closely. What attracted her attention is unknown but probably the linen was less than perfectly folded or perhaps a small spot caught her eye. She immediately summoned Charlotte, and through the inquisition discovered that her daughter had hosted a small party. The mother could scarcely contain her anger, and finally failing to do so, caustically commented that Charlotte's next social affair "would probably be her funeral."[102]

Elizabeth frequently vented her displeasure by giving voice to threats. In a home life defined by this behavior, Charlotte probably dismissed the affair as just another example of her mother's ranting. But a few days after Elizabeth's tirade, Charlotte became ill. The illness developed suddenly and produced violent waves of nausea and vomiting. The retching emptied her stomach and removed whatever offending agent caused the vomiting. Charlotte felt better, regained her appetite, and enjoyed her dinner. No sooner had Charlotte finished her meal than the symptoms returned with a vengeance, but this time instead of nausea, her stomach burned and her bowels writhed in agony.

Charlotte's father instructed Elizabeth to call a doctor. The mother did as she was directed and the doctor arrived a short time later. He found Charlotte ambulatory but in obvious discomfort. An examination revealed a rapid heart rate and a patient who, in spite of the pain, minimized the malady. The doctor prescribed several remedies, including Dover's Powder, and left unheeded instructions to call if Charlotte did not improve overnight.

Charlotte vomited many times throughout the night, never gaining relief. A family member comforted Charlotte all night but was powerless to stop the pain. Elizabeth prepared tea on several occasions and urged Charlotte to drink it. Each time Charlotte took more than a few sips, she was racked with abdominal spasms. With her energy ebbing, Charlotte found it difficult the next day to dress and she was unable to attend Sunday church services.

Elizabeth did not like rats around her house and a few weeks earlier had procured some arsenic to rid the premises of the pests. A couple of days after Charlotte became ill, she went to a different pharmacy requesting a stronger dose of arsenic. For reasons unknown, Elizabeth took the opportunity to get chatty with the druggist. During the course of their discussion, Elizabeth mentioned her daughter's failing health and casu-

---

102 Ibid., 8.

ally noted the similarities to Mary's fatal illness. The druggist harbored no apparent suspicions and Elizabeth left with her arsenic.

The day after the Sabbath, Elizabeth prepared a meal for Charlotte and a family member took it upstairs. Charlotte took a few tentative bites before experiencing a burning sensation in her mouth and throat. Naturally, she consumed no more. Fatigue, pain, and near starvation hastened Charlotte's demise. Her fevered mind wandered with incoherent ramblings, finally yielding to death. In due course, following the coroner's report, Elizabeth was arrested and charged with murder.

Mrs. Heggie's legal defense was insanity. Two doctors testified on her behalf. The prosecution was seemingly content to rely on one witness, Dr. John Gray. As a pair of witnesses for the defense, the two doctors did not move in tandem. Dr. Brown, a staff physician at the New York's Bloomingdale Asylum, believed the defendant insane while Dr. Cook, a staff physician at the Canandaigua Asylum in New York, initially waffled. Dr. Gray had not a scintilla of doubt in proclaiming Elizabeth sane.

Dr. Brown looked at Elizabeth's life and detected all of the hallmarks presaging insanity. He looked at her family history of insanity, the head injury as a child, the resulting change in her personality, a lifelong irritability, and her peculiar fondness for sameness all adding up to madness. The most compelling bit of evidence, though, was Elizabeth's irrational conviction that her daughters sought to unseat the mother from the household throne. Brown found nothing factual to support Elizabeth's suspicions and concluded that the defendant suffered from a delusion. The presence of a delusion, a fixed, false belief that would never yield to reason, was the sine qua non of insanity. When a doctor stamped a criminal behavior as delusional, it signified a lack of moral responsibility. Brown danced around the magnitude of Elizabeth's insanity. It did not quite fit traditional examples of insanity, and after much public deliberation the doctor settled on partial insanity.

Dr. Cook began his testimony with a lack of resolution. He ticked off the factors favoring insanity such as the lifelong eccentric behavior, a deterioration that accompanied her later years, a peculiar distrust of her daughters' growth and development, unrelenting insomnia, and a rapid heart rate. Despite the list, Brown remained unconvinced. The doctor believed the defendant did not fit the typical case of insanity and he spent some time deliberating the possibilities. Brown shrank from calling her insane, instead preferring to label Elizabeth as mentally unsound. The distinction was probably lost on the jury but perhaps more important was the doctor's unwillingness to identify a delusion. The attorney, no doubt exasperated, asked the witness to stay in the court room and listen to additional evidence. Cook was then recalled to the witness stand. The discursive Doctor Brown listened attentively, and crediting the additional information, confidently asserted an opinion of insanity.

Dr. Gray testified for the prosecution. He based his opinion on several interviews with the defendant and evidence presented at the trial. The same facts the other doctors uncovered, principally the family history of madness and Elizabeth's head injury, factored in Gray's analysis. He conceded that these events warped the defendant's personality, resulting in an irritable, disagreeable, suspicious disposition. Elizabeth's limited education left her uncultured and crude. The stunted intellectual development contrasted sharply with her daughters. Mary and Charlotte had received a liberal education, and to the mother, probably flaunted their superior knowledge. Any new ideas suggested by the daughters for managing the household inflamed Elizabeth, and seemed to her to highlight her deficiencies; she responded with increasing jealousy and quiet rage.

Gray looked at basically the same evidence as Drs. Cook and Brown but reached the opposite conclusion. Instead of finding mental illness, Gray saw only a petty, vengeful woman intent on punishing her daughters. There was no delusion; the mother knew exactly what she was doing when poisoning Mary and Charlotte. She also knew the behavior was wrong, given the furtive manner in which she carried out the criminal act over many days. There was time for reflection and perhaps revision of the murderous plan but Elizabeth never swerved from her determination to kill Mary and Charlotte. In Gray's calculation, the mother's behavior was bad, not mad.

The trial judge explained the legal definition of insanity to the jury. "Our law has fixed a standard and measure of intellect to which it brings all persons, and holds them responsible for the crimes they commit. Any person who has a capacity to understand the nature and quality of the act, and to know that it is unlawful and morally wrong, under our law is responsible, whatever perturbation or weakness of intellect there may be in the case."[103] The rather irresolute testimony of the defense doctors, which seemed mostly an effort to twist and turn the soft evidence of mental illness into insanity, failed. Gray took the position that Elizabeth's behavior was morally wrong. The jury agreed and she was found guilty. Her initial sentence was death by hanging but a subsequent appeal lessened the punishment to life imprisonment.

---

103 Ibid., 25.

In one of a myriad of similar cases, the story of Ann Barry turned on the role of alcohol. Just months after the Civil War ended Barry walked out of prison, freed after serving a sentence for theft and drunkenness. While imprisoned she gave birth to a child. The newborn infant was a burden and Barry fixed on an idea to relieve the weight. She drank heavily, and while under the influence of the intoxicating liquor, threw the baby into a canal. Barry was arrested but her demeanor, savage and staring, suggested insanity. Infanticide, an act so alien to human nature, attracted the attention of a number of physicians who testified on her behalf.

Ann Barry was known as a habitual drunk. In the normal course of events, most citizens of the time viewed inebriation as a moral deficiency. It was common knowledge that over indulgence with intoxicating spirits loosened the tongue, befuddled the brain, and wobbled the gait. As such, the use of alcohol rarely succeeded as a legal defense. Barry's case was a bit different though, she was a woman and she killed her baby. Both were novel and strayed far enough from conventional social sensibilities to suggest insanity. The legal trick was convincing a jury.

Chronic intoxication subjected the victim to varying degrees of scorn and sympathy. The two moral judgments even oscillated around the same person. Some doctors, and lay people, were struck by the compulsive nature of drinking. Even after suffering all sorts of negative alcohol related consequences, the person continued along the same destructive path. It was this seemingly mindless enslavement which suggested mental unsoundness. Dipsomania was a popular term of the nineteenth century employed in an effort to relive the social stigma of drunkenness by medically cloaking the conduct.

As a legal defense, dipsomania was not always successful. Nonetheless, Ann Barry had few other options. She also had three sympathetic doctors. In the main, the doctors all testified that Barry had dipsomania. They differed in whether they believed dipsomania was a primary disorder or the result of alcohol's deleterious impact on the brain's physiology. All three doctors believed Barry insane and a fit subject for an asylum. The Superintendent of the State Lunatic Asylum in Utica, New York disagreed.

Dr. Gray examined Barry and the charges lodged against her. He found no evidence of delusional thinking, the touch stone of insanity in nineteenth America. Gray also pointed to Barry's confession, and the selfish reason she cited for the murder, as tipping the balance decidedly away from madness. On cross examination, Gray disputed not only the diagnosis of dipsomania but the very notion of such a disorder. The prosecution's star witness stripped away the medical mantle of dipsomania and replaced it with the moral label, intemperance. The jury agreed, found her guilty, and Barry spent the remainder of her life in prison.

The Barry and Heggie cases unfolded in 1865. Dr. Gray was building a reputation as a steady expert witness, one who carefully reviewed the legal evidence, interviewed the defendants, and testified in a believable manner. In most of these legal contests Gray's credibility as the Superintendent of the State Lunatic Asylum in Utica, New York allowed him to tower over opposition doctors. Gray's confidence surely swelled as he vanquished his foes. In these early matches Gray clearly had the advantage, in terms of clinical experience with insanity and comfort in the court room. That changed as more doctors became expert witnesses. Slowly but surely, two distinct professional rivalries developed. The McFarland Trial showcased the coming tug-of-war.

The McFarland Trial captivated the public. It was a voluminous story saturated with romance, betrayal, and vengeance. As the tale of treachery unfolded, it seemed that most readers passionately split in their support or condemnation of McFarland. The drama challenged the conventional role of married women, their rights and prerogatives, with strong undercurrents that tugged the emotions of readers. Newspapers and periodicals reported the facts and then cultivated controversy by exploiting every conceivable twist and turn. The crime involved the staff of the New York Tribune, Horace Greeley's famous soap box. The debate over McFarland's sanity added spice to the saga.

Daniel McFarland was born in Ireland and immigrated to America in 1824. Tragedy struck when he lost his parents, forcing the twelve-year-old boy to fend for himself. Through a mixture of pride and pluck the young man steadfastly pursued legal scholarship. His studies were interrupted by a three year stint in the 13th Massachusetts Volunteers.[104] He eventually learned enough to pass the bar exam and plied his craft in Delaware. Not long after, while traveling through New Hampshire, McFarland had a chance encounter with an attractive, spunky fifteen-year-old girl named Abby Sage. A four year courtship culminated in marriage between the 36-year-old suitor and his 19-year-old betrothed.[105]

---

104   Charles E. Davis, *three years in the Army: The story of the Thirteenth Massachusetts Volunteers from July 16, 1861 to August 1, 1864* (Boston: Estes and Lauriat, 1893), 489.

105   Thomas Samuel Duke, *Celebrated criminal cases of America* (San Francisco: James H. Barry Company, 1910), 605.

The marital bliss withered as the romantic bloom faded. In later accounts of the marriage, Abby bitterly came to realize her husband's fraud. "Mr. McFarland represented to me that he had a flourishing law practice, brilliant political prospects and property worth $30,000, but while on our bridal tour he was forced to borrow money in New York..."[106] The disillusioned bride initially bore the deceit with a victim's badge of resignation. Abby's recollection of the marriage was heavily tainted by her later actions but always vigorously disputed by Daniel.

By some accounts, mostly sympathizers of Mrs. McFarland, the ten year marriage was a nightmare. Daniel drifted like an itinerant dragging the despairing wife from one failed venture to another. Always in debt and debilitated by her husband's drinking, the brave but proud Abby was often forced to beg for food. In memorializing her victimization, a receptive press cast Abby as the moral glue holding her family together. In spite of the desperate circumstances, Abby remained at her husband's side. In spite of the ordeal, the couple rejoiced in the birth of three children.[107]

While living in New York, Mrs. McFarland's fortunes took a turn for the better when she met Horace Greeley's sister. The pair formed a fast relationship, and joining with several other likeminded women, banded together for mutual support. This happy arrangement introduced Abby to the wide world of arts and entertainment. She soon was employed in the fine art of public reading and even managed to publish a few children's verses. Probably possessed of mostly mediocre talent, the sisterhood propelled Abby to greater heights. McFarland's wife soon gravitated towards the theater, hoping no doubt, to launch a stunning debut. She landed a small, unmemorable part in Shakespeare's Merchant of Venice. In so far as the trial of Daniel McFarland was concerned, the most important introduction garnered through the social circle occurred when Abby met the dashing Albert Richardson.[108]

Albert D. Richardson was a journalist for the New York Tribune. His lack luster career hit a zenith during the Civil War. As a battlefield correspondent, Richardson provided compelling eye witness documentaries. The peril of his position became apparent when he was captured at the Battle of Vicksburg in 1863. He escaped from Confederate confinement in late 1864. Like any reporter worth his salt, Richardson wrote of his ex-

---

106 Ibid.

107 Alfred Lewis, "The murder and the wedding at the Astor," *Pearson's Magazine* 24, no. 2 (1913):237-46.

108 Ibid., 239.

ploits as a war correspondent in a book titled, *Field, Dungeon, and Escape.* After the war ended the intrepid member of the press received an assignment from the Tribune to travel the rails of Western America. Richardson journeyed across the Western frontier and wrote colorful accounts of his many observations.[109]

Mr. McFarland piteously recalled that, "I lived harmoniously and happy with my wife for nine years—absolute happiness—until she formed the acquaintance of this man Richardson; from that moment my happiness was destroyed."[110] McFarland also darkly hinted at Richardson's friends in the press who fanned the flames of a libelous attack aimed at destroying his character. The imputation seemed to imply that Greeley's newspaper abandoned journalistic ethics in an effort to shield the reputation of Richardson. The embattled attorney took umbrage at claims of intemperance, insisting instead that he was a family man devoted to his wife and children. Meanwhile, Albert and Abby started spending more time together, much to the consternation of McFarland.

McFarland knew the routine. His wife left for the evening to attend the theater, accompanied by Albert Richardson. The discarded husband probably passed many nights fuming as he waited for Abby's return. On one ominous occasion, McFarland spent the night hiding outside his apartment. As the happy couple approached their apartments, McFarland sprang from some nearby bushes and fired three shots at Richardson. Apparently, he fired a bit low and struck Abby's suitor in the leg. Richardson and McFarland than engaged in close combat with neither man gaining much advantage. Abby's screaming brought the police and the threesome eventually made their way to a local police station. McFarland was arrested but was released without criminal prosecution. He made a convincing argument citing Abby's unfaithful behavior. The unrepentant wife left the city but maintained an ongoing correspondence with Albert. Abby's loyal friends sympathetically suggested a divorce. After weighing the matter for a short time, Abby moved to Indiana, and after fulfilling the legal residency requirement, filed for divorce. Apparently McFarland offered no objections. The Indiana Court granted the legal petition without any fanfare.[111]

---

109 "Lamentable tragedy," *New York Times*, Nov. 26, 1869.

110 Daniel McFarland, *The Richardson-McFarland tragedy: Containing all the letters and other interesting facts and documents not before published, being a full and impartial history of this most extraordinary case* (Philadelphia: Barclay & Co., 1870), 23.

111 "Lamentable tragedy," *New York Times*, Nov. 26, 1869.

In a rather surreal, detached manner McFarland later memorialized the events of November 25, 1869. McFarland recalled entering the Tribune building, apparently well aware of Richardson's scheduled arrival later in the day. Daniel was a fairly well-known figure to the staff at the Tribune so his lingering presence did not give rise to any suspicions. He whiled away the time, secretly awaiting Richardson, by striking up casual conversations with nearby employees. The fact that McFarland remained in the same basic position, partially hidden by a pillar, again stirred no concern in the busy office. Finally, Richardson arrived and, walking with an unsuspecting gait, approached the hidden McFarland. At this point, McFarland aimed a pistol and shot Richardson in the abdomen. Surely stunned by McFarland's assault, the wounded victim left the scene and stumbled off to another section of the building. An alarmed colleague desperately sought medical help.[112]

McFarland was arrested minutes later. He was calm and casual, smoking throughout the early phases of apprehension and interrogation. The police brought the assailant to the victim's bedside. During this brief encounter Richardson blamed the assault on McFarland. Later, at the police station, McFarland justified the attack after "being informed that Mr. Richardson was making preparations to leave the country, that he had sold his property in New Jersey, and believing that he contemplated taking with him his wife and child, he became frenzied, and committed the deed, which he claimed was but the law of nature." Unfortunately, the law of nature had yet to run its course as Richardson lay mortally wounded.[113]

Dr. Swan examined the critically injured man shortly after the assault. Richardson was conscious, enough so to point an accusing finger at McFarland as the perpetrator. The day after the attack, Richardson received sympathetic visits from hundreds of friends and colleagues. Even Horace Greeley stopped by. The great pain caused by the wound was relieved with morphine and the doctor taking care of Richardson signaled cautious optimism for a recovery. The outlook changed for the worse two days after the attack. Any remaining pretense of Richardson's lack of duplicity in seducing McFarland's wife was cast aside as the grim reaper approached. The ill-fated lovers exchanged marital vows, with the Rev-

112 Ibid.
113 Daniel McFarland, *The Richardson-McFarland tragedy: Containing all the letters and other interesting facts and documents not before published, being a full and impartial history of this most extraordinary case* (Philadelphia: Barclay & Co., 1870), 23.

erend Henry Ward Beecher officiating the ceremony and Horace Greeley acting as a witness. Abby's new husband lingered a few more days, finally succumbing to McFarland's treachery.[114]

The McFarland case ignited a tinderbox, the fuel for the resulting fire provided by social stresses as America grappled with women's rights, marriage, and divorce. No sooner had Richardson met his Maker than the controversy spilled forth in the tabloids. A self-declared, yet anonymous friend of Richardson authored a stirring defense of the deceased's behavior.[115] The friend dubiously declared that Richardson made no improper advances towards the wife of McFarland, always exhibiting the most decorous manner. Of course, Abby's divorce permitted the pair to openly and honestly pursue a romance. Richardson's friend denied as vile rumors any suggestion that he had seduced a married woman. He just as vigorously protested aspersions that Abby and Albert were proponents of "free love," a concept attacking marriage and promoting the most liberal interaction between the sexes.

Daniel McFarland had legions of supporters. The friends of McFarland deplored the unseemly conduct of Abby and Albert. To this group, Mrs. McFarland was morally bankrupt and selfishly abandoned her faithful and responsible mate. Richardson the seducer was cast as a vile home breaker who drove a wedge between a husband and a wife. A sermon at a New York Church verbalized the feelings of many in the pews by declaring that McFarland's crime "was but the expression of the love of a faithful husband — an act which every high-minded man could be induced to commit."[116]

Daniel McFarland was arraigned on a charge of first degree murder late in December, 1869. An impressive roster of attorneys, Eldridge Gerry, John Graham, and Charles Spencer, represented the accused man. After the charges were read, McFarland stood and pled not guilty. Court room observers were struck by the defendant's unkempt and exhausted presence. Whether intentional or not, the first whispers suggesting the defendant's mental unsoundness accompanied his appearance at the arraignment.[117]

---

114 "Richardson tragedy," *New York Times*, Nov. 27, 1869.

115 "The Richardson-McFarland case," *New York Times*, Dec. 8, 1869.

116 "Professor Graham on the Richardson-McFarland case," *New York Times*, Jan. 29, 1870.

117 "The Richardson homicide; Arrangement of Daniel McFarland in the Court of General Sessions," *New York Times*, Dec. 22, 1869.

The McFarland case started in earnest on the eighth of April, 1870. By now the steady drum beat of sensational news coverage caused a near stampede of townspeople hoping to get a seat in the court room. Most people were disappointed since few seats remained after the attorneys, family members, witnesses, and reporters crowded inside. The defendant was accompanied by his little son, an image of paternal sentiment that surely tugged the heart strings of men and women alike.[118] After everyone was settled, the judge sounded his gavel signaling the start of the trial.

District Attorney Gavin presented a dry, factual recitation of the crime. Witnesses dutifully described the events on the day of the shooting. Gavin apparently hoped to convince the jury that this was an open and shut case. Naturally, John Graham did not share the prosecutor's point of view. Instead, he mounted an aggressive counter attack. Through the course of cross examining prosecution witnesses, Graham developed the thesis that Richardson had a loaded pistol in a breast pocket. Graham intended to plant a seed of doubt in the jury's mind by inferring that Richardson expected McFarland and was prepared to engage his enemy in combat. Dr. Swan, the physician summoned to care for Richardson immediately after the assault, also felt the heat of Graham's blistering interrogation. The defense attorney drilled the doctor about the bedside marriage of Abby and Albert. Graham contended that the emotional ceremony undermined the doctor's prescription of rest and actually contributed to Richardson's death. Towards the end of the day's testimony Graham set the tone for the defense strategy when he commented that McFarland, "in a moment of frenzy and aberration of mind, innocently and unintentionally committed" the act in question.[119]

Charles Spencer, another of McFarland's attorneys, unfurled the next phase of the defense strategy. Confirming weeks of speculation, the defense attorney acknowledged that McFarland's insanity would be a central feature of the case. The marital scandal caused the accused endless embarrassment, anger, and wasted energy trying to contain his wife's behavior. The emotional excitement sapped McFarland's spirits. He became increasingly depressed, feverish, restless, and sleepless.[120]

Spencer was carefully laying the groundwork for the insanity defense. Even so, he probably recognized the jurors' skepticism. After all, McFar-

---

118 "The McFarland trial; Third day," *New York Times*, Apr. 7, 1870.
119 "The McFarland trial; Opening of the case for the prosecution," *New York Times*, Apr. 8, 1870.
120 "The McFarland trial; Opening address by Mr. Spencer for the defense," *New York Times*, Apr. 9, 1870.

land did not look insane as he sat in the court room, attentive to the trial with his young son seated nearby. Another factor weighing on the insanity defense was the Abraham Man. The public generally distrusted the insanity defense, often seeing it as a ploy to excuse criminal behavior. Insanity was easily faked, or so the populace believed. Spencer directly addressed this suspicion. "Gentleman of the jury, during the struggle this defense will not believe that this man was up to that time sane. He did not simulate sanity. Sanity is simulated oftener than insanity. The man whose sense of reason is departing or has departed struggles to appear sane ... and this man knew that if the state of his mind was discovered that all hope of obtaining possession of his children was gone."[121]

Charles Spencer called a number of witnesses, the collective weight an attempt to tilt the scales of justice towards insanity. McFarland's brother described a normal childhood, productive adult life, and a miserable marriage which consumed the congenial man. A fellow lodger at the New York residence commented on Daniel's odd hours and sad demeanor. A particularly interesting witness was Officer George Simmons of the Lunatic Asylum at Blackwell's Island. Simons produced a ledger, upon which patient admissions to the Asylum were carefully recorded. The witness pointed to an entry from 1847 which listed the name of Francis McFarland, one of Daniel's cousins. Another witness who knew Francis described the troubled man as irritable, intermittently incoherent, persistently jealous, and disconsolate. Francis became totally demented before death.[122]

Dr. John A. Ward personally knew both Abby and Daniel for about six years. He testified that prior to 1867, in a time period preceding Abby's affair, the marriage between Abby and Daniel seemed normal. Almost immediately after Abby started her flirtation with Albert, a striking change progressively overcame McFarland. He increasing manifested an extreme nervousness, mental distractibility, and a pervasive despondency. McFarland frequently expressed his dour disposition in suicidal terms. Ward recalled upwards of fifty visits with McFarland in the two year ordeal with Abby. The doctor was convinced that Daniel's symptoms were genuine, given the chronicity and degree of discomfort. In the weeks just before the murder, McFarland was a daily presence in the doctor's of-

---

121 Ibid.
122 Ibid.

fice. Ward vividly recounted the defendant's appearance, "his eyes were glassy and glaring and his general appearance extremely haggard..."[123]

Dr. Minor shared an office with Dr. Ward, and knew the defendant for about a year. Their first meeting occurred when Minor performed a simple surgical operation on Daniel. During the procedure, Daniel drifted into a lengthy ramble regarding his domestic difficulties. On subsequent visits, whenever the subject of Abby arose, he became exceedingly anxious and distraught. Daniel's unceasing perseverations led Minor to diagnose the disorder a monomania. He prescribed various nostrums such as codeine and caffeine but Daniel pointedly refused any medicinal alcohol.[124]

Among all of McFarland's caregivers, Dr. Egbert Gurnsey had the shortest relationship. Gurnsey met the defendant about one month prior to the murder. Even this short time span was sufficient to convince the doctor that the Abraham Man could never act this well. Gurnsey diagnosed nervous exhaustion, the result of a delirious brain twisted and tortured by Abby and Albert's two-timing interlude. To emphasize the point, Gurnsey testified that, "I discovered that the pulse was quick, nervous, and beating about 120 in a minute; when about half a minute had elapsed there was a muscular twitch; he turned his body and was unable to remain still...on looking at his tongue I found it flabby and generally unhealthy; his eyes were contracted, and his face haggard and bore the expression of internal suffering." Despite the graphic illustration of mental suffering, the doctor demurred in diagnosing a full blown case of insanity, settling instead for an incipient version. Nonetheless, his testimony added increasing weight to the ever stronger argument well calculated by the defense attorneys to prove McFarland's mental derangement.[125]

The physicians prescribed a variety of remedies to soothe McFarland's mind. None seemed quite as effective as morphine. This potent palliative helped bring slumber to McFarland. It also helped brighten his mood a bit and reduced the anxiety. Francis Edmond, a druggist, frequently filled the prescriptions for McFarland. Typically the doctor ordered one grain of morphine, divided into four daily doses. While waiting for the prescription McFarland always fretfully paced about the pharmacy, often muttering to himself in a low voice. On the few occasions where a

123 "The McFarland trial; Seventh day in the progress of the case," *New York Times*, Apr. 13, 1870.

124 Ibid.

125 "The McFarland trial; Progress of the ninth day in the case," *New York Times*, Apr. 15, 1870.

conversation passed between McFarland and the druggist, it usually gravitated towards the domestic discord. When cross examined by the prosecutor about the dose of morphine, the druggist expressed no concern, viewing one grain as a reasonable dose. Edmond maintained professional independence by suggesting that he would not have filled a larger dose without consulting the doctor.[126]

The trial was coming to a close but the defense had two strong witnesses waiting to testify. The first was Dr. Reuben A. Vance, an insanity expert. Vance was a graduate of Bellevue Hospital Medical College, where he also maintained an active practice. The doctor impressed the courtroom with his youthful appearance and sanguine manor. He testified with uncommon clarity, a compelling command of the language, and a singular conviction that captivated the jury. Vance was an exceptional witness, less for what he said then the drama of the delivery. McFarland's attorney questioned the doctor for about an hour.[127]

Dr. Vance interviewed Daniel McFarland at the City Prison in New York on three separate occasions. The first meeting was the longest, taking about three hours of the prisoner's time. During that first session Vance inquired about Daniel's family history, his religious beliefs, and his occupation. The doctor also conducted a physical examination. Vance, like many of his contemporary colleagues, believed insanity produced many physical signs which the astute diagnostician could easily detect. He carefully noted Daniel's high pulse rate racing along at one hundred and fifteen beats per minute. McFarland's skin was not flushed or warm to the touch, he responded appropriately to a pin prick, and there were no discernible gait abnormalities. Using an ophthalmoscope, Dr. Vance peered into McFarland's eyes. Vance's second visit was short, lasting about a half an hour. McFarland's heart rate was even faster this time, running along at one hundred and twenty-eight beats per minute. The doctor was struck by McFarland's blood shot eyes and exhausted expression. He told the prisoner he would return one last time. The third and final consultation focused on McFarland's family affairs. In his usual rambling style, McFarland shared his domestic distress with the doctor. Towards the end of the interview Vance once again examined McFarland's eyes with an ophthalmoscope.[128]

---

126 Ibid.
127 "The McFarland trial; Highly important testimony of a medical expert," *New York Times*, Apr. 26, 1870.
128 Ibid.

Dr. Vance had no doubts that McFarland was insane. The symptoms could not be the result of malingering. Using illustrated drawings, the doctor patiently explained to the jury the difference between a normal and an abnormal brain. According to Vance, cerebral congestion caused insanity. "Congestion of the brain is that condition where more blood is attracted to or circulates through the brain than there should be in its normal or proper condition ..." He further explained the inextricable link between chronic insomnia and insanity by testifying, "if sleep be lost, if a man be unable to sleep, an inordinate quantity of blood is supplied to and circulates through the brain, producing, to a greater or lesser degree, mental disorder".[129]

Aside from the physical stigmata of cerebral congestion Vance relied on the ophthalmoscope. Several decades earlier Hermann von Helmholtz invented the ophthalmoscope.[130] The ophthalmoscope allowed doctors to study the interior of the eye, focusing on the retina and the optic nerve. Vance brought one of the instruments to court and took a few minutes to demonstrate it. After the show and tell, Vance unequivocally claimed that a careful examination of the eye would always detect a swollen optic nerve, the consequence of cerebral congestion. The jury was probably impressed by this scientific tool which could unerringly upend the Abraham Man.[131] His testimony created quite a stir in the public's mind. A later gathering of oculists vigorously disputed Vance's sweeping conclusion.[132]

Dr. Vance mesmerized the court room audience. It seemed unlikely that another medical witness could outshine this star but McFarland's attorneys secured the services of the brightest luminary when William A. Hammond joined the team. Dr. Hammond met with Daniel McFarland on seven separate occasions scattered over several weeks.[133] On each visit he carefully conducted a physical examination and made numerous inquiries about Daniel's turmoil. Hammond was a man of science who loved tinkering with medical mechanisms. He used several of these de-

---

129 Ibid.

130 Thomas Hall Shastid, *The description of an ophthalmoscope: Being an English translation of Von Helmholtz's "Beschreibung eines Augenspiegels"* (Chicago: Cleveland Press, 1916; Berlin, 1851), 7.

131 "The McFarland trial; Highly important testimony of a medical expert," *New York Times*, Apr. 26, 1870.

132 "The ophthalmoscope and insanity," *New York Times*, June 26, 1870.

133 "The McFarland trial; Further important evidence of medical witnesses," *New York Times*, Apr. 27, 1870.

vices in the examination of McFarland. The use of these devices added scientific credibility to the diagnosis of mental disorders. In some legal cases, including McFarland's, the factual evidence supporting insanity was ambiguous. McFarland attorneys developed strong medical arguments, hoping to decisively obliterate lingering doubts of dissimulation. Hammond's use of novel medical instruments in the diagnosis of insanity reassured a skeptical jury.

Hammond spent two days testifying. The first day's interrogation was directed by a defense lawyer who allowed the witness considerable latitude. Through the use of charts and a display of scientific instruments, the witness dazzled the audience. Hammond patiently recorded his observations gleaned over the course of seven separate examinations of the defendant. The doctor's notes from the careful physical examinations recorded on one occasion how McFarland's pupils were of unequal size. Hammond felt the prisoner's throbbing temporal arteries, another sign suggesting cerebral congestion. The results of a sensory examination varied with some areas of the prisoner's body more sensitive to touch. Hammond monitored McFarland's pulse at every visit and each time it exceeded one hundred beats per minute. As an inveterate explorer, Hammond conducted an interesting experiment. He stunned McFarland by thrusting pictures of Abby in his face. The defendant became hysterical, sobbing, and agitated. Hammond took his hand and measured the heart rate, a pounding one hundred and forty-two beats per minute.

Like Vance, the former Surgeon General relied on the ophthalmoscope. The instrument allowed Hammond to identify the swollen optic nerve and spongy retina characteristic of cerebral congestion. Hammond used another tool, the dynamograph, to measure nerve strength. In fact, he pioneered the medical use of the device. The dynamograph was a mechanical contrivance which translated the strength of a person's grip to a line drawing. A healthy subject could squeeze the instrument smoothly, by applying a uniform pressure, which resulted in the pencil drawing a straight line. A patient who drew a crooked line showed the early signs of cerebral disease. Hammond firmly believed that insanity was an organic condition, the end result of a diseased brain. The dynamograph, when combined with the ophthalmoscope, offered concrete evidence of physical disease.[134]

---

134 William A. Hammond, "Medico-legal points in the case of David Montgomery," *The Journal of Psychological Medicine* VI (1872): 62-76.

The prosecution tried in vain to discredit Hammond's testimony. When the attorneys attacked by claiming that McFarland was faking, Hammond responded by arguing," It's easier for an insane man to feign sanity than for a sane one to feign insanity..."[135] Of course by now most court room observers and reporters were probably convinced that science could slay the Abraham Man. Hammond's use of the dynamograph and the ophthalmoscope were surely persuasive. Nonetheless, the prosecution continued the attack and contended that McFarland was not insane but committed the murder as a crime of passion. Once again Hammond countered. According to the unflappable witness, an insane person either remained at the crime scene or nonchalantly carried on as if nothing happened. Hammond contended that a person who committed a crime of passion understood the wrongfulness of their behavior and would undertake all manner of subterfuge to escape detection. The doctor stood his ground and resolutely proclaimed McFarland insane, a victim of chronic melancholia seized by a moment of violent mania.

After five weeks of court room maneuvering the trial was coming to a conclusion. John Graham, McFarland's passionate pleader, hypnotized his audience with a captivating, five hour summation. Many in the court room sobbed silently at particularly poignant moments, such as when Graham reminded the jury of Abby's infidelity. When the attorneys from both sides completed their arguments the drama shifted to the judge. It was his responsibility to provide clear instructions to the jury, explaining the relevant law so the twelve fact finders could properly adjudicate the case. The trial judge explained the insanity defense. "If upon the whole evidence in the case, the jury entertain a reasonable doubt as to the perfect sanity of the defendant at the time of the commission of the alleged act, they are bound to acquit him."

Armed now with all of the evidence in the case and the judge's instructions, the jury retired in mid-afternoon to begin their deliberations. Many court room observers expected a quick verdict favoring the defendant. Even the defense attorneys hoped the jury would decide the matter in thirty minutes. Unbeknownst to those remaining in the court room, ten jurors did quickly vote for acquittal but two stubborn hold outs protested. The thirty minute mark passed without a decision and the anxiety among the defense attorneys mounted. An ominous thunderstorm, perhaps portending a dark outcome, rattled both windows and nerves.

---

135 "The McFarland trial; All the testimony for the defense at last submitted," *New York Times*, Apr. 28, 1870.

About two hours after the jury left they somberly returned. A hush descended on the audience as the jury foreman pronounced the verdict — not guilty. The tension in the room immediately melted and gave way to raucous cheers. The judge let the jubilation continue for a considerable time. When quiet returned he performed the final act of freeing Daniel McFarland.[136]

The fireworks continued after the trial ended. Although the court exploded noisily in McFarland's favor, a disquieting social unease settled across America. It seemed most everyone found fault with the finding. The nascent suffragette movement lamented the public flogging of Abby. Other concerned citizens criticized the lack of punishment, bemoaning the fact that McFarland murdered an individual and got off scot-free. Still others wondered why a madman was roaming the streets instead of the hallways of an asylum.

The McFarland trial sparked a spirited, and at times, nasty debate among the elite group of insanity experts. The Medico-Legal Society of New York took the matter up about one month after the jury's verdict.[137] All of the members seemed to agree that the insanity defense was abused in the McFarland trial. They disagreed on the remedies, with some proposing legislative reform restricting either the jury's or the medical witness's role in determining insanity. Hammond was among the attendees, even though his presence probably stirred some resentment. After all, Hammond's testimony contributed to the unseemly outcome. Hammond still voiced his opinion in spite of any possible uneasiness among the other doctors. As a celebrity, even a controversial one, the assembled doctors still awaited his comments. Hammond expressed his displeasure with two facets of the insanity defense. Lawyers loved hypothetical questions and Hammond did not. His main objection was the crafting of a hypothetical question which was a one way street, leaving the medical expert with no room to maneuver. Hammond's second criticism touched on the unfettered release of McFarland. The doctor declared that insane men should not escape punishment. Even a death sentence could be justified by protecting society from the future insane man's progeny.

Six months later the rhetoric still ran hot. A leading medical journal published a lengthy opinion excoriating an unmentioned doctor who de-

---

136 "McFarland acquitted; Triumphant vindication of the defendant's action," *New York Times*, May 11, 1870.

137 "The plea of insanity in criminal cases: What should have been done with McFarland," *New York Times*, June 10, 1870.

clared the mind was, "a force developed by nervous action."[138] The oblique shot was aimed at William Hammond. In a sermon from the mount, the author of the article reproached Hammond's ungodly adoration of science. For many doctors, including John P. Gray, the soul and science did not mix. Science could never unravel God's Mysteries. The author's attack, surely sanctified by Gray, was an effort to pull the medical profession back from the yawning abyss of scientific atheism. According to this view, Hammond was a false prophet tempting the faithful with forbidden knowledge. The journal cautioned readers, "No true expert in insanity, qualified by long, special, and intimate observation and practice among the insane in all their moods and aspects, called as a witness, needs to resort to any such sophistical postulates to bolster his conclusion... and to be as positive as if he were dealing with a matter of anatomy or chemistry, instead of a subject that involves, in nearly equal degrees, questions appealing to our senses, and questions above both our senses and our reason; an insoluble compound of physical and moral science..."[139] Gray's group could not abandon faith, leaving science hobbled and the Abraham Man unfettered.

The McFarland Trial sensitized the public and the medical profession to the inherent inequities with the insanity defense. A compassionate society tempers retribution with reason. The insanity defense was a necessary legal hurdle preventing the unjust punishment of the mentally ill. McFarland's trial laid bare many of the disagreeable features of the insanity defense. Dueling medical experts, vague definitions of mental illness, and the ever present specter of the Abraham Man all conspired to undermine the controversial legal defense.

Dr. Gray resented the intrusion of Hammond and his like-minded colleagues. Gray considered himself and fellow asylum doctors the true insanity experts. Toiling in the cavernous asylums day after day exposed the asylum doctors to all manner of severe mental illnesses. Controlling the leading insanity journal allowed Gray and his friends to publicize their experiences, and through those efforts, achieve a prestige denied nonbelievers. Gray accepted a narrow definition of insanity, one which required a successful defendant demonstrate an inability to know the nature and quality of the criminal act because of mental illness. In actual practice this meant the defendant's criminal behavior emanated from a

---

138   TSC, "The McFarland trial," *American Journal of Insanity* 27, no. 3 (1871):265-277.

139   Ibid., 271.

delusion. The delusion preempted the defendant's judgment and forced a course of action dictated by the disturbed thinking A seemingly endless parade of self-professed experts commented on the responsibility of the insane for criminal behavior. Gray dismissed most of these pretenders as false experts. He wrote two lengthy journal articles discussing the responsibility of the insane for their murderous acts. In the first article he reviewed fifty-eight records of asylum patients admitted after committing a murder.[140] His purpose was to classify, through clinical vignettes, the various mental states of the homicidally insane person. Gray grouped the fifty-eight patients into discrete categories, including murders arising directly from a delusion, a paroxysm of insanity, epilepsy, and delirium tremens. He added two additional groups for insane patients who killed from base motives and for patients with no evidence of mental illness. The latter two categories might have been artifacts, representing successful insanity defenses based on persuasive legal arguments at the expense of sound medical opinion.

After carefully examining the asylum records, Gray concluded that thirty-nine cases of homicide were attributable to a delusion. The other nineteen cases included homicides resulting from epilepsy, paroxysms of insanity, and delirium tremens. Gray identified six sane cases, at least two of whom were malingering

Gray followed up his analysis of completed homicides with an article examining attempted homicides among the insane.[141] He used the same classification scheme to organize the sixty seven homicide attempts. Not surprisingly, the doctor traced fifty-six of the attempts to a delusion. Gray's two articles on homicidal insanity probably contributed more to his reputation than to science. His case studies included only asylum inmates, overlooking the larger population of murderers in prisons. Had Gray ventured beyond his turf, he might have discovered an entirely different view of homicidal insanity.

The court room spectacle of medical doctors debating abstruse concepts of insanity sold newspapers. Reporters added large doses of melodrama to the otherwise mundane testimony. The stories often created a faux controversy between the experts, who many times disagreed over minor points. Even so, doctors could make or break their reputations in court. The substance of their testimony often faded in comparison to

---

140 John P. Gray, "Responsibility of the insane: Homicide in insanity," *American Journal of Insanity* 32, no. 2 (1875): 1-57.

141 John P. Gray, "Responsibility of the insane: Homicide in insanity," *American Journal of Insanity* 32 no. 2 (1875): 153-183.

their poise and presentation. An inarticulate but accurate medical witness could lose the case to a confident, charismatic charlatan. Many doctors, particularly those ensconced in the asylums, wanted a large moat across which the pretenders could not pass. They vigorously supported a variety of plans insulating their guild from competition. The plan probably favored by Dr. Gray involved the appointment of a commission. The court would appoint the commission and select the members from among a small group of experts, vetted by the Asylum Superintendents as true experts. Once the commission received its charter the members would conduct the necessary assessment and report their results to the court. In Gray's world this scheme had several advantages. It excluded all but a favored few medical experts, ensured the most dependable testimony, avoided the public spectacle of dueling doctors, and perhaps most importantly, prevented competition. The case of Perrine D. Matteson was the first insanity commission in New York which fully satisfied Gray's idealistic canon of medical testimony.[142]

Perrine Matteson shot and killed his brother. The matter grew out of the most innocuous circumstances. Both brothers lived on separate farms, a geographic separation that reduced sibling rivalries. Charles lived alone while his brother shared the father's house. On a Sunday afternoon, most likely right after church services concluded, the three men gathered for an informal get-together. Charles and his father were casually talking near the barn. Perrine walked by without a word on his way to the house. A few minutes passed and Perrine left the house and entered the barn. While Charles and his father were talking, Perrine fired two shots at Charles. One shot went wild but the other struck Charles in the abdomen. The wound was not immediately fatal and death stayed its hand long enough for Charles to sign a sworn statement accusing Perrine. After the shooting Perrine fled the area, jumped aboard a local train, and was finally arrested many miles from the crime scene. Perrine signaled his intention to plead insanity at the arraignment.

The court ordered a commission to examine the mental state of the accused. The trial judge referenced a law providing the authority to delegate the examination of the defendant's mental state to the commission. John P. Gray, along with two colleagues, accepted the appointment. Dr. Gray probed the witnesses carefully and obtained a fairly detailed picture of Perrine. Perhaps the most important event in Perrine's life was

---

142 "Case of Perrine D. Matteson, indicted for murder in the first degree, plea, insanity," *American Journal of Insanity* 31, no. 3 (1875): 336-344.

a childhood bout of scarlet fever. The inflammatory disease left Perrine deaf in one ear and indelibly scarred his brain. He was henceforth subject to fits, nervousness, and irritability. The fever arrested his intellectual development. As he grew into manhood the disabilities prevented employment and contributed to a vagabond existence. In the fall of 1861 his meanderings led to an enlistment in the 14th New York Volunteer Infantry Regiment. After three months he was discharged with a mental disability. He returned home briefly but again began wandering off. His travels led to the Navy where he enlisted. This tour of duty was just as short as his army career. From this time until the murder, Perrine lived near his father and brother.

Perrine's life on the farm was not pleasant. His paranoia increased to the point where he believed his food was poisoned and his family conspiring to kill him. He repeatedly threatened to kill his brother. On one occasion Perrine shot Charles, inflicting a minor head wound. A few months before the murder Perrine started complaining that visions of ghosts were haunting him. The hallucinations taunted Perrine and urged him to kill Charles.

The sum total of the testimony convinced Gray that Perrine Matteson was insane. Gray arrived at this conclusion in spite of Perrine's repeated threats, fleeing the scene, and never needing mental treatment before the murder. The serious possibility of malingering was apparently never raised. The court accepted the Commission's report and remanded the defendant to Gray's Asylum. Gray extolled the virtues of the commission, particularly pleased with the efficiency and thrift of a procedure bypassing tedious testimony.

The concept of a lunacy commission favored the parochial interests of the asylum doctors. It further served to insulate the doctors from the discomfort of genuine disagreement. The Abraham Man also applauded the commission, pleased at the prospect of avoiding the glaring light of a cross examination. Perrine's case left unchallenged the legitimate question of malingering.

In the nineteenth century epilepsy was a mysterious malady still shrouded in superstition. An epileptic attack scared people with its sudden onset and uncontrolled flailing. As the understanding of epilepsy evolved from demonic possession to a physical problem one feature remained constant. The afflicted souls were not in control of their faculties which raised the arguable proposition that epileptic attacks left the victims criminally unaccountable. Doctors and lawyers seized on the possibilities. A convulsive disorder seemed like the quintessential brain disorder which could excuse criminal misconduct. Unfortunately, doctors found it difficult to diagnosis the fleeting disorder. The Abraham Man perpetually exploited convulsions which complicated the use of epilepsy for the insanity defense.

The murder of Dorcas Magilton created quite a stir in Philadelphia. She was well known, and the brutal manner of her death contributed to a sense of deep disquietude. The shocking slaughter took place on a sleepy Sunday afternoon. On the day of the murder Mr. Adam Magilton left the house on foot, walking to a nearby store. His wife, sitting in a rocking chair and sewing, bid him adieu. It was meant to be a quick visit to the store but Mr. Magilton struck up a conversation with the proprietor. He finally began his trek back home, perhaps sensing his tardiness. As he prepared to enter the house Magilton was momentarily perplexed by the locked door. In a time when doors could be safely left unlocked, this was a puzzle. After trying in vain to gain entry, the door was suddenly flung open and George W. Winnemore sought to make a hasty exit. Seeing Mr. Magilton, Winnemore exclaimed, "Your wife is murdered; come in and see."[143]

Dorcas Magilton lay sprawled on the floor near the rocker which moments before she contentedly occupied. The panic stricken husband ran out into the street crying for the police. George followed, seemingly engaged in the same activity, but in reality he sauntered on down the street with no such object in mind. When the police returned to the crime scene the full horror of the murder became evident. Mrs. Magilton was apparently approached from behind catching her totally unaware. Seven blows from a hammer crushed her skull. The murderer then cut her throat. Aside from the victim nothing else in the house was disturbed.

George meanwhile was arrested by the police, no doubt following Mr. Magilton's confession of the chance encounter with Winnemore. George was naturally the prime suspect but he told a good story. According to Winnemore, he entered through the unlocked door and discovered Dorcas dead. He then proceeded to lock the doors in a vain effort to trap the murderer. After failing to find the assailant Winnemore was on the verge of leaving the house when he ran into Mr. Magilton. George was a frequent visitor to the Magilton's house so his presence was not wholly unexpected. As the investigation unfolded a few incriminating bits of evidence turned up. The police discovered a pair of two dollar bills which

---

143 "Atrocious murder at Germantown, new Philadelphia," *New York Times*, May 27, 1867.

purportedly belonged to Dorcas. A sharp razor was found abandoned in a well on the Magilton's property. A witness later identified the razor as resembling one seen in Winnemore's apartment. Curiously, no blood was found on Winnemore. The most unusual item found in Winnemore's possession was a suicide note. The note was dated about five weeks before the murder and made reference to unstated accusations, "which are utterly false. God knows I am innocent of them..."[144]

George Winnemore was charged with first degree murder. A mere ten days after Dorcas was murdered the wheels of justice began moving. The prosecution moved swiftly. Witnesses explained that Winnemore knew the Magiltons for a few weeks, perhaps drawn by word of their interest in spiritualism. In fact, the Magiltons regularly met to hold séances. George was twenty-four years old at the time and enjoyed the motherly attention of Mrs. Magilton. On the day of the murder Winnemore actually visited around breakfast time but left soon after. He returned later in the day claiming the opportune discovery of Mrs. Magilton's murder.[145]

The legal counsel for Winnemore relied on the insanity defense. Reaching back to his childhood, the defense attorney revealed a head injury which left the young Winnemore senseless. From that point forward he suffered seizures, even having an attack during the trial. The fits warped his mind as he grew older. His brother recounted incidents where George imagined seeing dead people come alive. His sister was alarmed by his strange behavior; laughing without reason, dancing about foolishly, and speaking a strange language. Several physicians examined Winnemore and testified at the trial. The defense also deposed several spiritualists. The spiritualists commented on Winnemore's trance-like behavior and ability to see ghosts.[146]

An intrepid reporter secured a written statement from the accused. It was a remarkably odd account of the trial. Court room observers were struck by Winnemore's aloofness. For a man facing a possible death penalty he seemed detached and wistful. His written statement suggested otherwise. "It drove me mad to hear the witnesses against me, and none for me. I was then told that I stood very well under it. No wonder, when I was a magnet, drawing the magnetism of 800,000 persons about me, and was the central point for all these currents. It is a wonder it did not

---

144 Ibid.

145 "The scaffold; execution of George W. Winnemore, the murderer, at Philadelphia," *New York Times*, Aug. 30, 1867.

146 Ibid.

take me up from their presence and take me away..."[147] The remainder of Winnemore's statement dwelled on his lack of attention to the legal proceedings. He seemed mentally dissociated often daydreaming of the afterlife. He protested his innocence repeatedly finally proclaiming, "I am perfectly willing to leave this earth if it will be beneficial to mankind, for I know that happiness awaits me on the other side which I hardly ever felt or saw while on earth."[148]

The speedy trial came to a close with opposing counsel offering their summaries of the evidence. The jury retired for a few minutes deliberation and returned to announce the guilty verdict. As throughout, Winnemore retained a passive air of indifference with both the verdict and the accompanying death sentence. His attorney now resorted to various post-conviction relief efforts, all of which failed. In a final desperate gamble to save Winnemore's life the defense attorney asked Isaac Ray to examine the condemned prisoner. Along with two other colleagues, Ray did as requested. The esteemed doctor of medical jurisprudence met with Winnemore for several hours.[149]

Ray and his colleagues considered the relationship between epilepsy and homicide. They seemed unpersuaded by the prosecution's claim that the few dollars found in Winnemore's possession was a sufficient motive for murder. After all, Winnemore had no prior criminal history. The doctors speculated that Winnemore, if he did commit the murder, may have acted from an altered, seizure induced state. Based on their preliminary assessment of the prisoner, Ray and his colleagues made an appeal to the Governor of New York. In their request, the doctors asked for a stay of execution in order to perform a more in depth evaluation. That request was denied. The speedy trial, appeals, and clemency ran their course in matter of weeks.

Winnemore consumed his last breakfast on earth which consisted of eggs, bread and coffee. He spent a few moments with his family before ascending the gallows. The condemned man spoke his last words, "But one thing I want you to remember, and that is, that it is an innocent man's life you are taking...I did not get justice...As Christ died for a principle, so do

---

147   "The Magilton homicide in Philadelphia: Winnemore's statements," *New York Times*, Aug. 16, 1867.

148   Ibid.

149   Isaac Ray, "Epilepsy and homicide," *American Journal of Insanity* 24, no. 2 (1867): 187-206.

I die..." With a farewell to his family the trap was pulled and Winnemore met his Maker.[150]

Isaac Ray considered the trial of George Winnemore a travesty. The pell-mell rush to convict the accused limited the availability of defense witnesses and a careful medical examination by competent clinicians. The prosecution shredded the epilepsy story, contending that no medical authority ever diagnosed the condition. Unfortunately, the answer was literally in the mail. Shortly after his death, the defense counsel received Winnemore's army discharge certificate, prominently noting his release for epilepsy.

The Asylum Superintendents were on the ropes. The McFarland Trial and the Winnemore case shoved the esteemed alienists into a corner. It seemed the only time the Asylum Superintendents prevailed was when their opinion went unchallenged. The criminal responsibility of epileptics was a hotly contested subject with the asylum superintendents asserting exclusive professional expertise. Much to their chagrin, William Hammond challenged the asylum superintendents' presumptions when once again the former Army Surgeon General weighed in on the Montgomery case.

The case of David Montgomery once again raised the thorny issue of epileptic insanity. Of course the matter would never have come to the public's attention without a crime and Montgomery furnished that when he killed his wife. The marriage was troubled from the outset. Montgomery lived a sheltered life but somehow the eighteen-year-old man managed to woo a woman. By all accounts his wife was vile and coarse. She was discretely described as unchaste but more accurately painted as a prostitute. Even more so, she enjoyed her work and chafed at the restrictions marriage imposed. Naturally this became a point of contention between the newlyweds. The pair got along well enough, when not arguing about the merits of fidelity, to have a child. The birth of the child did not cement the relationship and Mrs. Montgomery eventually fled her husband, taking the son along.[151]

David Montgomery was grief stricken by the loss of his wife and child. At the intervention of a family member, efforts were undertaken to reunite the couple. The husband and wife appeared to reconcile their differences and even dined peacefully together after patching up the rela-

---

150 Ibid.

151 M.G. Echeverria, "Criminal responsibility of epileptics, as illustrated by the case of David Montgomery," *American Journal of Insanity* 29, no. 3 (1873): 341-425.

tionship. Despite the seemingly amicable armistice, Montgomery darkly hinted to a friend that he would never suffer his wife's bad behavior again. As the evening light dimmed over the convivial reunion the family slowly made their way home together. They arrived home about midnight. The only historian to the events that transpired over the next eight hours was David Montgomery.

The early part of the night apparently passed without friction. At some point, perhaps after an intimate encounter, Montgomery began pressing his wife. He cajoled and pleaded, hoping to convince the wayward woman to remain faithful to her marital vows. Mrs. Montgomery resisted her husband's request and pointedly reminded him that her lifestyle predated their marriage. Somewhere in the early morning hours, about six or eight hours after they returned home, Mrs. Montgomery drifted off to sleep. David, perhaps still fuming about his immoral wife, went outside to get an axe. Montgomery's murderous impulse wavered for several minutes, perhaps struggling with ambivalence before striking a deadly blow. Immediately after killing his wife Montgomery ran outside. His father and a brother saw the distraught husband running from the house. Montgomery confessed at this point and attempted to kill himself with a razor. A police officer later testified that Montgomery spontaneously spoke that "his wife would be a whore, and that he would rather see her dead than to be one, and for that reason he struck her."[152]

Shortly after his arrest and confinement in jail a number of observers reported disparate findings. In response to a police officer's investigation Montgomery frankly admitted killing his wife in a fit of rage and briefly considered an escape to Canada. A chaplain visited the prisoner in jail mere hours after the murder. Montgomery's flushed face and manic condition concerned the chaplain. The story Montgomery told was essentially the same rendition except now he inserted a comment about kissing his wife after he killed her. Montgomery's casual comment impressed the chaplain, showing an apparent tenderness towards his wife which somehow seemed to soften the crime. A local newspaper reporter finagled an interview during which Montgomery affected a memory loss. When queried by the reporter, the prisoner could not recall where he was, why, or even his age.

Montgomery's confused behavior, seemingly purposeless crime, and history of seizures provided sufficient justification for the trial court to order an insanity commission. Four physicians, including the ever pres-

---

152 Ibid., 348.

ent John Gray, accepted the court's appointment. After reviewing the evidence and interviewing the accused the commissioners' issued a brief report. All four doctors agreed that Montgomery's epilepsy started as a young child, was occasionally marked by violent behavior, and the history of repeated attacks had created a "slight dementia." Dr. Gray later testified that Montgomery was insane when he murdered his wife, a direct consequence of the seizures and the dementia.

At some point, perhaps after the Commissioners' released their report, the prosecuting attorney approached Dr. William Hammond. The prosecutor hoped Hammond would review the evidence and offer a medical legal opinion. Hammond obliged, and after examining the legal record, concluded that the evidence did not support the insanity defense. This was a preliminary opinion, which Hammond believed could only be strengthened by interviewing the defendant. The prosecutor made arrangements for Hammond to interview Montgomery on two separate occasions. The two interviews did not change Hammond's initial opinion.

According to Hammond, the essential feature of a seizure was unconsciousness. An individual could not remember any behavior that occurred during the convulsion. In closing the door on further discussion, Hammond noted, "There is no case on record of a crime being committed by an epileptic during a paroxysm, and the recollection of it being present."[153]

When called to the witness chair, Hammond dutifully detailed his opinion. The prosecution's star medical witness admitted the obvious. The accused did indeed suffer from epilepsy, although to a lesser degree and frequency than Dr. Gray believed. Hammond never directly declared that Montgomery was feigning but he obliquely hinted at the possibility. It seemed rather self-serving, and not at all like a seizure, for the sufferer to have such detailed memories of the event. Montgomery's account of the murder included thoughtful deliberation, as he held the axe over his wife's head and pondered the possibilities. In any event, Hammond's testimony helped the jury convict Montgomery of murder.

The verdict was barely pronounced before the defense requested a new trial. The principal reason put forth by the defense was the presence of Dr. Hammond. Apparently the defense could find little to nitpick besides the fee charged by the famous doctor. It took a certain amount of chutzpah to lambast Hammond's $500 fee as exorbitant. The defense re-

---

153   William A. Hammond, "Medico-legal points in the case of David Montgomery," *The Journal of Psychological Medicine* VI, (1872): 62-76.

lied on the expertise of three physicians, including Dr. Gray. Apparently the three witnesses for the defense were satisfied with their state salaries, as opposed to the privately employed Hammond. The defense lawyer's post-conviction character assignation of Hammond hardly seemed a reasonable legal basis upon which to grant a new trial. The trial court judge politely reasoned that expert medical witnesses' fees were common practice and even more importantly the jury members heard of the fees during the trial. The judge did not grant the defense request.

The asylum superintendents and the dejected defense counsel lost two successive rounds to Hammond. John Gray would fight the next battle on his turf, launching a rebuke of Hammond's testimony from the pages of the Journal of Insanity.[154] The article, written by Dr. M.G. Echeverria, contained a verbatim record of Hammond's testimony, conveniently excluding a similar treatment for Gray and the other medical witnesses who testified on behalf of Montgomery. Naturally, this left the reader with no comparisons. It also exposed a deep bias on the part of the author who considered the asylum superintendents' testimony above reproach.

Hammond focused on Montgomery's behavior before, during, and after the murder. He saw purpose, motive, and deception. Echeverria looked at the same facts and concluded that Montgomery suffered epileptic insanity, based on a formula of duration, frequency, and heredity. The blind application of the formula defied common sense. Montgomery admitted the murder, expressed some regret in killing his immoral wife, and sought to escape the consequences. All of these behaviors pointed to a man who knew right from wrong. The jury obviously agreed with Hammond.

After the verdict the Governor of New York appointed another Lunacy Commission. John Ordronaux joined two other colleagues and set about examining Montgomery. Not surprisingly, the Commission found the convicted man insane and recommended his removal to an asylum. Hammond prevailed at the trial but the indefatigable asylum superintendents upended the will of the people and had their way in the end.

A new lunacy law greeted the citizens of New York in 1874. The new law granted broad powers to a trial judge to appoint a lunacy commission, which in turn, would report their findings to the court. If the commissioners found the defendant insane, and the judge agreed, the bother

---

154 M.G. Echevernia, "Criminal responsibility of epileptics, as illustrated by the case of David Montgomery," *American Journal of Insanity* 29, no. 3 (1873): 341-425.

and expense of a trial was avoided. The new system displaced the deliberations of a lay jury with medical experts. Defendants found not guilty by reason of insanity were sent to an asylum. From that point forward the asylum doctors determined the person's fate, specially charged with deciding how long the person would remain at the institution. This transfer of legal authority to the asylum doctors sparked a fair amount of criticism. "Criminals, especially those indicted for capital offenses and anxious to set up the plea of insanity, "emotional," or otherwise will no doubt invariably apply for the appointment of a commission to test their mental condition. If found to be insane they would be sent to a lunatic asylum, and should it happen that after a few months' confinement they should suddenly become sane, no course would be open to the authorities but to let them loose upon the community they had outraged."[155]

Perhaps it seemed odd that some members of the public lacked much faith in the asylum doctors. Part of the distrust came could be traced to the difficulty detecting the Abraham Man. The medical jurists sought to dispel these doubts with heaping doses of hubris. A deep vein of public suspicion usually countered the doctors' conceit. To overcome the public resistance the asylum doctors lobbied for judicial reform which removed the ill-informed jury. The end result was a lunacy commission. Isabella Jenisch was the first person tried under the new and very liberal lunacy law. The horrible crime committed by this woman, ostensibly gripped by epileptic insanity, guaranteed an avid audience.[156]

John Ordronaux recited the story of Isabella Jenisch in a manner resembling a magnum opus, complete with sardonic repartee and philosophic badinage. Before commencing a description of Jenisch's atrocious act, the author penned a preamble lamenting the apathy that infected the disinterested populace. The public seemed emotionally numbed by the number of murders in New York City. Although dutifully reported by the newspapers, the murders sparked little interest and no outrage. It almost seemed like murder was an expected part of life in a large, crowded city. Isabella Jenisch's crime disturbed the status quo.[157]

Isabella Jenisch was a poor woman who scarcely rippled the waters of life as she silently struggled day to day. She was not a sympathetic figure, looking older than her thirty-five years, unpleasantly plump, and sporting a ruddy complexion. Her blotchy facial features hinted at a fondness

---

155 "The new lunacy law," *New York Times*, Jan. 19, 1875.

156 Ibid.

157 John Ordronaux, "Case of Isabella Jenisch: Epileptic homicide," *American Journal of Insanity* 31, no. 4 (1875):430-442.

for intoxicating beverages. Isabella quickly admitted the obvious and agreed that she drank ale occasionally. Her memory was impaired, no doubt from chronic alcohol indulgence, leaving in doubt the true amount consumed. When not drinking, Isabella occupied her time with typical domestic chores. She kept her apartment in reasonably good condition and prepared the meals for her husband and two young children. Isabella was in poor health most of her adult life suffering mostly from an alcohol induced seizure disorder. In spite of their impoverished existence, Isabella apparently adored her children. At least she did until one day late in November 1874.

Mr. Jenisch was a common laborer, congenial in his relationships and frugal to a fault. He returned home as usual one night late in November accompanied by his brother. Upon entering his apartment, the worn out worker immediately noticed the pungent smell of smoke. He discovered his wife near the stove acting in a confused manner, oblivious to his arrival. The husband suspected his wife was drunk and, no doubt in disgust, left the room to check on his children. His four-year-old daughter moaned when he entered the room. She was lying on the bed dressed in a clean white night gown. The father picked her up, noticed a strange odor, and was horrified to discover the lower half of her body burnt to char. As he ran out the door to fetch a doctor, the husband instructed the brother to monitor the room. The brother asked the little girl's mother what happened. Isabella did not initially respond but later quietly stated she felt ill, retiring to bed where she stayed for almost a full day. Isabella's daughter lingered through the next day finally succumbing to the awful burns.

A police investigation added some details. Just before the little girl was apparently burned, Isabella complained to a neighbor that one of her "fits" was starting. The neighbor was familiar with epilepsy and helped manage the seizure for a while. For some unknown reason the neighbor left Isabella still in the throes of the seizure. From this point forward the history became more speculative, mostly based on the eyewitness statements of the six-year-old son and circumstantial evidence. Isabella remembered nothing of the affair. The young son told police that his mother put the little girl in the stove. In fact, the son first alarmed the neighbors by pounding on their door. The noise alerted a nearby apartment dweller, who tried and failed to open the locked door. The neighbor ran to the back of the apartment complex and ascended the fire escape ladder. She witnessed Isabella holding the girl near the stove.

Isabella's attorney entered an insanity plea and requested the court appoint a lunacy commission. John Ordronaux and two fellow doctors constituted the commission. After examining Isabella on several occasions, and taking testimony from many witnesses, the Commission concluded that Isabella's actions were the direct result of a seizure disorder. The doctors speculated that Isabella's seizure produced a profound mental disorientation. Ordronaux believed that Isabella was tending to one of her common chores, starting a fire in the stove, when the fit started. With her mind fully fogged by the fit, Ordronaux speculated that Isabella usually gave her children a bath while waiting for the stove to heat up. Regrettably, Isabella confused the stove with the wash basin which helped explain why the burns were only on the lower half of the child. The Commissioners unanimously declared Isabella insane. The disturbing unanswered questions included how the child's clothes were changed, what happened to the charred clothing, and what role alcohol played. Clearly the commissioners believed Isabella incapable of subterfuge.

Hammond and Gray were dogmatic dueling doctors. As they and like-minded colleagues fought pitched battles, the Abraham Man quietly took advantage of the disarray. In short order the nascent field of medical jurisprudence was under siege, forced to confront an implacable foe that left the public questioning their medical ability to discriminate the fit from the fake.

Chapter 5: Supporting Cast

Charles H. Nichols was appointed by President Fillmore to the position of superintendent of the newly christened[158] Government Hospital for the Insane. Nichols remained in that position for a quarter century.[159] After leaving the Government Hospital, Nichols assumed a similar position at the Bloomingdale Asylum in New York. Nichols devoted a substantial amount of time to professional and community organizations. Although not a founding member of the Association of Medical Superintendents of Institutions for the Insane, he was an active contributor who rarely missed a meeting. Beginning in 1873, Nichols served as President of the group for a six year stretch.[160]

As a person, Dr. Nichols cast an imposing figure. He was a tall man with a quiet, deliberative manner. A common description usually referenced his genteel manners. Friends and colleagues admired his organizing efforts, a talent embedded in the structure of the asylums he built and ran. Typically, the doctor was not the first to voice an opinion on contested matters but after joining a debate, he resolutely held his ground. Religion played an important role in his personal and community life. Nichols disagreed with Dr. Gray's narrow definition of insanity, allowing mental disorganization to develop in the absence of physical disease.

---

158 *Preliminary report of the eighth census,* edited by U.S.C. Office (Washington, DC: Government Printing Office, 1862), 430-43.

159 A. H. Hare, "Obituary," *Medical News* 56, (1890): 26.

160 T. E. McGarr, "Proceedings of the Association of Medical Superintendents of American Institutions for the Insane," *American Journal of Insanity* 47, no. 2 (1890): 166-239.

This more permissive view of insanity offered an opportunity for Nichols to examine, and ultimately support, the legal defense of Lewis Thornton Powell, otherwise more commonly known as Lewis Payne, one of the Lincoln Conspirators implicated in the assassination.

The trial of Lewis Payne moved along speedily. An effort by Payne's attorney to cast a wide net for prospective witnesses was defeated by the prosecution. The Government attorneys dismissed the defense's effort as a delaying tactic, solely undertaken to drag the trial out. Ultimately, the defense counsel dropped the request and the trial quickly moved forward.[161] Payne's role in the conspiracy involved invading the home of Secretary of State William H. Seward, and while there, he stabbed the Secretary and four other individuals. Seward's wounds were tended to by Surgeon General Joseph K. Barnes, who later testified against Payne. As the Superintendent of the US Government Insane Asylum, it seems reasonable to assume that Nichol's participation in Payne's defense carried certain political risks. Despite his accommodating stance towards Payne's insanity defense, the attorney seemingly mishandled his witness by peppering him with "scores of hypothetical questions." The disgruntled witness repeatedly voiced his discontent ultimately leading to a request, which was granted, to leave the courtroom.[162]

Contemporary news accounts did not paint a flattering picture of Payne "as a wild and savage-looking man, showing no marks of culture or refinement – the most perfect type of the ingrain, hardened criminal. He is fully six feet high ... blue eyes, large, staring, and at times wild ... slightly twisted mouth, curved unsymmetrically a little to the left of the middle line of the face."[163] In reality, pictures of Payne show a young, serious, reasonably attractive man. Other factual inaccuracies reported by newspapers, such as the claim that Powell deserted from the Confederate Army, could have been the result of sloppy reporting or an effort to vilify his character. In any event, the real story began when Powell enlisted in the 2nd Florida Infantry in 1862. He served without any particular distinction until receiving a minor wound at the Battle of Gettysburg. At

---

161 "Trial of the conspirators," *Philadelphia Inquirer*, Jun. 1, 1865.

162 Edward Wasgate Markens, "Lincoln and his relations to doctors," *The Journal of the Medical Society of New Jersey* XIX, (1922): 44-7.

163 D. Herrold, "Resume of the evidence and personal description of the prisoners," *New York Times*, Jul. 7, 1865.

this point, the wounded Rebel became a prisoner of war. He eventually escaped from a Union Hospital.[164]

The conspirator's trial engrossed the war torn nation. The evidence against Payne was overwhelming, probably leaving insanity as the best, if however remote, defense. William E. Doster undertook the herculean task of defending the assassin. Doster was an accomplished barrister, and seeing the insurmountable mountain of incriminating evidence, sought the only available path by invoking his client's supposed mental imbalance. The gist of the defense was an effort to convince the military commission that Payne was an ideologue living in a fantasy world of chivalry, honor, and duty in the lost Confederate cause. That argument needed the authority of a medical diagnosis stamping the behavior insane. Doster hoped Nichols, the Superintendent of the US Government Insane Asylum, would provide that credible diagnosis.[165]

Nichols contended that Payne suffered from moral insanity. Moral insanity was a controversial concept among the insanity experts. Gray denounced the diagnosis but many of his colleagues, including Nichols, disagreed. The notion of morality and immorality, with its attendant choices, was held as a religious tenant by Gray. As such, it resided in the soul, a metaphysical region without form or substance. Many doctors took a less rigid approach and believed that brain disease could destroy a person's capacity to act with propriety, restraint, and decorum. Moral insanity spared the intellect while allowing various forms of antisocial behavior an unimpeded expression.

Doster meticulously questioned Nichols, systematically building the argument that Payne was insane. According to Nichols, military service increased the likelihood of insanity along with irritability, depression, suicidal tendencies, stealthy behaviors, and unprovoked violence. Not surprisingly, each of these attributes seemed to fit the defendant. The manner of Payne's arrest also stirred the concern of Doster. "If the sane person ... although in the possession of a sound horse, make no effort to escape, but should abandon his horse, wander off into the woods, and come back to a house surrounded with soldiers, would that not be additional ground for the suspicion that he was insane?"[166] Nichols quickly agreed with the proposition. Additional behaviors offered as proof of

---

164   *The assassination of President Lincoln and the trial of the conspirators* (New York: Moore, Wilstach & Baldwin, 1865), 161-8.

165   Edward Steers, *The assassination of President Lincoln and the trial of the conspirators* (Lexington, KY: University Press of Kentucky, 2003), 161-8.

166   Ibid.

insanity by Doster, and confirmed by Nichols, included Payne's request shortly after his arrest to be hanged, his incongruous laughter during the trial, and a nonchalant attitude towards his death sentence.

Doster continued asking hypothetical questions of Nichols until the opposing counsel objected. The attorney representing the Federal Government's case objected to the defense counsel's confused, rambling, irrelevant interrogation of Nichols. Nichols seemingly took this as an opportunity to extricate himself. The Superintendent complained that Doster's incessant examination based on imaginary facts left no room for an informed medical opinion. It was all guess work and Nichols would have none it. He asked, and the judge granted, his request to be excused from further testimony. This seemed an odd turn of events. Surely the experienced superintendent of the US Government Insane Asylum understood his role as a defense witness and the implications of his testimony. The use of hypothetical questions was standard fare in a court room and the grumbling complaints by Nichols seemed out of place. Perhaps the gravity of the case, and the potential political consequences, led to the fumbling retreat.

James C. Hall, the second physician to testify for the defense, began his testimony by explaining the physical condition of Payne. Hall carefully examined the defendant, in contrast to the esteemed asylum superintendent who made no mention of a physical examination. Nichols did not explain what sort of evaluation, if any, he conducted. Hall testified that Payne displayed "a remarkable want of symmetry in the two sides of his head," an abnormal pulse, and a tendency towards constipation.[167] Hall tested his subject's memory which he found sluggish. In the end, the best Hall could state publicly was a suspicion of Payne's insanity. This assertion was certainly more than Nichols provided and was at least based on an interview with the defendant. In the end it did not matter. Payne was convicted and hanged.

When doctors dared to enter the courtroom a few books provided some guidance on avoiding the common mistakes. Perhaps the most commonly consulted and cited reference was Isaac Ray's "*A Treatise on the Medical Jurisprudence of Insanity.*" Isaac Ray was a legend in his time, widely revered for his sage thoughts on the relationships between insanity and the law. The author of this widely quoted book was born in 1807 in Massachusetts. A mere twenty years later he left Harvard with a medical degree. Moving north, Ray traveled to Maine where he prac-

---

167 Ibid.

ticed his chosen profession. In 1838 he published "*A Treatise on the Medical Jurisprudence of Insanity*," quite a feat for a physician not among the inner circle of asylum superintendents. Ray joined that august group in 1841 when he assumed the post of superintendent at the Insane Asylum in Augusta, Maine. Three years later Ray joined with a number of his colleagues in founding the Association of Medical Superintendents of American Institutions for the Insane. Isaac Ray later took the helm as President of the organization in 1855. Ray's contributions from this point forward, while still influential, declined as poor health and family misfortunes took a toll.[168]

Isaac Ray was no stranger to the Abraham Man. In fact, Ray considered fabricated mental illness one of the greatest stumbling blocks preventing the law from accepting the insanity defense. "The supposed insurmountable difficulty of distinguishing between feigned and real insanity has conducted, probably more than all other causes together, to bind the legal profession to the most rigid construction and application of the common law relative to this disease..."[169] In other words, doctors could not reliably identify an easily counterfeited mental disorder. This left the two professions, law and medicine, in a precarious, distrusting posture. The law could not cede decisions of criminal or civil culpability to the whims of doctors. For their part, doctors were frustrated by a legal system wed to arcane, unbending rules that failed to take account of modern scientific theories of human behavior. Ray saw the problem and proposed solutions.

The Abraham Man thrived in the long shadows cast by ignorance. By the time Ray wrote his seminal medical legal book, the asylums were firmly invested in the business of treating all manner of mental illness. This concentration of cases at the asylums certainly provided the staff an almost inexhaustible opportunity to treat and study insanity. Country doctors had far less opportunity to treat insanity but courthouses leveled the playing field. Much to Ray's eternal chagrin, the testimonial rules governing the admission of evidence rarely excluded any clinician. Ray considered much of the controversy and lack of faith in medicine's ability to unearth the malingerer, directly attributable to the inexperienced doctor who presumed to challenge the vastly superior knowledge of the asylum staff. His point was clear — if attorneys wanted reliable testimony they must draw doctors solely from the ranks of the asylums.

168 *Proceedings of the American Academy of Arts and Sciences*, New Series, Vol. X (Boston: University Press: John Wilson and Son, 1883), 457.
169 Ibid.

According to Isaac Ray, a skilled doctor could unmask the Abraham Man. Perhaps the greatest mistake the faker made was overplaying his hand. The performance, to the eyes of a knowledgeable doctor, was often too dramatic, too violent, too wild, or just too bizarre. A malingerer monitors the audience and adjusts the act as necessary. A truly insane person is indifferent to the public and deliberately downplays his insanity. Memory loss is a favorite tactic of the faker. The Abraham Man might proclaim vast swaths of their life as beyond recall, including their identity. According to Isaac Ray, an insane person has no memory loss; in fact the power of recall can be extraordinarily detailed. In mania one of the chief features was a seemingly inexhaustible supply of energy. Individuals feigning mania, unlike those with the real disorder, were hard pressed to stay awake for days on end. Ray cautioned physicians to carefully consider the longitudinal course of insanity. In most all cases, insanity had a lengthy period of decline preceding the frank display of delusions and hallucinations. Madness that conveniently coincided with malevolent behavior and immediately receded, suggested the presence of the Abraham Man. According to Ray, only the asylum doctors had the keen power of observation and the frequent association with madmen necessary to detect many of the subtle signs of insanity. A particularly difficult task involved disproving a claim involving hallucinations. Anyone could claim visions unseen by others or voices only reaching their ears. Ray understood the importance of defeating this simple ploy. A thorough evaluation and a lengthy period of observation often tripped up the faker.[170]

Ray devoted many pages to the subject of malingering. This was a necessary step to bolster the law's confidence in medicine's ability to accurately detect feigned behavior. Even as early as 1839, Ray must have known that the medical expert witness faced a bleak future in the court room unless the omnipresent Abraham Man was reliably exposed. In the beginning, the doctors' mere presence and presumed authority probably seemed sufficiently persuasive. An attorney's pointed questions, the doctor's arrogant responses, and the jury's general skepticism quickly eroded that credibility. Physicians soon realized that the scientific study of insanity polished their testimony to a new brightness.

John Ordronaux was somewhat in the mold of William Hammond, at least in terms of being a prolific author. Ordronaux was born in New York City in 1829. He studied law at Harvard and graduated with his degree in 1852. After a very brief period of practicing law, Ordronaux

---

170 Ibid.

temporarily cast aside his legal interests and pursued the study of medicine. Ordronaux graduated from the National Medical College in Washington, DC in 1859. Leaving the Nation's Capital, he returned to New York City later that same year. Upon returning to his hometown, Ordronaux fused his two professional degrees and was appointed a Professor of Medical Jurisprudence at Columbia University.[171] His expertise in medical jurisprudence led to academic appointments at Trinity College and Dartmouth. Although not an asylum superintendent, Ordronaux served in a somewhat similar administrative capacity as New York State's first Commissioner of Lunacy from 1873-1882.[172]

Ordronaux contributed to the Civil War effort by performing medical examinations on recruits from a Brooklyn office. Towards the end of the conflict, he was appointed an assistant surgeon of the Fifteenth Regiment, of the National Guard of New York. As a result of these two military experiences Ordronaux had the perfect perch from which to observe, and promote, best clinical practices. Ordronaux wrote two important books, *Hints on Health in Armies and Manual of Instructions for Military Surgeons on the Examination of Recruits and Discharge of Soldiers*, both of which served as professional field manuals. His interest in academic medicine produced two other books, the *Jurisprudence of Medicine* which appeared a few years after the war ended and the *Judicial Aspects of Insanity* which he wrote nearly a decade later.[173]

Although Ordronaux shared a passion for writing and lecturing like Hammond and Gray, the personalities of the threesome stood at opposite poles. Hammond and Gray were bombastic souls who willing waded into controversies. Both seemed to thrive on conflict. Ordronaux avoided conflict at all costs, and when unavoidable, emotionally retreated to minimize injury. "He was so very sensitive that the slightest physical hostility, or even opposition which savored of hostility, caused the doctor, like the leaves of a sensitive plant when touched, to fold up within himself. If, when he was testifying as expert in court, the cross-examination became of an overbearing or brow-beating character, he could scarcely (as

---

171   G. T. Chapman, *Sketches of the alumni of Dartmouth College: From the first graduation in 1771 to the present time, with a brief history of the institution* (Cambridge, MA: Riverside Press, 1867), 385.

172   "Deaths," *New York State Journal of Medicine* 8, no. 3 (1908): 168.

173   H. A. Kelly, *A cyclopedia of American medical biography: Comprising the lives of eminent deceased physicians and surgeons from 1610 to 1910.* Vol.II (Philadelphia: W. B. Saunders Company, 1912), 227.

he often informed his friends) refrain from bursting into tears."[174] The man's appearance did not inspire much fear, instead probably provoking derision. He was short, thin, boasted a crop of red hair, and was normally ponderous in thought, as if weighing the consequences of his words before carefully releasing them out of his mouth. He was deeply religious, acquiring a vast storehouse of knowledge on the subject. Ordronaux never married and was frugal to a fault. The man seemed a caricature of the bespectacled academic, counting as his preferred friends the words in books and otherwise venturing forth timidly in life.

The *Manual of Instructions for Military Surgeons on the Examination of Recruits and Discharge of Soldiers* expanded on the subject matter in *Hints on Health in Armies*. Military service offered one of the main stages for the Abraham Man. Ordronaux recognized this and took care by noting in the preface, "Many passages in the manual bear an impress of obscurity, which, it is almost needless to say, has been purposely given them, in order not to furnish any instruments of deception to those, who might seek here for assistance in accomplishing themselves in the art of malingering. While keeping this possibility constantly in view, it is believed that nothing of real importance to surgeons has been omitted."[175] Having said that, the author then described various methods of malingering often foisted by recruits. For example, some recruits tried to avoid military induction by faking hemoptysis. The actors would "prick the finger, forearm, or any other part of the body accessible to the lips, and by suction, fill the mouth with blood, which they void immediately after having feigned a spasm of coughing. Others prick the gums and pharynx,—while some conceal under the tongue or the hollow between the teeth and cheeks, Armenian bole, or a sponge saturated with blood, from which they express variable quantities, and thus redden the saliva. The cheat is easily discovered by passing the fingers through the mouth, and rinsing it out with acidulated water."[176]

The malingerer's creativity knew no bounds. Goiter could be faked by injecting a slight amount of air in the neck, bleeding from the stomach simulated by carefully hiding a quantity of blood in the mouth and "vomiting," skin disease by applying caustic solutions, lost teeth willfully removed, and a wobbly gait the result of a deliberate deceit. Ordronaux admitted that the most skilled and observant surgeons would occasion-

---

174 Ibid.

175 John Ordronaux, *Manual of instructions for military surgeons on the examination of recruits and discharge of soldiers* (New York: D. Van Nostrand, 1863), 10.

176 Ibid.

ally get duped by the Abraham Man. Whether from fear of the conse-quences, or simply from offering sensible advice, Ordronaux cautioned his colleagues about the risks of prematurely charging a recruit with malingering.

John Ordronaux's experience in the military sharpened the accuracy of his clinical observations, introducing the many faces of the Abraham Man, and possible left an indelible disdain for dissension. It seems curi-ous that a man so avoidant of controversy would devote the rest of his life to medical-jurisprudence. Ordronaux clearly seemed more comfortable in his arm chair than the witness chair. Perhaps the intellectual stimu-lation of jurisprudence attracted his interest more than the practice. In any event, after the war ended Ordronaux spent the next several decades lecturing, writing, and occasionally testifying about the relationship be-tween the law and madness.

As a physician and a lawyer, Ordronaux was uniquely qualified to define medical jurisprudence. Medical jurisprudence grew out of the overlapping interests between the two professions. Ordronaux set about early in his career to establish the ethical foundation of the new field. The ideal medical jurist is "a counsellor retained not in the interest of one par-ty, but in the truth generally..."[177] In reaching that lofty goal, Ordronaux set forth a number of injunctions, such as advocating the abolition of the term moral insanity. There seemed to be no advantage to using a term which had such a halo of controversy hovering above it. Ordronaux also suggested that medical jurists resist compartmentalizing insanity into convenient labels such as partial insanity and instead educate the court on the degrees of insanity present in the accused. In a similar fashion, Ordronaux chafed at the restricted legal definition of insanity. The pre-vailing legal definition of sanity required the defendant understand the difference between right and wrong. Ordronaux believed that insanity existed along a continuum, some cases devoid of reasoning while others seemed nearly normal. Further complicating the matter were the typical oscillations of the disorder that occurred over time in the same person. As a consequence, Ordronaux balked at the all or none legal concept of insanity which maintained that an insane person could commit a crime and still understand the wrongfulness of their behavior. For Ordronaux, the tiniest glimmer of insight was irrelevant since the defendant still had a persisting physical disease of their brain.[178]

---

177 Ibid.
178 John Ordronaux, "History and philosophy of medical jurisprudence," *American Journal of Insanity* 25, no. 2 (1868): 173-212.

Another raging debate of the day involved moral insanity. Ordronaux held firm, immovable views on religion. In fact, the doctor who was formally trained as an attorney had informal religious education on par with leading academic clerics. On the subject of moral insanity Ordronaux had no conflicts, expressly asserting man's separate moral and physical realms. According to the doctor, people could make bad moral choices which led to bad outcomes. Such choices did not constitute insanity. "It can never be other than blasphemous to assume God in condemning sin did not know the difference between it and disease, and that He could commit the injustice of permitting that very sin to convert itself into a physical disease for the purpose of eluding punishment ..."[179] Ordronaux carved out an opinion on moral insanity in opposition to Isaac Ray, almost ridiculing the concept as a medical cover excusing human depravity. Of particular concern to Ordronaux was the growing acceptance of moral insanity by criminal courts, which undermined broader spiritual efforts to proscribe bad behaviors. Science had its limits and could never unravel the soul.[180]

When it came to the written word, Ordronaux was a veritable pit bull. He vigorously scolded a system of justice which relentlessly excused all criminal behavior. Ordronaux was addressing a legal trajectory he feared, which seemed bent on divorcing morality from all bad behavior. He ridiculed his critics who believed, "Every vice, every crime is disease, nothing short."[181] According to the pious doctor, the utter descent into this folly was best illustrated by reformers attempting to redefine habitual drunkenness as a disease. Once classified as a disease, the morality was stripped from the behavior and the person excused from all consequences. In a methodical manner, the author explained the fallacy of alcoholism as a disease. In perhaps his most poignant attack, Ordronaux wondered what other disease required an exercise of will power as a cure. It was a valiant but doomed effort to blunt the advance of science and retain man's holy soul.[182]

Another interesting study in contrasts was the imposing personality possessed by Eugene Grissom. Where John Ordronaux went to the greatest lengths to avoid conflict, Grissom seemed to relish the role as a

---

179 Ibid.

180 John Ordronaux, "Moral insanity," *American Journal of Insanity* 29, no. 3 (1873): 313-40.

181 Ibid.

182 John Ordronaux, "Is habitual drunkenness a disease?," *American Journal of Insanity* 30, no. 4 (1874): 430-43.

medical pugilist. One of his best remembered publications was a withering diatribe in an article discussing, "True and False Experts".[183] Grissom,
lecturing from his days as Superintendent of the North Carolina Insane
Asylum in Raleigh, lambasted what he declared were "false experts." The
righteous superintendent indicted physicians who produced, according
to his view, misleading, contradictory, and flamboyant testimony. Even
worse, these false experts were not part of the close knit brotherhood of
asylum physicians. As such, these pretenders, and agents of the Abraham Man, did not have the experience gained from treating thousands of
inmates crowded in cramped institutions. The territorial breech of the
asylum superintendent's authority was insufferable. As a professional
servant receiving a salary, and expending vast sums of the public treasury on a hospital teeming with insane inmates, Grissom begrudged doctors in private practice the fees they charged. Although thinly veiled in
the literary edifice of "True and False Experts," Grissom was expressly
attacking William Hammond. In the most vitriolic language imaginable,
Grissom compared the false expert to "a moral monster whose baleful
eyes glare with delusive light; whose bowels are but bags of gold to feed
which, spider-like, he casts his loathsome arms about a helpless prey".[184]
The literary hit piece, "True and False Experts," soon found itself in print.
Grissom could count on his former classmate from their days in medical school at the University of Pennsylvania, John Gray, to publish the
article.

Grissom hardly needed to invite the inevitable counter attack from
Hammond and his friends. The asylums in America, first envisioned as
wholesome and humane soon suffered embarrassing setbacks. The over-
crowding caused concern as well as periodic accounts of poor treatment.
The use of mechanical restraints to subdue violent patients also upset a
segment of the populace. Grissom wrote a spirited defense of the practice,
taking swipes at his ill-informed critics, and supporting his fellow superintendents.[185] Roughly a decade after defending the use of restraints and
the venomous attack on Hammond, Grissom stood accused of "gross immorality, cruelty, and misappropriation of property at the asylum." Two
doctors brought the charges which led to a month long trial. Grissom
prevailed, in part by producing a letter written by one of his accusers to

---

183 Eugene Grissom, "True and false experts," *American Journal of Insanity* 35,
no. 1 (1878): 1-36.

184 Ibid.

185 Eugene Grissom, "Mechanical protection for the violent insane," *American
Journal of Insanity* 34, no. 1 (1877): 27-58.

a former female patient. His vindication was muted by three minority votes supporting the charge of "gross immorality".[186]

The list of physicians who shaped the nascent field of medical jurisprudence included Edward Spitzka. Spitzka rallied the Hammond contingent after the asylum superintendents' proxy attack with Grissom's "True and False Experts" article. The real battle brewing between Hammond and Gray was a power struggle between competing philosophies of insanity. Spitzka joined the battle and laid bare the hidden agenda behind Grissom's nasty attack. According to Spitzka, the Association of Medical Superintendents felt increasingly challenged by public perceptions of inhumane treatment in their institutions. Instead of addressing the concerns, the asylum leaders attacked Hammond who they blamed for stoking the public discontent. Spitzka directly raised charges of mismanagement and medical incompetence with a withering broadside by noting that, "a certain proportion of patients who die from the results of excessive restraint and violence at the hands of attendants, or from poisoning by narcotics, are knowingly reported to have died from incidental affections, in contravention of both the truth and the law. How closely entrenched superintendents are behind the veil of secrecy which covers most of the transactions in an asylum ..."[187]

Grissom's offensive article appeared in the Association of Medical Superintendents' flagship journal. Since Gray was the editor, the article naturally had his approval. The whole affair cast an unseemly light on insane asylums. By publishing the article, Gray allowed his enemies to respond with populist attacks. The lay press sensationalized accounts of poor care in the asylums. Spitzka joined the criticism by accusing the Superintendents' of financial corruption, barbarous care of the inmates, and lacking interest in scientific research. The merging of Spitzka's professional indictment with popular suspicions of the institutions only served to weaken the superintendents. "True and False Experts" was just another skirmish in the long running battle between Gray and Hammond. Most of the battles took place in the court room as each side sought judicial anointment as the undisputed insanity expert. The Abraham Man was lurking in the shadows determined to defeat and embarrass the dueling experts.

---

186 G. P. Shrady, "Dr. Grissom acquitted," *The Medical Record* 36 (1889): 129.
187 Edward C. Spitzka, "Merits and motives of the movement for asylum reform, In *Journal of nervous and mental disease*, edited by J. S. Jewell, H.M. Bannister, W.A. Hammond, and S.W. Mitchell (Chicago: G. P. Putnam and Sons, 1878), 703.

CHAPTER 6: CONTESTED WILLS

The earliest battles between medical experts involved disputed wills. In was during these encounters that attorneys and doctors took the first steps towards the growth and development of medical jurisprudence. The novel nature of the legal cases attracted the attention of the public. Newspapers favored the subject, since the stories typically involved the rich and famous.

Oliver Smith's contested will was an early example that bore all the hallmarks that would define many future cases. Smith left behind a valuable estate, and disinherited, disgruntled heirs, when he bequeathed his fortune to charity. The case attracted the attention of Rufus Choate and Daniel Webster, two of America's greatest lawyers. Supporting these two lawyers were some of the ablest physicians of the time, including Isaac Ray and Luther Bell. The drama unfolded in the mid nineteenth century and was a testament to creative legal thinking.

Oliver Smith was a rich man. During his life, through shrewd real estate transactions, he managed to accumulate nearly $400,000. The will was signed in mid-July, 1844 and Smith died shortly thereafter. His surviving heirs, incensed by Smith's generous donation of the estate to charity, sought the services of Rufus Choate, one of the best legal minds in America to overturn that decision.

Rufus Choate was born shortly after the America Revolution, and until his death in 1859 he steadily developed impeccable credentials as a lawyer, politician, and impassioned orator. His life and trials seemed inexorably intertwined with Daniel Webster, a fellow attorney and politician from Massachusetts. Both alternately served as US Senators with roughly similar political views.

Daniel Webster was a constitutional scholar who argued important cases before the US Supreme Court. He had a richer public life than Choate, serving as a US Senator, Secretary of State, and three-time presidential contender. Like Choate, Webster was a skilled orator, highly respected for his dramatic and influential arguments.

In the courtroom, even though both Webster and Choate occasionally stood across from each other when advocating different positions, they remained respectful and friendly towards each other. Perhaps the best testament of Choate's fondness for his occasional rival was the poetic eulogy delivered upon Webster's death. In any event, Oliver Smith's heirs recruited a most ardent, and innovative, barrister to handle their grievance. The preservation of the will, or more specifically the interests of the charity, fell to an equally astute lawyer, Daniel Webster. The stage was set for a grand legal drama.

The heirs sought the legal skills of Rufus Choate after suffering a stinging rebuke in probate court when the will as written was upheld. Marshaling their resources and demonstrating their resolve, the heirs promptly appealed the probate court decision. Choate and Webster argued the case on appeal.[188]

Rufus Choate challenged Oliver Smith's will in a most unconventional manner. Instead of attacking the testator's mental state, or some obscure codicil, Choate argued that one of the attesting witnesses, Theophilus P. Phelps, was insane and therefore incapable of determining Smith's mental soundness. In the span of three days Choate presented his case, Webster rebutted, and the jury decided.

Rufus Choate was determined to portray Theophilus as insane. If he was successful, the will would be judged invalid, lacking the two requisite signatures from competent attesting witnesses. The court heard testimony from Charles Phelps, his father, and various other witnesses commenting on Theophilus' strange behavior. Charles recollected a rather slow decline in his brother's behavior starting with a youthful predilection towards social isolation, poor physical health, and culminating in 1843 with a pervasive paranoia. In the summer of 1843, fear took a tight hold on the mind of Theophilus, leading him to suspect that various friends and family members were actively plotting to injure him.

---

188 "Oliver Smith's will," *American Journal of Insanity* 4, no. 3 (1848): 226-46.

His social isolation intensified, he disappeared for long periods without explanation, complained of unrelenting headaches, and was exceedingly restless and dysphoric.

The father of Theophilus endorsed much of what Charles related. It seems that the precipitating factor accelerating his son's descent into madness closely followed his father's accident. Late in the summer of 1843, the father broke his leg, after which Theophilus seemed to grow ever more irrational. Another brother, acting at the behest of the concerned family, finally persuaded Theophilus to seek medical attention.

Dr. Woodward examined Theophilus in August, 1843. During his testimony, the doctor recalled the intense fearfulness he observed in Theophilus. Although Theophilus complained of a headache, on closer questioning, the patient admitted that a feeling of "oppression" better described the discomfort. As noted by family members and friends, Theophilus was constantly scanning his surroundings, apparently responding to invisible persecutors. Theophilus admitted that he feared being "dissected" by these unknown tormentors. After a careful examination, Dr. Woodward concluded that Theophilus was delusional, a situation either aggravated or caused by dyspepsia. The chronic poor health accompanying the dyspepsia also contributed to a melancholy state, lassitude, and insomnia.

The subject of the trial, Theophilus P. Phelps, took the witness stand towards the end of the first day and "his testimony was given with remarkable clearness and precision. He gave a minute and lucid account of the transaction of attesting the will." Naturally, both Webster and Choate spent considerable time exploring the events as portrayed by the witness.

Theophilus responded to the probing inquiry calmly but with an uneven memory. Although Theophilus remembered his father's injury, he did not recollect the episode as particularly traumatic. Instead, he placed greater emphasis on a slow but steady decline in his physical health. Theophilus reasoned that his poor health affected his mind, causing nervousness, an unfounded fearfulness, and persistent headaches. The symptoms intensified towards the end of his last year at Amherst College and finally led to his visit with Dr. Woodward. A few months later, the mental confusion and depression lessened, leaving only the headaches unimproved. On cross examination by Daniel Webster, Theophilus claimed, "I think I have had no fears the past two years." Such an admission satisfied Webster, since it suggested that Theophilus was fully recovered, at least sufficiently to act as a competent witness to Oliver Smith's will.

The testimony provided by Theophilus seemed to favor Webster's position but Rufus Choate offered another twelve witnesses. These twelve additional witnesses included family physicians, Amherst College classmates, a pair of eminent ministers, and chance acquaintances, all of whom commented on peculiar aspects of his behavior. One witness, no doubt offered as proof of Theophilus' current insanity, testified, "he saw Theophilus sitting in a sleigh, in pretty cold weather, at the time of the Probate Court, for two hours..."

The parade of medical experts consumed much of the second day. Their appearance, and their prominent stature in the medical community, underscored the seriousness Webster attached to winning this case. All three physicians called as expert witnesses formed their opinions solely based on the evidence revealed during the trial, without benefit of an independent evaluation of Theophilus. For the time period, this sort of detached observation, and subsequent analysis of a witness' behavior, motivations, and mental condition, sufficed to offer expert testimony.

All three expert medical witnesses were superintendents of state lunatic asylums. The stature attached to the position enveloped the occupant with considerable influence. The first of the trinity to testify was Luther Bell, Superintendent of the McLean Asylum in Massachusetts. Dr. Bell readily conceded that Theophilus was acutely insane in 1843, but after a few months of mental confusion the condition gradually dissipated, restoring the victim's sanity. Bell summed up his testimony by declaring that, "My conviction is, that Theophilus P. Phelps was equal to such a transaction, as the attesting of a Will, in July, 1844.

Rufus Choate carefully developed the history of headaches as incontrovertible evidence of insanity. Theophilus also attached great weight to the headaches, even relating his insanity to the chronic pain. Since Theophilus still complained of headaches, even while performing his legal duty to Oliver Smith, it offered Choate the ideal argument connecting the insanity of 1843 with events two years later. Dr. Brigham, Superintendent of the State Lunatic Asylum in Utica, New York, minimized the headaches. In the doctor's experience, patients with insanity rarely complained of headaches. Brigham confidently declared, "Judging from the testimony of the different witnesses, and of the gentleman himself, I find nothing, that brings conviction to my mind, that he was insane in 1844."

Webster presented his most important medical expert when Isaac Ray, Superintendent of the Butler Hospital in Rhode Island, offered his opinion. Ray was the author of *A Treatise on the Medical Jurisprudence of Insanity*; a contribution accorded the highest medical accolades. The respected physician arrived at his opinion like his colleagues, through his attendance at the trial and through his reasoned interpretations. Dr. Ray equated the delusions Theophilus spoke of as evidence of insanity in 1843 and the utter lack of delusions in 1844 as proof of his restoration. Having arrived at this observation, Ray testified, "I have no hesitation in saying that Theophilus P. Phelps was perfectly competent to attest the will in 1844..."

The third and final day, "the court house was crowded to its utmost capacity ... to listen to the arguments." Closing arguments represented the last opportunity for an attorney to influence the jury.

Rufus Choate reminded the rapt jury members that Oliver Smith was a bachelor and his relatives expected to share in his wealth. From the law's perspective, this natural right to inheritance could be denied but only when legal procedures were strictly followed. According to Mr. Choate, the will in question failed this test by not providing three competent attesting witnesses. Through a methodical analysis of the evidence, and a reliance on legal authorities, Choate insisted that Theophilus P. Phelps lacked the capacity to judge the mental state of Oliver Smith.

The disenfranchised heirs could not hope to prevail if the eminent asylum superintendents' testimony went unchallenged. Choate spent considerable time attacking and disassembling the physicians' opinions. Choate reminded the jurors that, " medical men who were called hither, as experts, rely upon the fact that the family did not notice insanity, as evidence, almost conclusive, that none existed; but it is not; they constantly avoided probing him ... Insanity unquestionably existed in 1843, yet none of the family suspected it." Perhaps the asylum superintendents cringed a bit as Choate attacked the shallow basis of their opinions. After all, none of the three medical experts had conducted an independent assessment of Theophilus, instead relying solely on the information revealed in the acrimonious, adversarial court room setting. Clearly, Choate intended to impress the jury by the ease with which medical experts could be deceived by the Abraham Man.

Daniel Webster took his opponent's place scarcely five minutes after Rufus Choate finished his eloquent argument. Webster restated the matters in contention, at the same time trivializing the dispute. "This case turns a good deal on the character of a young man. The property is large. The heirs are disappointed ... Things have been presented in a dramatic form." Webster reminded the jury members that Oliver Smith was a bachelor and also emphasized that without brothers or sisters, the surviving nephews and nieces hardly qualified as natural heirs.

At the conclusion of the closing arguments, the judge took center stage and reminded the jury that the heirs had no rights if the will was properly executed. In this case, the question confronting the jury centered on the mental competency of one of the three required witnesses. Broadly paralleling the definition of competency offered by Daniel Webster, the judge instructed the jury members that "absence of interest, of infamy, and of imbecility of mind" was sufficient to attest the will. The jury members left the court room for about an hour and decided the case in favor of upholding the will of Oliver Smith.

The Oliver Smith case was sensational both in terms of the sizeable estate and the professional talents put forth in deciding it. The asylum superintendents took some hits but prevailed in the end. A raft of other legal contests followed Smith's case, some even achieving a greater fame. Each case touched an important testamentary issue, challenged the expertise of medical jurists, and collectively, although progressively, undermined the public's faith in expert medical witness testimony.

Many a will has foundered because of hastily crafted, bizarre, or simply unreasonable codicils. One of the most important cases of the nineteenth century addressed a will's three codicils, and in the process of litigating the matter, some of America's foremost physicians testified. The dispute enveloped the last will and testament of Henry Parish. It took nearly six years for the controversy to wind its way through probate and appellate courts.

Henry Parish was fifty-four years old, married but without children, when the original will was drafted under the able supervision of a respected attorney.[189] Parish was a successful merchant with a business office in New York City. He was known for his meticulous attention to financial details, regular habits, and reliable exercise of judgment.

Parish signed the original will in 1842 and carefully listed the legatees of his three-quarter million dollar estate. Approximately half went to his wife with the remainder distributed amongst various family members. The sore point that eventually led to the protracted litigation centered on a clause bequeathing the residue of the estate to his brothers. Parish directed that any future properties, or deaths of named beneficiaries, should enrich the residual portion of the estate, which went to his brothers. Several family members did pass away, and Mr. Parish consulted with his attorney. He was reminded that their portion of the estate now

---

189   Pliny Earle, MD, *Medical opinion in the Parish will case* (New York: John F. Trow, Printer, 1857).

passed, through the residual clause, to his brothers. Mr. Parish made no changes to his will, suggesting his interest in maintaining the status quo.

Catastrophe, in the form of a severe stroke, felled the vigorous merchant in 1849. Parish was left without his voice, the use of half of his body, and although the subject of immense debate, a diminution of mental acuity. The residual value of the estate had increased by nearly $300,000 during the seven years between the signing of the will and the stroke. Following the debilitating stroke, Mrs. Parish assumed an informal, but practical role, as her husband's guardian. Family members chafed at her control and criticized her self-imposed isolation. Once socially gregarious, Parish now received only occasional visitors.

Mrs. Parish was instrumental in amending the will with the first of three codicils written roughly one month after her husband suffered a stroke. Her portion of the estate increased in value by nearly half. Four years later, in the fall of 1853, the second codicil again revised the will. As before, Mrs. Parish was influential in recommending the change and benefited by yet another substantial financial gain. About nine months later the third and final revision revoked the brothers' residual legacy, awarding the bulk of the estate to Mrs. Parish. Parish died in 1856, and a short time later his contested will began its six year journey through probate and appellate courts.

The protagonists, chiefly pitting Mrs. Parish against her husband's disinherited brothers, fought an expensive and exhausting battle. An indisputable fact, that Parish suffered a massive stroke, was uncontested. Instead, the court battle focused on the degree of mental impairment suffered by Parish and the extent to which this precluded his capacity to alter the will. Related to this key question, thousands of pages of documents recorded the testimony of family members, friends, business partners, family physicians, and renowned medical experts. All the witnesses pretty much agreed that Parish lost the power of speech, the use of the right side of his body, and underwent a rather profound change in his personality. Faced with these facts, the attorneys for Mrs. Parish argued that her husband adapted to the stroke using alternate means of impaired but essentially effective communication. Naturally, the opposition took a different view and forcefully suggested the stroke left Parish a helpless mental invalid.

The Surrogate Court of New York City heard the first arguments contesting the Parish will case. A number of lay witnesses described the stroke and the sequelae. Immediately following the apoplexy, Parish suffered a right sided hemiplegia, loss of speech, and confusion. A few months later he could move his right leg somewhat and his mental confusion lessened. His previous silence gave way to a few guttural and garbled words that approximated "yes" and "no." Parish attempted to supplant his lost speech with vigorous gesticulations. Once an avid reader, the former merchant lost all interest in the written word. Nonetheless, some members of the family spent each day reading the newspaper to Parish. Whether he understood what he heard was a matter of conjecture but the family seemed convinced that the stimulation might improve his cognition.

Mrs. Parish remained tirelessly at her husband's side throughout the ordeal. She tried in vain to improve his communication. Efforts were undertaken to have Parish write with his left hand, point to phrases in books, or use alphabet characters. None of the efforts were particularly successful even though samples of his primitive writing were introduced as evidence of his mental capacity.

The stroke reduced Parish's social life dramatically. Previously accustomed to travel and hosting social activities, he now lived the life of a recluse. His isolation necessarily followed his mental and physical deterioration. No longer could Parish dress himself, eat without some assistance, or bathe alone. Even so, family and a smaller circle of friends, still maintained a daily vigil. Their frequent observations of Mr. Parish in the years after the stroke formed an important, and contradictory, picture of his impairment.

Of all the changes wrought by the stroke it was the change in his personality that most people commented on. Prior to the stroke Mr. Parish was universally portrayed as a calm, caring, and courteous man. After the catastrophe, nearly the opposite ensued. Parish was belligerent, short tempered, and occasionally violent. Evidence emerged at the trial suggesting Parish had struck his wife several times. Fits of deep despondency often preceded a seizure, after which Parish regained his equanimity. The seizures were frightful spectacles that convulsed his body in violent tremors and left him breathless for extended periods.

The mountains of medical testimony all addressed the "mental soundness" of Mr. Parish following the stroke. The term "mental soundness" was a legal concept derived from English Case Law and subsequently enshrined in American jurisprudence. As applied to testamentary capacity, the "mental soundness" of any testator was presumed to be present. In cases where the mental soundness was questioned, probate courts did "not measure the understanding of the testator, but if he have any at all, and be not an absolute idiot, totally deprived of reason, he is the lawful disposer of his own property, and his Will stands as a reason for his actions."[190] All parties in the Parish Will Case structured their arguments to accommodate this definition of mental soundness. It was an imperfect definition with no clear boundaries distinguishing an "absolute idiot" from a more functional "idiot." Nonetheless, a series of medical experts, all supporting dissolution of the later codicils, accepted the challenge.

Seven physicians reviewed the lengthy probate transcripts and unanimously agreed that Mr. Parish was 'mentally unsound" when the later codicils were written. The opinion of Dr. John Watson weighed heavily on the Surrogate Court's ultimate verdict, perhaps in part reflecting his exhaustive testimony which consumed three hundred and fifty pages of the legal record. Watson was a surgeon at the New York Hospital, an influential member of local and national medical societies, and co-founded the *New York Medical and Surgical Journal.*

Dr. Watson explained in excruciating detail the physical consequences of catastrophic bleeding in the brain. The right sided hemiplegia resulted from the injury to the left hemisphere of the brain. Watson, and his like-minded colleagues, went further in unambiguously asserting that the right side of the brain did not escape unscathed after the stroke. The seven differed only in the degree to which they believed the right brain suffered. Watson testified that "No brain can be extensively diseased on both sides ... without impairment of mind sufficient to be at once recognizable by the medical observer." Watson's testimony seemed to suggest that the resulting impairment was relatively feint and detectable only by skilled clinicians. Subtle, minimal, or even moderate intellectual impairment clearly did not meet the legal standard of an "absolute idiot" required for testamentary incapacity.[191]

Dr. Luther Bell, considered "one of the ablest and most experienced American experts in insanity," agreed in principle with Watson. Like his colleague, Bell reviewed the legal record in arriving at his opinion. None of the expert witnesses conducted an independent inquiry that might have broadened their investigation beyond the highly partisan nature of the probate hearing. In any event, Bell was entranced by the testator's post-stroke violent convulsions and seized on this history as confirming damage to both sides of the brain. It was important to emphasize global brain impairment, and minimize adaptive coping, to meet the legal test of "mental unsoundness".

---

190   "The Parish will case," *American Journal of Insanity* 19, no. 2 (1862): 210-27.
191   Ibid.

Even the venerable Isaac Ray joined the group of seven in concluding that the testator lacked the means of expressing his will. Ray's opinion typically carried great weight since he was a well-known authority on medical-legal issues.

Pliny Earle was also among the seven physicians who collectively opined that Mr. Parish lacked sufficient mental acuity to author the will's codicils. At the time Earle publicized his analysis of the Parish will case he was employed as a physician at the Bloomingdale Asylum for the Insane, in New York.[192] Earle was also an active member of the Association of Medical Superintendents of American Institutions for the Insane.

Dr. Earle memorialized his opinion of the Parish will case in an extensive review published in 1857. Like all the other experts, Earle received a copy of the probate proceedings with the expectation that after reading the transcript he would apply his knowledge of mental illness to the testimony. Before issuing his opinion, Earle realistically noted that the definition of "mental unsoundness" was imprecise. Nonetheless, Earle approached his task with a serious resolve and a comprehensive structure designed to touch on all known aspects of mental illness. In setting forth his opinion, Earle explained the two step methodical process leading to his conclusions. Earle first delved into the "Relationship of the testator's condition subsequent to the attack on the 19th of July, 1849, to his condition antecedently to the attack followed by an analysis of the antecedent, attendant, and collateral facts and circumstances." These two broad areas canvassed hereditary influences, prior brain injuries, instances of peculiar behavior before and after the stroke, family relationships, and a detailed review of Parish's personality. Earle's structure was a useful tool to organize information but it seemed to offer little benefit in answering the ultimate legal question.

Earle rather begrudgingly acknowledged that Parish had a limited capacity to communicate. His mannerisms and indistinct utterances forced his family to exert extra efforts to understand him, often leading to a pleasant outcome. Parish was judged not by his limited success in communicating but more harshly measured in terms of lost abilities. The fact that Parish could not write, seemed little interested in reading, and was socially isolated weighed heavily in favor of "mental unsoundness." In an apparent display of thoroughness, Earle carefully cited the observations of family physicians long familiar with Parish. One physician testi-

---

192   Pliny Earle, MD, *Medical opinion in the Parish will case* (New York: John F. Trow, Printer, 1857).

fied that "the condition of his mind appeared to be clear, sound." Earle dismissed his colleague's account since the physician's consultation extended only to an examination of Parish's eye. Another family physician stated, "he appeared to understand simple questions regarding his health." Yet again, Earle dismissed the testimony as irrelevant since "the same may be said of a large majority of the inmates of the hospitals for the insane." Dr. Earle seemed determined to find Parish mentally unsound. After hearing all of the evidence the Surrogate Court declared the codicils following the stroke invalid, inviting the inevitable appeal.

The New York State Court of Appeals was the final stop in the seven year litigation of the Parish Will case. The Court's majority opinion sustained the will but reversed the last two codicils. In doing so, the majority overruled previous legal decisions holding that a will's provisions could only be reversed if the testator's mental state matched that of an "absolute idiot." Clearly, the majority could not sustain their ruling using that rigorous standard. The judicial majority removed that burdensome obstacle by rejecting previous legal precedent and rewriting a new standard. Henceforth, a valid will required the testator possess, "sufficient capacity to comprehend perfectly the condition of his property, his relations to the persons who were, or should, or might have been the objects of his bounty ... and He must have sufficient active memory to collect in his mind, without prompting ... the business to be transacted ... and to hold them in his mind a sufficient length of time ... and to be able to form some rational judgment in relation to them."

The medical witnesses obviously influenced the majority's opinion. Each received a respectful deference, were extensively quoted, and their credentials wrapped in lofty superlatives. Two appellate judges, who constituted the minority opinion, were less enthusiastic. Their views, while not openly hostile to the parade of medical experts, bordered on the dismissive. A number of witnesses, including a physician who maintained daily contact, a politician holding a high state office, an affluent merchant, and the Superintendent of the Military Academy at West Point all testified that Parish was able to "understand himself perfectly." The dissenting jurists expressed disbelief that men of this stature would confuse Parish with an "absolute idiot."

Parish, and a close business associate, often met together to decide which stocks and bonds to buy or sell. Throughout these complex negotiations Parish always seemed engaged and directed specific transactions. In a matter more directly related to the codicils, several witnesses testified that Parish long resisted a specific charitable donation. After much haranguing from several family members, Parish finally relented and left a small legacy to the charity. The two appellate judges writing the minority opinion took this and many other examples, as proof of Parish's intact intellect.

The decision in the Parish will case raised the intellectual requirements for testamentary capacity. It also signaled a relatively enthusiastic acceptance of medical testimony. The doctors' contributions in upending the Parish will guaranteed future medically-assisted assaults on testamentary capacity. A trickle of lawsuits soon gave way to a flood of litigation.

The legal definition of testamentary capacity was evolving in America when the Angell will case came before the probate court in 1862. The disaffected heirs challenged the will claiming Eliza Angell was insane. At this point in American jurisprudence, a successful challenge of this sort required proof of severe mental illness, such as "congenital imbecility," advanced dementia, or habitual intoxication. The law gave great deference to a person's last bequest, even allowing retribution to be exercised beyond the grave. Disgruntled heirs maneuvered around that obstacle by challenging the testator's sound memory and judgment, both of which were legal predicates for a valid will. Generally, a person who could honor any legal contract and "transact the common business of life" passed the law's test to create a valid will. This doctrine slowly changed and was replaced by a higher standard. The new legal standard for testamentary capacity tied mental agility to the estate's value. Probate courts adopting this approach reasoned that large estates demanded a fiscal and intellectual prowess well beyond that necessary to dispose of a miniscule inheritance. The prosperous testator's aberrant behavior, not just their memory or judgment, now came within the scope of testamentary incapacity. Eliza Angell was indeed strange and her unhappy family members produced endless examples to back their claim that she was insane.

The natural heirs challenged the will in probate court on three occasions. The first two trials resulted in a "hung jury." The third trial reached a different conclusion. The two sides squared off against each other in the third trial. The disinherited family members brought forth a litany of evidence demonstrating Eliza's insanity. The main thrust of their case centered on a twenty year unfounded claim that family members had stolen a valuable piece of real estate from Eliza. The family members also noted that "she believed without a tittle of proof" that her relations hated her and were constantly making her life miserable. "One witness testified that Eliza believed everyone wanted to rob her – except the milkman."

She claimed that the servants stole her food, neighbors stole her chickens, and more ominously, believed that various people tried to poison her food. She kept a pistol under her pillow and two more on the floor should any one attempt to harm her. Sometimes Eliza dressed in a rather reckless, revealing fashion that shocked the neighbors. Dr. Tyler of the McLean Asylum added to the testimony by "unhesitatingly expressing the opinion that" Eliza was insane.

The beneficiaries of the will countered this testimony. They noted that an attorney prepared her will, "another was her advisor," and several physicians that treated her over the years all uniformly found "nothing strange or unusual in her conduct or conversation, dress or demeanor".

The standards for deciding the effect of mental illness on testamentary capacity were evolving but the Angell will case helped move the process along. Until this time, insanity sufficient to overturn a will required severe mental derangement referred to as "congenital imbecility, paralysis or the decay of old age." To help gauge the impact of illness on capacity, "courts were always seeking some standard by which the testamentary capacity could be measured. In the case of imbeciles, the ability to count to ten, to tell the day of the week, or measure a yard of cloth..." Eliza was not this impaired but the probate court set a different standard by requiring a greater mental capacity "when disposing of a large amount of property to various persons..." The Angell will case also dismissed the time honored notion that distant family members had no legal standing to contest a will. And finally, the case severed the previously required link between a delusional mind and the creation of the will. "It is not necessary to show that the will was the legitimate offspring of that delusion." The mere fact that Eliza had a long history of a mental disorder was sufficient to invalidate the will.

The long accepted social sentiment expected that a person's accumulated wealth would pass to close family members. Any deviation from this practice, such as a charitable distribution, increasingly raised the possibility of a posthumous legal intervention. "Last wills have been a prolific cause of imputed insanity. Many excellent people have gone with tainted memories among their posterity..."[193] Attorneys honed their legal arguments and physicians refined their definitions of insanity.

When determining the impact of mental disease on testamentary capacity, American Courts of the 1860s generally considered insanity as

---

193 "Last wills – Unsound mind and memory," *American Journal of Insanity* 25, no. 2 (1868): 213-35.

either active or passive. Passive insanity lumped all forms of congenital mental disease under the banner of idiocy. For the most part, individuals with passive insanity could not create a valid will. Active insanity on the other hand created a fertile field of medical-legal dissension.

Physicians and jurists generally accepted a nomenclature which classified active insanity as either moral or intellectual mania. Individuals with moral or intellectual mania could suffer the disease in two stages, referred to as general when the full range of symptoms were present or partial in less severe cases. General examples of intellectual mania produced far less legal controversy than moral mania of any type.

Asylum superintendents, the self-appointed experts of mental disease, equated the label intellectual mania with reasoning insanity. Intellectual mania, a form of active insanity, arose from a disturbance in the person's reasoning faculties. The *sine qua non* of intellectual mania was delusional thinking. An individual afflicted with intellectual mania, and exhibiting delusional thinking, would adopt a patently false or ludicrous viewpoint which no amount of reasoning could dislodge. In the general form, the disordered thinking spanned a wide range of aberrant behaviors. Partial intellectual mania, also known as a monomania, preserved much of the intellect and created a disturbance involving only one discrete behavior. Popular novels of the time, including Herman Melville's Moby Dick which highlighted the obsessive behavior of a ship's captain in pursuit of an elusive whale, brought the monomaniac to life.

The asylum superintendents unequivocally associated intellectual insanity with a lack of mental responsibility. If the mental footprint of delusional thinking was evident in the creation of a will, the disaffected heirs stood a good chance of prevailing. The same medical authorities took a much dimmer view of moral mania. In fact, almost without exception they derided the notion of a moral insanity. While intellectual mania distorted rational thinking, moral mania perverted the normal emotions. In moral mania the normal person's emotional ups and downs gave way to disabling exaggerations. Acting under the throes of deep despair, morbid melancholia, or excessive excitement, a normally stable person's behavior became widely erratic. Champions of moral mania pointed to the person's singular preoccupations to explain the existence of a mental disease.

Moral mania preserved the intellect along with the capacity to reason. As a consequence, victims of moral mania could make proper judgments and decide right from wrong. A popular description of moral mania encapsulated the religious overtones, "The man retains his intellectual powers unimpaired, but he sets his heart fully to evil. He refuses to yield to the demands of his conscience. He practically discards the obligations of moral responsibility. He has the powers of free moral agency, but persistently abuses them. He has a reason which affirms obligation, but he refuses obedience to its affirmations... Since the Bible affirms it to be a fact that sinners are mad in heart, we may naturally expect to see some manifestations of it."[194]

Both general and partial versions of moral mania found little legal traction when disputing a will. On the other hand, partial intellectual mania produced convulsions in the legal system with episodes of acceptance alternating with rejection. During the Civil War era, some legal theorists argued that any evidence of delusional thinking whether temporally related to a will's construction or not, unquestionably proved testamentary incapacity. Some states, including New York, gradually adopted a different approach and invalidated a will only if the monomania left distinct traces negatively affecting the interests of the natural heirs.

Charles Hopper wrote his will on October 28th, 1861 and died four days later. He was sixty-seven years old and left behind an estranged widow, a sister, and an assortment of more distant relatives. By all accounts, Hopper was a course, vulgar, profane man with a penchant for the bottle. He bullied his way through life, but he made a fortune as a butcher in the Franklin Market of New York, and invested the proceeds shrewdly in real estate. Even those individuals who disliked Hopper commented favorably on his business skills, devotion to work, and headstrong ways. Hopper was illiterate, but when necessary, as in writing his will, called in learned advisors to fill in that deficiency.[195]

Hopper left the bulk of his $100,000 estate to twin charities, the American Seaman's Friend Society and the Ladies' Union Aid Society. The will provided for his wife, left various tokens to family members, and handsomely rewarded a home nurse. Despite the will's superficial generosity, Hopper's widow and certain family members took exception to the charitable legacy. A few months later the New York City Surrogate Court declared the will invalid. The two charities sought to reverse that decision and appealed. The New York State Court of Appeals reviewed the matter carefully.

The family insisted that Hopper was insane and his legacy a demonstration of foolish beliefs. With some consistency, most witnesses de-

---

194   Charles G. Finney, "Moral insanity," *Oberlin Evangelist*, Sep. 10, 1856.
195   "The Hopper will case," *American Journal of Insanity* 22, no. 3 (1866): 285-307.

scribed a change in Hopper's behavior around 1856. Hopper's distinctive truculence transitioned in an ominous fashion from bearable irritability to an irrational mistrust. In the succeeding months and years, Hopper's suspicious nature intensified. He alternately quarreled, condemned, and accused his wife and family of various nefarious schemes. Hopper lived in perpetual fear, always vigilant, awaiting with dread an uncertain fate at the hands of his family. A particular incident absolutely cemented in Hopper's mind the evil intentions of his family.

Whenever family member's challenged Hopper's paranoia he resolutely indicted them all with the steamboat affair. Always on the lookout for trickery, Hopper's fear no doubt spiked when the family arranged a leisurely steamboat trip. Once on board, Hopper's anxiety fueled his imagination. Convinced that his family awaited the proper moment to throw him overboard, and then divvy up his estate, Hopper took the initiative and apparently sought protection from the ship's officers.

The Surrogate Court records listed other examples of Hopper's suspiciousness. Chloroform played prominently in one of Hopper's more persistent accusations. He was convinced beyond reasoning that his family was poisoning him with chloroform. Odd tasting food, fatigue, and an occasional tumble all served as evidence to Hopper of the ill effects of chloroform. Business associates were shocked when Hopper took them aside, spoke of the family conspiracy, and sought their support in his struggle.

In 1859 Hopper was arrested. The arrest followed a particularly vicious argument with his wife, during which Hopper apparently threatened his wife's life. By this time, Hopper's wife had endured three years of ever-increasing belligerence, but now citing concerns about her own safety, she left the ill-tempered husband. Her departure, far from motivating any rapprochement, led to even greater recriminations as Hopper now concluded that his wife's separation stemmed from infidelity.

Following his wife's parting, Hopper accused her of adultery. When pressed to name the men, Hopper accused several well-known and respectable members of the clergy. Unlike him, Mrs. Hopper was devoutly religious and maintained close ties to a local church. Such familiarity apparently preyed on Hopper's feverish mind eventually bubbling forth with an insane jealousy. In a further response to his wife's betrayal, Hopper would frequently accost strangers on the street and accuse them of supporting the marital separation. Towards the end of his earthly existence Hopper complained of scattered body pains and non-healing sores. Despite medical reassurance, Hopper claimed the physical ills came from his wife's unfaithful activities.

The Court of Appeals framed the Hopper Will Case along two opposing lines. As the Court reasoned, was Hopper's behavior the product of bad-temper liberally saturated by intemperance or was his behavior irrational and delusional? The court considered additional testimony before deciding between the two viewpoints.

Dr. Downs was a family physician familiar with Hopper's final year. He listened with patience as Hopper ranted relentlessly about the family conspiracies. Downs eventually concluded that his patient suffered from a monomania, entirely distinguished by a venomous preoccupation with his family. Despite the Doctor's diagnosis of insanity, he nonetheless attested his deranged patient's will.

Another peculiarity the Court of Appeals looked at concerned Hopper's choice of legatees. Long before his death Hopper accused a nephew with a blatant and malicious assault. Family members could never unravel the mystery and dismissed the story as yet another fabrication of Hopper's distorted psyche. A rational person would scarcely consider such an act worthy of a bequest yet that is precisely what Hopper did to the amazement of friends and family. In a similar act of perplexing beneficence, Hopper left a tidy sum to his nurse. The nurse shared many of Hopper's worst traits, a rude, offensive woman who drank excessively. Hopper snubbed several gentle and compassionate family members.

Weighing all the evidence, the Court of Appeals logically arrived at the conclusion that Hopper was insane; the victim of a moral mania, and the will was declared null and void. As a consequence of the Court's action, the disposition of Hopper's estate followed New York's definition of intestacy.

John Ordronaux, a giant in the world of Civil War era medical-legal practice, cited the case of William Winter as the perfect example of what comes from a poorly informed legal system. Instead of attacking the author of the will, the contestants sparred over the mental capacity of the executor. The facts, at least according to Ordronaux, could only lead to one outcome.

Gabriel Winter and his wife died in 1862 and left a sizeable estate to their only son, William. Gabriel Winter's two grandchildren petitioned the court to invalidate the will because William was considered an unfit trustee given his long standing mental illness.[196] William was indeed a strange person. For as long as the family could remember, William stood

---

196 John Ordronaux, "In Re William Winter," *American Journal of Insanity* 27, no. 1 (1870): 47-80.

apart from the rest of his family – quite literally. William would never eat with his family, always insisting on a separate area in the kitchen. In fact, this space was his dominion. William ruled in a peculiar manner over the staff from his self-appointed perch in the kitchen. "His orders to servants were usually given in a loud, peculiar, screaming or howling tone, and in a way to alarm every person who heard it." Other habits disturbed the family. William's bedroom was filthy, he wondered about in a sullen, depressed state, and had erratic sleep.

William was suspicious of nearly everyone but his distrust morphed into a passionate hatred of his father. Often times these verbal attacks escalated for no apparent reason into violence, directed at any nearby property. William's behavior took a decided turn for the worse around the age of nineteen when he was a student at Columbia College. During the next few years he tried various professions such as law and medicine but failed at each. William also suffered from other oddities. He mindlessly collected scraps of paper and most ominously "became addicted to the practice of the secret vice of onanism..."

During these wandering years, William fell under the spell of an attorney who was unknown to the other family members. The relationship between this attorney and the future trustee of a large estate caused further alarm. Shortly after William met his attorney friend he left home to live with him. In the first nine months of their life together, the attorney received over two thousand dollars from William for various legal services. Naturally, the family believed the attorney was a scam artist taking advantage of William's mental infirmity.

Not content to stand idly by, the family petitioned a lunacy commission to examine William. The commission duly assembled and took the testimony of many witnesses – all for the purpose of determining William's mental fitness to serve as the trustee of his father's estate. Ordronaux points to the absence of a single medical expert on the lunacy commission as evidence of a wholly inept judicial proceeding. In any event, these lay commissioners listened to many witnesses, including seven physicians who testified against William. This group of seven pretty much agreed that "it was unsafe to entrust a mind as weak as Winter's with the charge of a large estate." The jury, obviously unimpressed with the doctors' testimony, dismissed all these concerns and concluded that William could handle the estate. Ordronaux was vindicated by the rest of the story. Several years after the verdict, William's peculiar habits accelerated while his attorney friend now gave "evidence of a wealth somewhat rapidly accumulated..."

Sometimes a contested will revealed a neglected chapter in a famous person's life. Such is the case of Horace Greeley's will. Greeley is a legendary figure celebrated in history for his contributions to journalism, politics, and various social causes.[197] His early life was remarkable for demonstrating, even at the youngest age, a manifest destiny.

Horace Greeley was born in 1811 and spent his early years in New Hampshire.[198] Contemporary accounts credit the young Greeley with learning to read before talking. Greeley passed many hours under a shade tree, as early as the tender age of six, totally absorbed in some literary work. Another favorite pastime was spelling and Greeley would spend hours honing his vocabulary through the process. The future orator canvassed all homes in the area, sometimes walking up to seven miles, borrowing every book he could find. Although he devoured books, the young Greeley's favorite reading material was the local newspaper. Greely's parents fretted that about their son's obsession with books and lack of interest in other youthful pursuits.

Greeley's early childhood changed dramatically when the creditors came calling. After they left, the bankrupt and discouraged family relocated to nearby Vermont. Greeley quickly restored his balance and resumed his voracious literary appetite. A short time later Greeley left home after accepting an apprenticeship at a newspaper. Greeley took his most important step when he left for New York City in 1831. With ten dollars to his name, the intrepid journeyman printer continued his labors for six dollars a week, working exceedingly long hours for that sum.

Innovation flourished in the heart of Greeley and soon after arriving in New York his entrepreneurial spirit motivated the launch of a penny newspaper. His audacious venture failed but Greeley persisted and in 1841, ten years after arriving in New York, succeeded with The New York Tribune. The New York Tribune was a penny post in a city already saturated with twelve daily newspapers. A competing newspaper responded by attacking The Tribune's news carriers, which actually backfired, and spurred sales.

The Tribune grew to become a respected voice of public opinion. From that carefully cultivated platform, Greeley promoted Fourierism, a socialist theory of government. The notoriety gained from the editorial pulpit of The Tribune served Greeley's political interests, which led to a

---

197 James Parton, *The life of Horace Greeley* (Boston: Houghton, Mifflin, and Company, 1889), xiii.
198 Ibid.

brief term in the US House of Representatives and his nomination in 1872 as a presidential candidate.

A combination of factors led to a precipitous decline in Greeley's mental functioning. He vigorously campaigned for President but ultimately was rejected by the voters. The rigors of the election, and the loss, sapped his vital energies. His wife died around this time further destabilizing his tottering psyche. After his defeat at the polls, Greeley resumed his editorial work at The Tribune. A visibly fatigued and wasted Greeley alarmed his friends and co-workers with previously unseen behavioral eccentricities. His rambling speech dramatically emphasized the mental decline and eventually led to a touching retirement to a private sanitarium.

George Choate, a nephew of the famous attorney Rufus Choate, was a physician with a private sanitarium in Pleasantville, New York. It was here that Greeley spent his final days. Soon after arriving, Greeley's insanity intensified into excitable spasms of maniacal behavior. Choate's famous patient refused to eat and the lack of nourishment further weakened Greeley, eventually culminating in the editor's death on the 29th of November, 1872.[199]

Horace Greeley resurfaced, at least in name, when an unhappy heir contested the probate proceedings. The heirs originally presented a will written in 1871 to the surrogate court. Unfortunately, Greeley apparently wrote another will in the succeeding year which led to the legal controversy. The will of 1871 left the bulk of the estate to Ida and Gabrielle Greeley although the Children's Aid Society received a generous bequest. Among other changes, the revised will of 1872 neglected the Children's Aid Society, leading the executors' of the earlier will to protest the changes. In deciding which of the two wills to honor, the surrogate court in White Plains, New York investigated various irregularities in the construction of the 1872 document along with an in depth review of Greeley's mental state.

Friends and personal acquaintances of the respected editor were shocked by Greeley's aberrant behavior, recalling the onset around the first of November, 1872. The situation only worsened over the next week and during a period of obvious confusion, Greeley apparently rewrote his will. As the surrogate court noted, a number of irregularities cast doubt on the legal authenticity of the 1872 will including the mystery surrounding where the document was written, found, and most importantly, the

---

199 George Shrady, *Medical Record*, Vol. 50 (New York: William Wood, 1896), 19.

extent of Greeley's contributions. The court was further frustrated by the witnesses' "very meager and unsatisfactory" evidence bearing on Greeley's mental state when the second will was written. Despite that obstacle, the court pieced together sufficient information to question Greeley's testamentary capacity.

Greeley wrote the amended will on the 9th of November 1872, during which "no word was uttered by the dying man other than the monosyllables 'Well', 'Yes', and 'No' in response to questions put to him." When first asked if the paper was his last will and testament, "he, it would seem, with his eyes closed, said 'No,' and on the question being repeated in a different form, he opened his eyes slightly, raised his head, looked at it, and said 'Yes'..."[200] In another example of odd behavior, Greeley repeatedly said "no" when asked if a close friend could serve as a witness. Despite being hobbled by evidentiary gaps, such as the lack of testimony from Dr. Choate on the mental condition of his famous patient, the surrogate court reasoned that Greeley lacked the proper mental soundness to execute the will of 1872.

The wills of celebrated individuals such as Horace Greeley served as magnets attracting attorneys and doctors. Both groups benefitted from the publicity as careers blossomed. Other individuals, basically unknown figures, slowly but surely built a fortune through a mixture of pluck and luck. Their sizeable estates, and the ensuing controversies, produced a posthumous fame.

Thomas Duncan, an immigrant from Ireland, rose from humble beginnings and realized the American dream. Duncan gambled that riches awaited intrepid souls willing to join the rush for black gold in northern Pennsylvania. Duncan traveled roughly a hundred miles north from Pittsburgh to the developing oil fields in Alleghany County. At first, fortune eluded his every step but a partnership with George C. Prather reversed that trend. Just weeks after the country suffered the traumatic loss of President Lincoln; oil was discovered near Pithole Creek. Duncan and Prather, with the former doing much of the wheeling and dealing, procured land rights to important swaths of the oil rich region. Their successful partnership, joined by legions of fortune hunters, fueled the growth of Pit Hole City.[201]

---

200 "Horace Greeley's will," *Chicago Tribune*, Feb. 14, 1873.

201 John J. McLaurin, *Sketches in crude-oil: Some accidents and incidents of the petroleum development in all parts of the globe*, 2nd ed. (Franklin, PA: John J. McLaurin, 1902), 157-61.

Pit Hole City grew from unpretentious farmland to boomtown and back at dizzying speed. Shortly after the first oil well gushed forth a flood of fortune seekers, charlatans, bandits, and speculators scooped up every speck of land. As the oil derricks sprouted like weeds, several bona fide developments delivered respectable amounts of crude oil. Several wells excited the community by producing gushers exceeding five hundred barrels of oil daily.

Land leases were even more valuable than oil. Duncan and Prather traded real estate and made a fortune. In one particularly lucrative deal, the famous duo received 1.3 million dollars in exchange for a thirty day lease on the richest oil producing land. Oil fever inevitably attracted the con artists. Although Duncan and Prather were basically honest speculators, the allure of quick wealth proved too tempting for others. In at least three cases, unsuspecting investors purchased seemingly valuable property only later to find a pipe connecting a well with a hidden tank of oil.

Pit Hole City prospered for a short time. The oil bonanza attracted thousands of dreamers along with hotels, saloons, banks, theaters, and social clubs. In the fall of 1865 nearly sixteen thousand adventurers populated Pit Hole City. Roughly one year after oil was found, the number of inhabitants had rapidly dwindled as nearly twelve thousand people moved elsewhere. A series of devastating fires and increasing numbers of dry wells doomed the city. By 1870 only a few hardy souls remained.

It was against this back drop that Thomas Duncan accumulated an estate valued at $400,000. Along with Pit Hole City, Duncan soared to stratospheric heights but just as quickly faded away. Duncan's downward trajectory began in 1864 when a chronic respiratory ailment robbed him of his vigor, leaving behind a pallid and weak shadow of his former self. Despite his disability, Duncan persisted in the oil business and profited handsomely. In August of 1865 Duncan suffered a blow to his head when an errant piece of lumber struck him. The injury left the victim unconscious for nearly two days. Afterwards, Duncan was plagued with withering, incapacitating headaches. The lancing pain was a major force in Duncan's life, creating inattention, irritability, and fatigue. Duncan hoped to retire in Battle Creek, Michigan and enjoy his wealth but his physical condition steadily deteriorated. In a desperate bid to quell the pain, he journeyed back to his home in Ireland and, remarkably, experienced a recovery. The relief proved temporary and the pain returned with a vengeance until death brought peace in 1871.

Thomas Duncan wrote his will eleven days before he died. Almost immediately, his natural heirs contested the will citing Duncan's mental

instability. The will was litigated in Marshall, Michigan two years after Duncan's death. Duncan generously provided for his mother, brother,
various family members and friends. As a devout Methodist, the will left
large sums to support the church. What riled the natural heirs was a
provision warning against challenging the will. Any such attempt automatically deprived that person's legacy and placed the money in a residual account benefiting the church. The disgruntled heirs seized on that
"very singular" language and mounted an aggressive effort to undermine
Duncan's will.[202] As a newspaper eagerly noted, the unhappy relatives
hired "the best lawyers in the state." The impressive cadre of counselors
counted three attorneys arguing in favor of maintaining the will as written while an equal number contested that claim.

The attorneys contesting the will painted an unflattering image of
Duncan. Following the blow to his head, and amplified by the chronic re-
spiratory malady, the attorneys presented a series of witnesses designed
to demonstrate mental instability following the injury. A variety of witnesses testified that Duncan's memory often failed him, that chronic incapacitating head pain distracted his attention, and a deep suspiciousness invaded his relationships. One witness recalled an incident when
Duncan, for no apparent rational purpose, accused his physician of trying
to poison him. Another witness thought it peculiar that "He would pace
up and down the room, holding his hand to his head, and never seemed
to notice people then."[203]

The attorneys must have figured that the lay testimony was weak
for they relied heavily on the medical testimony of eight physicians to
prove Duncan's mental aberrancy. Surprisingly, much of the medical testimony focused on Duncan's asthma. A rather creative line of reasoning
proposed, "The office of the lungs ... is to purify the blood by eliminating
such portions as no longer fit to be used, and receiving fresh supplies of
oxygen from the air. The testator's lungs were found after death to have
been rendered by disease incapable of performing their special function
to such an extent, that the blood could not have been properly purified
and that the brain, which received it, must have been poisoned by it..."
Eight respected physicians representing the claimants must have nodded
in agreement.

---

202 "The Duncan estate; A large property and a singular will, *New York Times*,
Nov. 7, 1873.

203 Isaac Ray, "The Angell will case," *American Journal of Insanity* 20, no. 2
(1863):145-86.

Not to be outdone, the attorneys countering the claimants assembled nine physicians to challenge the medical arguments. This impressive crew's credibility centered on the revered contributions of Isaac Ray. Ray and company scoffed at their medical adversaries and sought to shoot them down with a popular theory of the day. In a lengthy dissertation, the medical witnesses explained the process by which the human body compensated for impairment in one area by shifting responsibilities to another organ system. In fact, Ray considered the lungs a perfect example of physiologic adaptability. Abnormal byproducts normally removed by the lungs were effectively removed by the skin when disease prevented full pulmonary action.

Although the medical testimony assumed a certain prominence in Duncan's case, other facts proved more important. Even though Duncan created the will shortly before his death, inarguably at a time of physical and mental strain, he had received legal counsel. A witness to the will recalled Duncan's concern that "my brothers have treated me badly, and there will likely be litigation with respect to my will, as I am sure they will be displeased."[204] This prescient comment presaged the protracted dispute but also provided a glimpse of Duncan's astute mental faculties.

A physician in close daily attendance with the testator described no untoward behaviors during Duncan's final days. Other evidence documented a rational basis for Duncan's lifelong dislike of his brothers, a belief not predicated in delusion but in reality. Despite Ray's persuasive arguments, and broadside criticism of his medical colleague's fanciful lung poisoning theory, the jury favored the contestants. After further jury deliberation and legal wrangling a compromise was eventually reached among the disputing parties, which probably pleased no one.

The Duncan will case showcased the spectacle of seventeen doctors, apparently handpicked, to support their respective attorneys' legal argument. Neither side scored a persuasive knockout leaving the value of medical testimony in tatters. Despite this setback, doctors continued to stream into the courtrooms.

A fine line separates delusional belief and religious fervor. Harriet Douglas Cruger, a feisty octogenarian, challenged that boundary with a will written towards the end of her life. By all accounts, Cruger was quick witted and smart well into her late seventies. Cupid struck at this time and Cruger, much to her later regret, married. The union proved a disaster and its dissolution mired the mature romance in years of legal

---

204 Ibid.

wrangling. A silver lining of sorts accompanied the protracted dispute with Cruger developing good relationships with several attorneys. This would come in handy when she sought their help in crafting a will.

Cruger's life took a turn for the worse when she stumbled and fell in 1865. Almost immediately after the tumble, the lively and energetic woman's behavior shifted towards a pervasive distrust, religious pre-occupation, and tiresome penchant for quarreling. Friends and family lamented the change, always hoping for improvement. During this difficult time, Dr. Parker kept a frequent medical vigilance. Parker was no doubt dismayed when his patient started exhibiting more organized but frankly bizarre behavior. Cruger looked and acted petrified, and when questioned, would blame satanic influence. Sleep eluded Parker's patient, no doubt impeded by a fire, lit by the devil, directly under her bed. No amount of reassurance could quiet the woman's fears.

Cruger's pastor, Reverend Paxton, sorrowfully observed her delusions. Paxton was probably mostly disturbed by her senseless agitation, profane language, and incessant pacing. The matter took a different sense of urgency when Cruger took steps to write a will. The attorney initially consulted to draft the document took counsel with Dr. Parker and both agreed that Cruger was insane. No action was taken on the will for several months when once again the elderly woman, now 79 years old, repeated her demand. The second time around proved successful and a will dividing the estate between her relatives, the American Bible Society, and the Board of Foreign Missions was created. Reverend Paxton still objected noting that Cruger's bequest to the American Bible Society and the Board of Foreign Missions arose from a delusional belief that such a tithing would provide relief from the Devil's incessant torture. Despite repeated assurances that salvation lay in religious conviction and the money would be better left to her family, Cruger rebuffed her Pastor's advice.[205]

Harriet Cruger's estate was valued at roughly $250,000 when she died in 1872. Shortly after her death, family members challenged the will claiming Harriet was insane at the time of its execution. Legal counsel for the American Bible Society and the Board of Foreign Missions objected. The facts in the case seemed to favor the family with both Reverend Paxton and Dr. Parker being credible witnesses to Cruger's insanity. The fly in the ointment that served the interest of the American Bible Society

---

205 "The Cruger will case," New York Times, Jun. 6, 1874; and "The Cruger will case; The contested instrument not admitted to probate," New York Times, Jul. 3, 1875.

and the Board of Foreign Missions developed when Dr. Parker testified that while he believed Cruger was indeed insane in March 1866 he also believed she had recovered in the following six months when the will was apparently written.

A strange series of missteps accompanied the writing of Cruger's will. Her attorney, initially convinced that his client's insanity forbid a will, later agreed to construct the document. Apparently poor communication between Dr. Parker and the attorney allowed the will to be signed in spite of their shared reservations. The attorney assumed that his request for Dr. Parker's services as a witness to the will would include an assessment of his client's mental state. Dr. Parker testified that during the time in question, when the will was signed, Cruger had physically improved. During the same testimony the physician admitted that he never examined his patient's mental condition, only assuming it improved along with her general health. The attorney never specifically requested Parker determine the mental competency of Cruger. Numerous lay witnesses regaled the Probate Court with endless examples of Cruger's odd behavior, totally embarrassing both attorney and physician.

In setting aside the will, the probate court judge set forth the expectation that cases involving insanity, when a remission seemingly intervenes, require medical testimony to prove the existence of a lucid interval sufficient to competently execute a will. Finding this lacking in Cruger's case, the judge applied the rules of intestacy which naturally favored the family.

The cavalcade of contested wills led to a willing and enduring embrace between medical witnesses and eager attorneys. Both professions benefited from these early collaborations. Through the process, attorneys became more adept at using medical expert witnesses to buttress legal arguments. The public cast a wary eye on the merger, even at this early stage of professional cooperation. Constructing synthetic insanity seemed just too simple and medical experts, exchanging the scientific for the supercilious, seemed oblivious to malingering. The controversial Vanderbilt will case was an illuminating moment in medical legal history, fully exposing the vanities and vagaries.

The Vanderbilt will case had all the drama necessary to captivate the public attention. An unbelievable fortune drew so many moths to the shining gold that it seemed to eclipse its brilliance. Family members sparred with each other and attorneys lobbed incendiary accusations. In time, the testator's mental acuity was questioned, stimulating a demand for medical testimony. America's best, seeking fame and fortune, offered learned opinions. In many ways the Vanderbilt will case is a dismal social commentary exposing human greed, the lust for fame, and the means by which untold fortunes perpetuate the folly.

Cornelius Vanderbilt, otherwise known as the Commodore, was born in 1794 and soon thereafter developed the personal characteristics that built an empire.[206] The confinement of a classroom held little attraction for the young Vanderbilt who soon swapped the stiff chairs for the open waters off Staten Island. Barely two decades passed in Vanderbilt's life before he was married and a steamboat captain. Not content with his small stake, Cornelius soon expanded his interests further along the east coast. Perseverance and patience permitted the empire builder to construct a vast and profitable steamship business.

Just prior to the outbreak of hostilities heralding the War Between the States, the Commodore took a fancy to railroads, building the Staten Island Railway and purchasing the Harlem Railroad. Vanderbilt purchased the Harlem Railroad at a bargain price, and in a few years, saw his original investment grow nearly forty times. By steadily withdrawing assets from his steamship, and plowing the money into the railroad industry, the Commodore soon became the driving force bringing the power of the locomotive to America.

The Commodore was a taskmaster, pretty much what would be expected of such a human dynamo, with great expectations placed on the shoulders of his sons. His favorite son was George, a West Point graduate and veteran of the Civil War, who died shortly after the fighting ended. Cornelius, Jr. the second oldest son, disappointed his father and the pair drifted apart. William Vanderbilt, the first born son, struggled at first. Much to the displeasure of the Commodore, William took a fancy to farming. To his father's later delight, the farming venture returned very handsome profits. The elder businessman remained a skeptic until his son revived the dissipating fortunes of the Staten Island Railway. William proved himself worthy and upon his father's death ascended to the presidency of the vast railroad network. In addition, the Commodore left the majority of his one hundred million dollar estate to the capable administration of William. Incensed family members almost immediately contested the will.

---

206 E. Walker, F. Johnson, J. Rusk, and A. Fowler, *Leaders of the 19th Century* (Chicago: A. B. Kuhlman Company, 1900), 195.

The Commodore died on the 4th of January 1877 in New York. His last will and testament was written nearly two years earlier and consumed twenty-four pages of text. Four witnesses affixed their signatures to the document. Even though the will was prepared with legal guidance, only William and the Commodore could accurately value the estate which was estimated to be worth 100 million dollars. The wealthy railroad magnate left his wife $500,000 in bonds, his house, and all the furnishings except the portraits of his first, long deceased, wife. The will also provided for his daughters and son Cornelius, Jr. William received most everything else and was named the will's executor.[207]

The first public inkling of discontent bubbled to the surface about six weeks after the Commodore's death. Rumors were circulating that Cornelius, dissatisfied with a legacy of income from a $200,000 investment, was seriously considering contesting the will. Cornelius received advice and counsel from three respected attorneys, Ethan Allen, Jeremiah Black, and Scott Lord.[208] The Commodore's will was now headed to court.

Delano C.Calvin, Surrogate of New York, began the official proceedings at 10 am on 27 February, 1877. Henry L. Clinton represented the interest of William Vanderbilt in preserving the will as written. Ethelinda V. Allen and Mary A. La Bau joined Cornelius in contesting the will. With the main players and their respective roles now publicly identified, Surrogate Calvin allowed the contestants two weeks to refine their initial legal arguments.[209]

The three unhappy family members returned two weeks later claiming William Vanderbilt had exerted an "undue influence" on the Commodore. According to the contestants, the Commodore "was laboring under a morbid and mental delusion and mania at the time the will was made, inducing an absence of natural affection..." In other words, the combination of old age and illness left the Commodore incapable of writing a rational will.[210]

Another week passed and the cast reassembled to press their respective positions. Apparently in the brief interim period the disgruntled

---

207 "Mr. Vanderbilt's will; The instrument filed in the surrogate's court," *New York Times*, Jan. 9, 1877.

208 "Local miscellany; Commodore Vanderbilt's will," *New York Times*, Feb. 23, 1877.

209 "The heirs dissatisfied; Commodore Vanderbilt's will," *New York Times*, Feb. 28, 1877.

210 "The Vanderbilt will case; Action of counsel for the contestants," *New York Times*, Mar. 9, 1877.

family members had a change of heart and surprised the court by abandoning their claims on the testator's will. Adding a dramatic flourish to the announcement, the contesting attorneys and their clients rose en masse and left the court room. The battlefield was completely ceded to Mr. Clinton who now proceeded to offer evidence of the will's authenticity. The first witness was Judge Rapallo who claimed a close relationship with the Commodore dating back at least two decades. Rapallo was the will's architect, both its current version and many prior editions. The jurist testified that the contested will bore major similarities with older versions, explicitly highlighting the consistency of the Commodore's wishes spanning many years. The Reverend Dr. Sidney A. Corey joined Rapallo in claiming an intimate knowledge of the Commodore's behavior, never observing eccentricities. A particularly interesting witness began his relationship with the Commodore as a business adversary. Edwin D. Worcester later joined forces with his antagonist and testified that throughout the years of their, at times tumultuous relationship, the Commodore always maintained a predictable pattern of habits. Mr. Clinton presented a strong case and the probate judge appointed William the executor of a vast estate.[211]

Months passed, during which a simmering discontent once again bubbled to the surface in the summer of 1877. Family members had a year to raise any objections to the will, an option exercised by daughter Mary A. La Bau. The court reconvened in July to hear the contestant's claim. Ms. La Bau contended that her father suffered mental instability evidenced initially through a belief in spiritualism and later worsened by age and medical maladies. Mr. Clinton, still representing William's interests, reprised much of his early case but, even at this early stage, countered Ms. La Bau's arguments. Francis P. Freeman, a witness to the will's execution, testified that in nearly two decades of contact with the Commodore the subject of spiritualism never arose. William probably hoped this would end the matter but this time around the opposition pressed forward.[212]

The court convened late in 1877. A huge mob surged forward when the doors opened with police turning away many of the curious. From this point forward, most of the legal wrangling turned on medical testimony and the titillating testimony involving the Commodore's belief in the spirit world. Physicians literally dissected the Commodore. Dr. Sattorthwaite, and his reluctant colleague Dr. Louis Stimpson, testified in

211 "Vanderbilt's will intact; The objections withdrawn the testament admitted to probate," *New York Times*, Mar. 14, 1877.

212 "Law reports; The Vanderbilt will case," *New York Times*, Jul. 13, 1877.

mind numbing detail about the Commodore's autopsy. Reporters faithfully recorded all the details leaving absolutely nothing to the imagination. According to the doctors, the Commodore died from peritonitis but much of their testimony dwelled on the condition of his kidneys. The bickering attorneys dwelled on the testator's renal health alternately suggesting and refuting the link between kidney disease and mental illness.[213]

Medical testimony continued through the spring of 1878. Dr. Ellsworth Elliot contradicted the contestant's claims. Elliot attended to the Commodore's physical infirmities in the months preceding his death. Throughout this close relationship, Elliot never observed irrational behavior nor did he believe that the Commodore's chronic pain caused insanity as claimed by Mr. Scott Lord who aggressively represented Ms. La Bau. Lord also insinuated that only insanity could account for the Commodore's abject rejection of his son Cornelius, a claim disputed by Elliot.[214]

Scott Lord opened up a second front by attacking the Commodore's belief in spiritualism. Spiritualism was a vibrant, although controversial, religion sweeping across society in nineteenth century America. The Fox Sisters, Kate, Leah and Margaret, popularized the movement in 1848 when they claimed direct communication with a previously unknown murder victim through a series of "raps." Their house near Rochester, New York was considered a haunted abode, later confirmed by Kate who began communicating on a regular basis with the spirit. The "raps" from the spirit world resonated in a society familiar with the Morse code which transmitted more worldly messages across telegraph wires. A receptive and respectable segment of American society greeted the Fox Sister's amazing abilities with uncritical acceptance.

Family members contesting the Commodore's will surely hoped traditional religious views, perhaps shared by the Surrogate, would trump the cult of spiritualism. In fact, the contestants went even further equating a belief in spiritualism with mental illness. Over the next few months, Scott Lord brought forth a parade of witnesses claiming attendance at séances hosted by the Commodore.

Helen S. Clark, a magnetic physician, testified at the Vanderbilt Will Case in the spring of 1878. Magnetic physicians practiced at a boundary

---

213 "A fight for a million; A dead father's secrets exposed," *New York Times*, Nov. 17, 1877.

214 "The Vanderbilt fortune; Was the Commodore a kleptomaniac?," *New York Times*, Mar. 23, 1878.

between science and faith, perhaps more of the latter in actual practice. Magnetism and electricity were new concepts, invisible, demonstrable, and powerful. Fusing the science of magnetism with biblical accounts of healing from "laying on of hands," the Civil War Era magnetic "physician" now had an influential clinical technique. Textbooks explained that "there are those who possess the healing power in a considerable degree..."[215] A magnetic physician like Clark enjoyed particular success relieving a sufferer's chronic pain.

The Commodore met Helen Clark in 1860, and over time the pair met on a regular basis. Apparently Clark possessed the magic touch, and by pressing her hands on the Commodore's head, she relieved his chronic pain. At one point in their relationship the subject of the afterlife came up and, perhaps at Clark's urging, the Commodore agreed to attend a séance. The medium conducting the séance conjured up the presence of the Commodore's first wife but the famous industrialist waved her aside insisting instead on learning stock tips from the spirit world. Clark passionately supported Scott Lord's efforts to overturn the will but her testimony was frequently attacked and often excluded.[216]

Much of the testimony during the summer of 1878 veered away from spiritualism and returned to all things medical. Dr. Robert L. Weir, commenting on the Commodore's kidney ailment, sagely proclaimed, "a disease which prevents the carrying off of impure blood from the system necessarily produces depressing mental as well as physical effects." Neither Weir nor the contestant's counsel proposed a mental disease like insanity but instead they suggested that the Commodore's infirmity promoted a singular fixation on the accumulation of wealth. According to Weir, this myopic and obsessive need to build vast riches suggested a monomania, a sort of light insanity which manifested its irrationality more subtlety.[217]

Another medical witness, Dr. Frank H. Hamilton, took a slightly different approach. Hamilton testified that brain dysfunction often arose from kidney diseases and "makes a man capricious, irritable, and easily

---

215 A Magnetic Physician, *Vital magnetic cure: An exposition of vital magnetism, and its application to the treatment of mental and physical disease*, 7th ed. (Boston: Colby & Rich, Publishers, 1890), 22.

216 "Vanderbilt's rich estate," *New York Times*, Apr. 10, 1878.

217 "The Vanderbilt will contest; The Commodore's susceptibility to influence more medical testimony," *New York Times*, Jun. 22, 1878.

influenced"[218] The good doctor sprinkled his testimony with many examples of "capricious" behavior, most all centering on the distant relationship between the Commodore and Cornelius.[219]

Perhaps the approach of Halloween influenced Lord's decision to revisit the Commodore's spiritual beliefs in the fall of 1878. Eleanor Bishop testified that the Commodore frequently sought mental and physical help from the spirit world. Lord, no doubt aware that many important people believed in the paranormal, made clear he was not attacking the religion but instead suggested that the Commodore's beliefs were irrationally introduced into the will making process. Lord's attempt to respect, and at the same time attack spiritualism, no doubt left many court room observers bewildered. The Surrogate, responding to complaints from William Vanderbilt's attorney, promised a ruling on the admissibility of further testimony regarding the Commodore's belief in sprits.

Surrogate Calvin was in a bind. All the testimony so far submitted clearly demonstrated the testator's active, thoughtful involvement in the will's construction. Nonetheless, the Commodore's belief in spiritualism strayed from conventional religious doctrine. Perhaps the judge harbored some doubts as to the mental stability of a successful businessman who adopted such a fringe faith based system. In any event, Calvin permitted such testimony, opening the floodgates to a parade of clairvoyants, charlatans, and mystics.[220]

Helen Clark, a star witness for Ms. La Bau, expanded her previous testimony. Clark described herself as a "magnetic rubber," possessed of special healing powers manifested through a "laying on of hands." She testified about frequent séances attended by the Commodore during which he would write a stock related question on a piece of paper and submit the inquiry to a psychic medium. The Commodore apparently never fully trusted the financial tips received from spirits in the afterlife, often waiting to see if the stocks appreciated as predicted. In most every psychic encounter, the Commodore sought to use the séance as means to gain a

---

218 "The Vanderbilt contest; Testimony of A. Oakey Hall and medical experts," *New York Times*, Jun. 27, 1878.

219 "The Vanderbilt will contest; Expert medical testimony the case postponed until September," *New York Times*, Jul. 4, 1878.

220 "Spiritualistic influence; Its effect upon Commodore Vanderbilt," *New York Times*, Oct. 5, 1878.

business advantage. Such worldly interests seemed entirely consistent with Vanderbilt's ambitious exploitation of any potential advantage.[221]

James B. Mansfield, casting himself as a doctor, was a writing medium. Although much of Mansfield's testimony was barred by Calvin, his role as a spiritualist stood. The witness described his special talent, "...when a question is placed under my hand in an envelope, I place my hand on it; then my hand begins to move, and the index finger of my left hand begins to move, and the index finger of my left hand is the medium through which the message comes like a telegraph message; it is received through the left hand, and I write it with my right hand; can receive it and write it just as well blindfolded; I cannot explain what the signs indicating these messages are; they are palpable only to my feelings; I cannot place myself in the condition to receive them at will, but when I do answer questions through the spirit medium I'll stake my life on the accuracy every time..." Through this mechanism, Mansfield answered the Commodore's stock questions. William's attorney conducted a spirited cross examination during which the witness admitted the "doctor" was a self-imposed label, that his former occupation was a dry goods merchant, and perhaps most condemning, forced the witness to confess that spirits may indeed lie.

As the court case dragged on into the late months of 1878, the public's fascination with the afterlife waned and Scott Lord turned his arguments back to more worldly medical testimony. In between the testimony of two medical experts, La Bau launched a broadside against William claiming witness tampering. Naturally, the favored son dismissed the allegations.[222]

Dr. Edward Petzold resurrected monomania, again making the claim that a single minded devotion, such as the Commodore's obsession in building an economic empire, could only be the product of a disturbed mind. Mr. Lord surely enjoyed the doctor's clever reframing. Instead of seeing perspicacity, persistence, and patience as noble virtues, Petzold redefined the Commodore's character traits as exemplars of insanity. This distorted but medically sanctioned testimony conveniently converted a brilliant business career into a mental malady. The Abraham Man surely chuckled at the doctor's twisted logic. Extending Petzold's reasoning to any singular preoccupation raised the specter of insanity

---

221 "Vanderbilt and the mediums; Testimony that he asked James Fisk's spirit about stocks," *New York Times*, Oct. 12, 1878.

222 "Law report; The Vanderbilt will case; How time is consumed," *New York Times*, Oct. 23, 1878.

being affixed to habitual drunkenness, recidivistic criminal acts, arson, gambling, and even "excessive" achievement.

A colleague of Petzold, Dr. Edward H. Dixon, discovered even more evidence of madness in the Commodore's entrails. Dixon believed the Commodore's small liver was incontrovertible physical proof of a dissipate lifestyle made worse through the overindulgence in tobacco. In response to hypothetical questions posed by the clever Scott Lord, Dixon testified that the Commodore was partially insane, most notably demonstrated by his unhealthy family life. While Petzold relied on a metaphysical theory of monomania entirely constructed from impressions and wrapped in a doctor's integrity, Dixon added the pseudoscientific gloss of the autopsy. In any event, both doctors testified that the testator was not of sound mind when the will was executed.[223]

The Vanderbilt will case entered its third and decisive year of debate in 1879. After months of attack, William and his attorneys forcefully responded. John P. Gray, arguably one of the most famous and respected physicians in America, testified next. Gray's presence was a significant coup for William and his attorney wasted no time discussing the doctor's impressive credentials.

Dr. Gray was Superintendent of the State Lunatic Asylum in Utica, NY. He ascended to that post in recognition of his clinical expertise, developed after studying over ten thousand cases of lunacy. Gray reviewed the autopsy and concluded that no evidence of mental unsoundness existed and furthermore, the purported anomalies of the liver or kidneys could exist without any adverse effect on the brain. Drawing on his vast storehouse of knowledge about insanity, Gray ridiculed the notion of "insanity for riches".[224]

The closing days of the great trial offered little in the way of public drama. Those contesting the will tried in vain to rattle Dr. Gray. The doctor withstood hours of grueling cross examination, but never strayed from his conviction that the Commodore was mentally sound. As spring took hold in 1879, the Surrogate Calvin settled the long contested will. As the judge noted, the central issue in contention revolved around a testator's legal right to discriminate among family members when fashioning his legacy. To reach this point, the contesting family members exposed

---

223 "The Vanderbilt will case; An author of medical works on the stand, the Commodore's deficient liver," *New York Times*, Nov. 7, 1878.

224 "The Vanderbilt will case; Testimony of President Bishop, of the New-Haven railroad, and Superintendent Gray, of the Utica insane Asylum," *New York Times*, Feb. 8, 1879.

every conceivable facet of their father's life. In his final analysis the judge decided that the Commodore's desire to keep his fortune intact, and under the control of William, was not an "unnatural ambition." The long case was settled in William's favor and the contestants, no doubt, again deeply disappointed.[225]

Another highly celebrated case involved the will of a newspaper magnate. Henry Carter was born in England in 1821 and started life's journey with the presumption, and strong encouragement, that he would take up his father's trade. Henry had other ideas, but given his father's unyielding insistence, he took up his passion in art quietly and secretly. The London Punch, and other magazines, recognized the artistic talent and purchased his illustrations. Henry published his illustrations with the nom de plume of Frank Leslie. Commercial success was no match for the siren call of gold in California. Henry left his native land and traveled to a new world in search of vast wealth. Shortly after arriving in America, Henry abandoned his real name and henceforth was known as Frank Leslie. California was not kind to Frank, but far from defeated, he traveled to New York where vast riches awaited. In 1855, the former gold digger started one of America's most famous publications, Frank Leslie's Illustrated Newspaper.

In the 1850s newspaper production was a laborious task. Nowhere was this more pronounced than with newspaper illustrations. The emerging art of photography had not yet found its way into publications. Editors illustrated their articles with woodcuts and engravings, truly works of art in many instances, but requiring weeks of preparation. As a result of the time intensive engraving process, newspapers could not illustrate current events. The genius of Frank Leslie changed this and brought contemporary news images to a receptive public. Before Leslie's transformational approach, one engraver tediously and slowly created one large illustrated block. Leslie divided the large block into 32 units, assigned one engraver to each section, and through the process created a full page illustration in one day. The illustrations tremendously expanded Frank Leslie's newspaper circulation. In addition, the capacity to render contemporary pictures of the Civil War brought the realities of the conflict home to every reader and further broadened the appeal of Frank Leslie's Illustrated Newspaper. The success of the newspaper

---

225 "The Vanderbilt will case," *New York Times*, Feb. 26, 1879.

led to other publications including the first widely circulated illustrated magazine, Frank Leslie's Popular Monthly.[226]

Frank was less successful in his personal life. He divorced his first wife and married Miriam Folline in 1875. The new Mrs. Leslie worked alongside her husband at the newspaper, later expanding her journalistic reach to other literary endeavors under her husband's banner. The financial panic starting in 1873 spared few businesses and by 1877 Frank was teetering on the edge of insolvency. Leslie named an impartial administrator to manage the newspaper empire during this difficult time. His wife continued to be indispensable, providing comfort for Leslie as his health declined and leadership for the company he had built. The great entrepreneur died in 1880, leaving behind a mountain of debt and a will rewarding the loyalty of Mrs. Leslie.[227]

Frank Leslie's will set in motion a brief but intense battle. A longtime confidant of Leslie, Edward Dickerson, drafted the testator's will following detailed discussions between the two. The disputed document was signed on December, 27, 1879. Leslie left his entire estate to his faithful second wife. Perhaps more importantly, Frank bequeathed the future use of his name to his wife for her sole exclusive use in marketing the media empire. Leslie's two sons, both born from the first marriage, expressed out-rage and promptly contested the will. The disaffected sons angrily alleged that Mrs. Leslie exerted an undue influence over their father, resulting in the unfair bequest. Both siblings also attacked their father's mental soundness in a further effort to explain the unnatural and immoral disinheritance.[228]

Leslie's two sons, Harry and Alfred, filed their joint objections in the waning days of January 1880. Both set forth a potpourri of grievances, complaining on one hand that Mrs. Leslie took advantage of their father's insanity and contrived, through artful manipulation, to disinherit them while also alleging that the widow was not a lawful wife. Surrogate Delano C. Calvin administered the legal proceedings, keeping ex-Judge

---

226 "Thirty years backward and one forward," *Leslie's Monthly Magazine* LIX (1905): 358-9.

227 Henry Woldmar Ruoff, et al., *Woman her position, influence, and achievement throughout the civilized world* (San Jose, CA: King-Richardson Company, 1902), 450.

228 "Frank Leslie's will sustained," *Frank Leslie's Illustrated Newspaper*, Dec. 18, 1880.

Fullerton, representing the interests of the will as written, and ex-Judge Curtis representing the sons, in line.[229]

Leslie was intent on redrafting his will. The matter grew more urgent when Harry, according to his father's interpretation, started a rival publishing business.[230] This act of betrayal angered Leslie and cost both sons their inheritance. Another act in the family drama unfolded between the former and current leading women in Leslie's life. The disagreeable state of affairs between the two women was on public display as the ex-spouse prominently positioned herself near her two sons in the courtroom. Part of the attack on the will included a number of broadsides directed at Mrs. Leslie. In the opening days of the trial, the former wife lamented the home wrecking siren who took her place. Once ensconced in Frank's life, Mrs. Leslie, or so it was claimed, did her utmost to seed discontent between father and sons. It seemed a weak argument, but the contestants seemed to imply some sort of magical enchantment possessed by Miriam Folline which clouded Frank's mind and led to the disinheritance. As proof, the sons submitted numerous examples of Mrs. Leslie blocking access to their father.[231]

Henry testified in the spring and started raising the subject of insanity. To build his case, the son reached back into the family tree and resurrected an allegedly insane uncle who committed suicide. In an effort to bolster his testimony, Henry proclaimed that his father was indeed, "a little light headed".[232] Howard Browne followed the disgruntled son and offered his learned opinion about Leslie's mental soundness. Browne, an employee and confidant, often advised Leslie on important business matters. It seemed all was well except when Leslie rejected Browne's suggestions. Browne recalled several such incidents, although one in particular seemed more important. The witness recalled recommending the closure of several non-profitable publications but was overruled because one of the magazines in question belonged to his wife. Browne took this as an example of insanity with Frank succumbing to the irrational influence

229 "Frank Leslie's will; To be contested by his sons Harry and Alfred," *New York Times*, Jan. 27, 1880.

230 "Frank Leslie's will; The contest opened before the surrogate," *New York Times*, Feb. 15, 1880.

231 "The Leslie will contest; A divided family before the court," *New York Times*, Apr. 15, 1880.

232 "Secrets of the Leslies; Tracing the taint of insanity in the family," *New York Times*, Apr. 22, 1880.

exerted by his wife. Other lay witnesses came forth and provided testimony painting Leslie as impulsive, absentminded, and gullible.[233]

The medical experts came next. Dr. James Kiernan, a lunacy specialist, proclaimed that inconsistent business directions and multiple revisions suggested an impaired mind. Once again, an influential medical witness reinterpreted the otherwise normal ups and downs of any business venture as evidence of insanity. Kiernan expanded his testimony by connecting Leslie's mental vulnerability with his wife's wily manipulation. It just so happened that this sort of testimony conveniently connected the dots between Leslie's presumed mental illness and his wife's domination.[234]

Another physician, with the rather ironic name of H.W. Quackenboss, testified that Leslie maintained a totally unfounded belief that he had Bright's disease of the kidneys. During this time period, medical doctors often linked Bright's disease with insanity. In Frank's case, his allegedly delusional conviction in the medical ailment satisfied Quackenboss' definition of insanity.[235]

After roughly a year of legal bickering, Surrogate Calvin presented his verdict. The judge dismissed the contestants' claim of undue influence. In dismissing the sons' argument, Calvin commented on the various efforts extended by Mrs. Leslie to appease the warring parties. In the end, the judge concluded that Frank obstinately, but willfully, refused to reconcile the relationships. Much of the acrimony between Leslie and his sons stemmed from Frank's unflagging conviction that his sons were undermining the family business. As proof, the Judge noted the similarity between the son's unauthorized use of the "Leslie & Co" mast head and their father's "Frank Leslie's Illustrated Newspaper." The Judge pointed to other examples of trademark infringement, aggressively adopted by Harry and clearly designed to deceive the public. Calvin's one hundred and sixteen page opinion dismissed the medical experts' insanity case. Instead, the judge placed greater weight on lay testimony by noting, "Expert testimony in doubtful cases, if intelligent and unbiased, may be very valuable, but it would be unsafe, save in some exceptional cases, to permit such testimony to override that given by intelligent daily observers of the conversations and conduct of those persons whose mental condition may be under investigation."

---

233 "The Leslie will contest; Mrs. Leslie's influence over Mr. Leslie – indications of unsoundness of mind," New York Times, May 12, 1880.
234 Ibid.
235 "The contested Leslie will," New York Times, Sep. 9, 1880.

The judge's reasoned decision in the Frank Leslie case seemingly placed a premium on common sense. Not surprisingly, seasoned medical doctors came forth and equated domestic squabbles with mental unsoundness. In the politest possible language, the judge dismissed the doctors' inventive testimony.

Several decades of medical legal wrangling over disputed wills tattered the image of medical testimony. The specter of doctors publicly disagreeing about mental illness did little to advance the public's faith. At the same time, criminal cases offered even more opportunities for doctors to discuss mental illness and misconduct. As they did so, the Abraham Man complicated their task of distinguishing the fit from the faking.

Chapter 7: Fit or Faking

America's Civil War presented the perfect opportunity for the Abraham Man. After the initial patriotic fervor died away, and recruiting waned, the need for soldiers escalated. Any thoughts of quickly vanquishing the Confederacy faded as the Southern Armies mounted a stiff resistance. The number of wounded and killed in action shocked both sides but at the same time solidified the resolve of political leaders to fight on and on. The will of an unknown number of recruits and soldiers wobbled, leading to rising rates of desertion. Another group, no doubt fearing the consequences of desertion, chose a different route to avoid the rigors and risks of war. These individuals were tempted by the Abraham Man.

John Ordronaux dedicated his *Manual of Instructions for Military Surgeons on the Examination of Recruits and the Discharge of Soldiers* to William Hammond. Both men were familiar with the scourge of malingering, a cowardly act consciously undertaken to avoid military duty. Ordronaux described three classes of malingering, one involving the dissimulation of voluntary muscle action or mental functions, another class involved the introduction of some prop such as blood, and the third category came about when the actor ingested or applied a chemical intended to produce some obvious injury or illness. The first group might fake insanity or limb paralysis, the second group might cough up a previously concealed quantity of blood, and the last group could create painful blisters by injecting caustic agents in the skin. The creativity, skill at concealment, and degree of real injury varied considerably among the practitioners. In all suspicious cases, Ordronaux advised the surgeon to assume malingering, leaving the doctor the difficult task of determining whether the soldier was really fit or faking.[236]

Exposing a fraud was difficult but not impossible. For the most part, the actor relied on a limited amount of medical information which left the doctor in a decidedly superior position. A lengthy period of evaluation would wear many malingerers down. Distraction was also useful. The doctor could divert the suspect's attention to another matter, and closely observe the person's behavior. In this manner, a person pretending paralysis might momentarily forget the act and use the affected limb. Sometimes detection required more aggressive actions. Epilepsy was the Abraham Man's favorite act. It provoked a mixture of fear, revulsion, and sympathy which almost guaranteed a get-out-of-the-military ticket. Military surgeons often suspected that recruits faked the condition. Epilepsy caused a fairly predictable range of physical symptoms, many of which were difficult to simulate. The more expert malingers certainly tried to fool the doctor. The characteristic foaming from the mouth could be replicated with a piece of soap. Faking the insensibility of epilepsy exposed the pretender to the discomfort of a wet cloth placed over their mouth, irritating snuff deposited in the nose, or a feather tickling their feet.

The Civil War sharpened the diagnostic skills of many physicians, forced to sift through the wheat and chaff of real and phony medical problems. This was a valuable skill for doctors who treated another favorite haunt of the Abraham Man, insanity. Mental illness was easy to fake. It seemed difficult to disprove the actor's simple claims of hearing voices or seeing phantoms. In reality, the doctor's knowledge of insanity and the associated dysfunctions substantially tilted the game against the malingerer.

The value of medical expert testimony was another area that benefitted from the focus on malingering. In some cases the expert witness relied on their medical authority but opposing attorneys soon made that approach untenable. Blistering interrogatories laid bare the physician's vulnerabilities. Insanity experts responded with increasingly sophisticated testimony, delivered through the fog of scientific explanations or esoteric, untested hypotheses. Newspapers seized on the entertainment

---

236 John Ordronaux, *Manual of instructions for military surgeons on the examination of recruits and discharge of soldiers* (New York: D. Van Nostrand, 1863), 30-1.

side of high drama court cases and breathlessly reported the antics of the lawyers, doctors, quacks, charlatans, families, friends, and foes.

Scammers and schemers knew no bounds in their contrivances to avoid military service. Some of these artifices suggested severe desperation even approaching suicidal depths. In a small town in Connecticut four prospective recruits deliberately severed their fingers in hopes of being medically disqualified. In some successful masquerades the outcome was a sorry commentary about the doctor. A New Hampshire man applied to a local physician hoping to get a medical exemption. The ruse was simple and consisted of a brief demonstration of a wobbly gait. To ensure success the faker removed the heel from one of his shoes. The physician, perhaps consciously driven to undermine the war effort, gullible, or stupid, seemingly spent more time issuing the exemption certificate than performing a competent exam. Other men, who no doubt feared any pain, acted the roles of habitual drunks or quickly converted to a pacifist religion. In both cases, once free of the hooks of Uncle Sam, the drunk quickly reformed and the pacifist dumped the new congregation.[237]

Malingering contributed to a corrosion of trust. It was so common in the Army that every illness or non-combat related injury invited suspicion. A surgeon reminiscing about the war recalled, "I remember when the first man died, the report was spread about the camp in this apparently unfeeling form: there is a man up at the hospital playing dead." Army Officers often suspected malingering. In one case, a soldier affected leg paralysis for a prolonged period of time. Suspicions of faking seemed to melt way as time passed by and the soldier still piteously limped about the camp. The soldier brought the curtain down with a particularly dramatic display after a long march, stumbling about with painful groans. Sensing success, the malingering soldier eagerly anticipated a medical discharge and the obliging surgeon was poised to grant the wish. The commanding officer had different thoughts and approached the soldier casually remarking that the surgeon had decided to remove the leg. The commander's threat had a remarkably curative effect. In less than twenty-four hours the soldier's gait was fully restored.[238]

A good dodge would spread like a wildfire. Soon, the less creative soldiers would mimic the illness du jour hoping to end their hardships. A surgeon recalled an incident of hoarseness which swept through his unit. The first practitioners thoroughly hoodwinked a beleaguered sur-

---

237 "Schemes of the shirks," *Chicago Daily Tribune*, Aug. 27, 1862.
238 "Malingering in the Army," *Chicago Daily Tribune*, Apr. 5, 1890.

geon and gleefully returned home with a medical discharge. An epidemic of laryngitis engulfed the unit and made every case suspect. In one particular case, a soldier stood a late night picket detail in a drenching rain. Returning to camp the following morning, the soaked soldier soon discovered his voice was audible only as a whisper. The regimental surgeon examined the sufferer and prescribed a soothing gargle. Unfortunately, the soldier's condition did not improve, prompting a referral to a doctor at the brigade hospital. The brigade surgeon was skeptical. A complete examination of the soldier's throat revealed nothing unusual. Convinced that the soldier was shamming, the surgeon set a trap. The hoarse Abraham Man was directed to a private room to recuperate. Before the patient arrived at the room, the surgeon had drilled a small hole through which the soldier could be surreptitiously monitored. A few days passed before anything happened. What excited the observer's interest was a partially written letter casually left on a table. After the soldier left the room the letter was seized. The author of the letter alerted his brother that he would soon be medically discharged from the Army following a successful campaign fooling the doctors. The Brigade Surgeon swung into action, determined to turn the table on the tricky trooper. The patient was sent on an errand to a distant camp, but unbeknownst to the soldier, was purposely detained until darkness fell. Returning to his camp, the duped private encountered the security picket. Naturally, the sentries demanded a password. The befuddled whisperer attempted sign language to no avail. The sentries opened fire, rifles and pistols lighting the night sky. Fearing for his life, the schemer screamed. After a brief and quite distinct dialogue, the soldier passed unharmed into the camp. By now the gig was up and the forlorn actor forced to suffer his critics' scathing reviews.[239]

It seems reasonable to speculate that successful malingerers in the military continued their dramas after receiving a medical discharge. A favorite target of the graduates of military malingering was the railroads and steamships. The transportation system was prone to accidents, resulting from failed battles with nature's elements, the difficulty in maintaining man's mechanical contraptions, and careless personnel. In spite of this, the railroads and shipping lines made scads of money and became prey for the Abraham Man. Every transportation accident seemed to spawn a spate of pretended injuries, all in hopes of winning life's lottery through a display of daring deceit. William Hammond encountered a young man who claimed a debilitating paralysis after suffering a fall

---

239 "Getting out of the Army," *Chicago Daily Tribune*, Sep. 26, 1886.

when leaving a railway car. The man consulted Hammond to substantiate the injury, in preparation for a large lawsuit against the transportation company. Partway through the medical examination, Hammond asked the man to ambulate about the room. In complying with Hammond's direction, the patient affected great pain and a wobbly gait. Hammond kept up a distracting conversation while the man bumbled around the room. After a few minutes the patient's gait improved, unable to keep up the act as Hammond peppered him with questions. Never a shrinking violet, Hammond accused the patient of malingering. The faker eventually admitted that his performance was staged under the eminent direction of an attorney.[240]

After Hammond left the military he remained en guard for the Abraham Man. Not all cases of malingering involved prisoners or military recruits and Hammond recalled such a case.[241] A young woman, obsessed with the prospect of trapping a potential husband, faked a pregnancy. She padded her abdomen, slowly enlarging the thickness over time. The family, alarmed by the growth of what they supposed to be a tumor, consulted a local doctor. The woman kept the appointment and revealed a shocking story to the doctor. She was indeed pregnant but coyly refused to name the man. Perhaps the woman's emotional presentation, along with her sordid tale of debauchery, blinded the doctor who documented the pregnancy while sparing the victim an embarrassing examination.

The family nearly collapsed when the doctor confirmed the pregnancy. As might be expected, the young girl's parents sought the villain's name. For quite a while, the young woman refused but then one day dramatically presented her father a written account of the affair. The man was well known to the family which only deepened the insult. Naturally, the angry father confronted the man, who in turn denied the accusation. Keeping a cool head, the alleged seducer asked for an audience with the young woman. The man was an attorney, and arguing perhaps the most important case in his life, adroitly challenged the woman's story. The woman eventually recanted, admitting the whole affair was faked, leaving a puzzled family struggling for answers.

The cat and mouse game between malingerer and doctor inspired endless efforts at outwitting each other. Neither side fully knew the in-

---

240 William Hammond, "Pretending to be crippled: A class of malingerers who seek to recover damages from railroads," *Atchinson Daily Champion* (Kansas), May 13, 1888.

241 James Kiernan, "Hysterical accusations: An analysis of the Emma Bond case," *The Journal of Nervous and Mental Disease* 12, no. 1 (1885): 13-8.

---

tentions of the other but skepticism fueled wariness. Any whiff of compensation or litigation certainly put the doctor on notice. In another transportation accident, a middle aged man was struck by a horse drawn wagon and suffered some scrapes and bruises. Despite the relatively minor injury, the victim's condition apparently worsened. He developed a partial paralysis in the right leg and pitifully moved about with the help of a large stick. As the story of the injury unfolded it became clear that a lawsuit was pending. The doctor continued the medical examination, conscious of the legal claim in question. A curious discrepancy arose when the accident victim claimed numbness in an area that did not match the neurologic distribution pattern associated with a presumed spinal cord injury. The inconsistent physical findings aroused the doctor's suspicions. In an effort to trick the presumed imposter, the doctor settled on a shocking experiment. Using an electrical induction machine, the physician applied the electrodes to the paralyzed limb. The doctor released the current, and much to his surprise, received no response from the patient. The induction machine packed a wallop and it seemed inconceivable to bear it without emotion. Still unconvinced, the doctor placed the electrodes on the non-paralyzed leg, released the current, and watched the patient shriek in agony. No normal person could fake this, or so the physician concluded. At the trial, the doctor supported the accident victim's ultimately successful lawsuit.[242]

Some people spent their entire lives moving seamlessly between madness, malingering, and malfeasance. No bright lines illuminated the transition between the three phases. It usually remained a matter of considerable conjecture for the average physician to decide whether the madness, the malingering or the malfeasance dominated the clinical picture. All three conditions could overlap to varying degrees and fluctuate over time. The devious malingerer exploited this human tendency.

Edward H. Rulloff seemed to glide with effortless ease between madness, malingering, and malfeasance. At various points in Rulloff's fifty years on earth, he moved between crime, faking illness, and approaching frank irrationality. Two broad themes dominated his life, brutality and brilliance. It seemed odd that a man capable of vicious violence could at the same time show a fondness for, and some talent, in scholarly matters. Reconciling these two extremes eventually landed Rulloff within the purview of Dr. Gray's decidedly far-sighted powers of observation.

---

242 Thomas Buzzard, "A medico-legal case of injury to the nervous system," *American Journal of Insanity* 25, no. 4 (1869): 514-8.

Rulloff was a vain man. He stood just over five feet tall, weighed 180 pounds, possessed a broad chest, deep brown hair, and gray eyes. He prized his stocky build which projected strength. Despite his weight and girth Rulloff had a cat like agility. The latter attribute probably came in handy when robbing stores.

A bungled robbery at a dry goods store bore all the hallmarks of Rulloff. The store was a well-known fixture in Binghamton, New York. Rulloff always traveled with two other confederates who supplied the muscle for the break-ins. The trio apparently did their homework casing the store. Two clerks typically slept in the store, a hazard the robbers planned for. Rulloff, along with his two accomplices, stealthily entered the store late one night and rendered the two clerks senseless with chloroform. They then proceeded to loot the store. The clerks awoke from their chemically induced slumber and quickly sized up the situation. In a most embarrassing turn of events, the two clerks subdued Rulloff's muscle men. Rulloff returned from another room and quickly responded to the emergency by firing his pistol at one of the clerks. The bullet missed its mark and slammed into a wooden stair sending splinters flying into the clerk's face. Rulloff took no chances with the second clerk, placing the pistol's muzzle next to his head before pulling the trigger. For their effort, the robbers collected little more than their senses, leaving behind incriminating evidence as they fled the store. Rulloff left his shoes, no doubt removed to aid his sneaky movement. This proved to be a fatal mistake since the robber had a foot deformity which left behind a telltale presence in the shoe. Like Cinderella, the shoes could only fit one person.

The authorities in Binghamton charged Edward Rulloff with robbery and murder. His two friends both drowned while trying to escape after the break-in. Although he had two attorneys, Rulloff trusted his own powers of elocution and persuasion. As a result, Rulloff conducted much of his own defense, even cross-examining the surviving clerk. The prosecution presented a more plausible case, as evidenced by the jury's brief spell of deliberation before finding the defendant guilty of first degree murder. Dismayed but not dissuaded, Rulloff turned his attention to an appeal. His attorney appealed to the Governor of New York, requesting a lunacy commission examine the mental and physical health of the frail inmate victimized by a prolonged incarceration. Rulloff had a different idea.

Rulloff was a master of several languages but his linguistic skills shined when he turned his attention to philology. The condemned criminal had spent considerable time perfecting a treatise titled "Method in the Formation of Language." Through a complicated discourse, the author claimed to have discovered the key that unlocked all languages. He built the claim on a solid foundation of Greek words, impressive for a person with no formal training in the language. Rulloff had presented the manuscript to the American Philological Association just prior to the robbery for which he now stood convicted. He vainly hoped the manuscript would find favor among the group and lead to publication. Unfortunately, the book was panned and the author dismissed.

As he pondered his recent conviction and potential appellate strategies, it seemed odd that Rulloff would waste precious time by sending copies of the "Method" to newspapers. A local paper, somehow smitten by the literary endeavors of a murderer, published extensive tracts from the "Method." The obtuse work was a hit and a number of New York newspapers jumped on the bandwagon trumpeting the brilliant contribution. Editorials extolled Rulloff's linguistic genius, and lamenting the pending loss, implored the Governor to intervene. These tabloid opinion makers weighed Rulloff's ruthless crimes against his purported philological prowess and cast their vote in favor of sparing his life. For many people familiar with Rulloff's shrewdness, the real genius in the "Method" was its value as a philological dodge. The skeptical crowd claimed that the crafty conniver invented the whole scheme, hoping against hope that gullible dupes would rush to his defense. The Governor of New York cast the deciding vote in asking Dr. John Gray to examine Rulloff's sanity.

Dr. Gray accepted the assignment from the Governor and asked a colleague; Dr. Oakley Vanderpoel to join him. The pair departed immediately and took as their prime directive the need to conduct a thorough evaluation of the condemned man. They also assumed an imperative obligation to assess the literary value of the "Method," the darling of the news media. Gray and his companion spent several hours interviewing Rulloff and many more reading the "Method." The history they gathered from Rulloff painted an interesting picture.

Rulloff was born in 1819 and passed his early years without incident. He left home at a young age and began working as a store clerk. A series of robberies nearly decimated the store, and while the owner suspected Rulloff, it took an act of stupidity to arrest the culprit. Rulloff was seen strutting about town in garments clearly purloined from the store. The clothes cost Rulloff two years in prison. After the short stint in stir, Rulloff bounced from job to job, at various times working on a canal, as a clerk in a drugstore, as a school teacher and as a botanical physician.

While tending school, Rulloff married one of his young students and a few years later a child was born into the dysfunctional union.

Apparently botanical physicians were in great demand for Rulloff's practice grew quite large. In the midst of success, his extensive knowledge of herbal medications facilitated a dark side. A family member urgently requested Rulloff's assistance caring for a child. The botanical doctor did as bid but the child rapidly succumbed to a minor illness. The mother suffered a strange malady and died a few days later. Not long after these mysterious deaths Rulloff got into a major tiff with his wife, an event observed by a neighbor. His wife and child then vanished without a trace. Naturally, friends and family questioned Rulloff who responded with a tangled web of lies. Ensnared by his prevarications, Rulloff was arrested on suspicion of murder.

A good deal of circumstantial evidence suggested Rulloff murdered his family and then disposed of the bodies in a nearby lake. The jury found the defendant guilty of kidnapping, apparently unable to agree on the murder charge but unwilling to completely exonerate the scoundrel. Rulloff was sent to prison where he distinguished himself as a determined malingerer. To avoid back breaking work, the prisoner carefully calibrated his food intake to lose nearly 50 percent of his body weight, eating just enough to survive. For nearly a year he pitifully assumed the posture of a cripple, with one leg seemingly paralyzed. Yet another time, the inmate complained of partial blindness. The prison doctors, suspecting malingering, were nonetheless impressed with Rulloff's nearly flawless performances.

After serving ten years in prison, Rulloff was released and then promptly arrested and charged with the murder of his family. It was a curious turn of events driven by citizens still convinced after ten years that Rulloff was guilty. Rulloff pretended to mount a serious defense but tiring of the affair or perhaps sensing the outcome, escaped from jail and remained at large until apprehended for the bungled robbery and murder in Binghamton. In the intervening period Rulloff paid tribute to the Abraham Man by adopting numerous disguises. In one city he presented fraudulent credentials hoping to receive an academic appointment to teach languages, while in another location he bilked funds from gullible investors. In every district Rulloff passed through merchants coincidentally reported a spike in the number of store thefts.

Dr. Gray minced no words in describing Rulloff. "He stands forth as one more, and a conspicuous example of the utter worthlessness of high intellectual endowments, severed from moral culture".[243] The doctor carefully reviewed the "Method" and came to the conclusion that the work was neither unique nor useful. The author wove an impressive number of Greek words together and then, employing an idiosyncratic formula, sought to explain the universality of language. It was not quite gobbledygook for a thread of logic knit the subject together but it fell far short of the author's lofty claims. Gray was also amused by Rulloff's crude attempts to feign physical exhaustion. Apparently the condemned man reckoned that he could not fake insanity and at the same time make a credible claim of being a linguistic genius. The ever nimble con man tried one last ploy in hopes of convincing Gray that he was too physically unfit for punishment. Gray was unmoved by the performance and in the end believed Rulloff was malingering. The "Method" was essentially dismissed as a peculiar form of trickery designed to play on the emotions of gullible reporters and their unskeptical readers. Rulloff played his last part and was executed shortly after Gray submitted his report to the Governor.[244]

The timing of the Abraham Man's appearance varied. In some criminal cases, the first act did not open until all hope for reprieve was exhausted while in other cases the play began much earlier. The emergence of odd behavior as the trial unfolded certainly suggested trickery. In many cases, the looming Sword of Damocles unnerved the cowardly con man who resorted to malingering in a desperate effort to avoid punishment. Confounding this conclusion was a reality that some prisoners with a proclivity for mental illness actually succumbed to insanity. Distinguishing between the two tested the diagnostic skills of the best physicians.

Joseph Waltz murdered Herman Holcher.[245] The two men had a casual relationship, distant enough that no friction existed. Holcher spent his last night on earth peacefully going to sleep in the Waltz's family home. For most of his adult life Joseph was a troubled man, for reasons he could not fully comprehend. The night that Waltz spent in the Holcher home seemed to destabilize Joseph. His tortured mind could not shake a horrible impulse to kill Herman. To calm his turmoil Waltz sought comfort reading the Bible and praying. Neither cooled his restlessness nor slackened his resolve. Something beckoned, an evil spirit according to Waltz, and overpowered his resistance. He soon secured an ax, and qui-

---

243 "Edward H. Rulloff," *American Journal of Insanity* 28, no. 4 (1872): 463-514.
244 Ibid.
245 "Feigned insanity – Case of Joseph Waltz," *American Journal of Insanity* 31, no. 1 (1874): 50-72.

etly entering Holcher's room, murdered the sleeping man. After recovering from a brief but intense period of numbness and nausea, the killer hid the body.

It did not take authorities long to find the body and pin the blame on Waltz. In his few final days of freedom no one noticed anything unusual about the killer. After his arrest Waltz seemed to melt, confessing the whole affair and even took authorities on a guided tour identifying the incriminating evidence. No one seemed particularly curious about a random act of violence.

Waltz was twenty-four years old when he was arrested. Life on his father's farm was good and the young man was healthy and strong. Not a hint of rough behavior tainted his life. He passed his leisure time reading, when not otherwise engaged in the labors of farming. The usual history of mental illness in the family was absent and the prisoner was free of head injuries. The only event punctuating an otherwise humdrum life was the murder.

The prisoner started acting strange a few weeks after being jailed. Jailors responded to the change in behavior with disbelief. The clever guards concocted their own trick to smoke the suspected fraud out. A piece of paper, with a phony description of insanity, mysteriously appeared in the prisoner's cell. As if on cue, Waltz studied the script and played his part in court. Those in the know must have silently congratulated themselves. The trial judge was part of the experiment and asked an accommodating prison doctor to instruct Waltz that his case would be more convincing with a frenzied display. Waltz again played the role assigned, sealing his fate as a malingerer. Apparently no one questioned the propriety of a doctor, prosecutor, and judge all conspiring to trick the prisoner.

At the conclusion of the evidence phase of the trial the judge issued meticulous instructions to the jury. The instructions prevented the jury from excusing Waltz's behavior because of a belief in spirits. Apparently, all that mattered was a strict application of the facts to the prisoner's capacity to distinguish right from wrong. Even if Waltz was compelled by a delusion involving evil spirits that was deemed irrelevant. Not surprisingly, after a few minutes deliberation the jury found the defendant guilty.

Following the verdict, for inexplicable reasons, the trial judge requested an audience with the Governor of New York. At this meeting the judge, who stubbornly maintained that the defendant was sane, nonetheless requested that a group of medical experts examine Waltz. Perhaps this strange turn of events arose from some lingering doubt of guilt given the judge's duplicitous behavior. In any event, the Governor approved the request and assigned the task to Drs. John Ordronaux and John Gray.

The dynamic duo of Gray and Ordronaux spent a day interviewing Waltz, speaking with jailors and medical doctors familiar with the prisoner and reading the trial transcripts. During the doctors' visit, Waltz acted bizarre, spoke irrationally and jumped about. Tiring of the performance, the two doctors challenged the whole act as fraudulent. The accusation bounced off Waltz who continued nonplussed. Waltz interspersed fragmented memories of the murder with nonsense, frequently gesturing to meaningless art decorating his cell. The doctors were unswayed. In rendering their opinion of malingering, Gray and Ordronaux placed considerable weight on the prisoner's good physical health, ability to describe the crime in detail, and his response to the repeated tricks so adroitly played by the trial judge and jailors.

Asylum superintendents never missed an opportunity to promote their institutions. In the process, they sometimes exposed fissures in their philosophy which often formed the basis for ridiculing their competitors. Isaac Ray was a sage mentor advising fellow asylum superintendents, a position achieved following the publication of his landmark book on medical legal practice. Even the esteemed doctor of jurisprudence occasionally, no doubt unwittingly, professed a standard of medical care which exposed contradictions in forensic practice among his colleagues.

Michel Trimbur landed in prison after taking criminal liberties with a young woman.[246] A partner in the crime soon shared Trimbur's cell. The pair seemingly tolerated each other's company without any obvious bickering. One morning as the guards made the breakfast rounds, Trimbur drily noted that only one tray was necessary. When questioned by the guard, the surviving cell mate declared his partner dead. With virtually no prompting Trimbur confessed the murder, motivated by the victim's criticism of the killer's mother.

The ever vigilant and suspicious guards dismissed as a crank Trimbur's erratic behavior after the murder. The inmate's rowdiness and visual hallucinations did not fool the astute jailers. Trimbur's attorney took a different view and petitioned for a mental examination. Isaac Ray entered the scene at this point, never fully disclosing the purpose of his visits to the inmate.

---

246 Isaac Ray, "Homicide: Suspected simulation of insanity," *American Journal of Insanity* 31, no. 2 (1874): 241-53.

Ray spent about an hour with the prisoner during the first interview. Nothing unusual passed between the two men as Trimbur faithfully and rationally recalled the murder. The next visit revealed a new facet when the prisoner suddenly shifted gears and began a rapid nonsensical monologue. Ray was impressed, believing that no actor could so genuinely replicate the pressured speech of insanity. Over the next few months the doctor briefly visited Trimbur a few more times and in each instance the babble issued forth. The actor's steady performance was slowly eroding the doctor's skepticism.

Ray hesitated in confirming the inmate's insanity. He openly debated the possibilities. The prisoner's artless first effort to deceive the jailers was a point favoring faking. On the other hand, Trimbur was not very smart, making the chances of a successful simulation less likely. Ray also prided himself on not fully disclosing the purpose for visiting the prisoner, as a consequence of which a pretender could not adapt the performance for his audience. Despite any misgivings he harbored, the well-known and widely respected asylum superintendent tilted towards sanity and so testified. Naturally, the jury found Trimbur guilty. All was not lost though when his attorney successfully argued for a new trial. Roughly a year passed during which Trimbur stayed in jail, still exhibiting the same oddities that Ray previously equivocated about. At the second trial the court, now convinced that Trimbur was insane, retuned an acquittal.

In recounting this case Isaac Ray almost seemed apologetic when justifying his faulty diagnosis and subsequent testimony. The somewhat chastened doctor, perhaps recognizing his inadequate preparation, confidently stated that all doubts about Trimbur could have been removed with an extended period of observation at the local insane asylum. Many of Ray's fellow asylum superintendents rejected this prudent proposition. Even when their testimony virtually guaranteed a death warrant, his colleagues firmly stood their ground, never trembling, when providing opinions based on the shakiest foundation.

The medicalization of mental illness placed a good part of the responsibility for protecting society on physicians. An emerging class of doctors specializing in psychological medicine embraced the role. Many relished the fringe benefits which included authority, prestige, and empire building. Doctors devoted to medical jurisprudence became celebrities with their names frequently appearing in newsprint. In time, the luster started to fade as mental illness defied efforts to abolish it. Asylum doctors increasingly fell victim to a restless public disillusioned by stories of patient abuse, managerial incompetence, and the increasing cost of institutional care. The number of criminals claiming insanity exploded and medical experts routinely lined up on both sides. High profile cases commonly counted a group of three or four doctors opposing each other on the question of insanity. In many of these cases the Abraham Man loomed large and the medical testimony was inconclusive.

William Barr joined a new class of criminals who seamlessly, and repeatedly, moved from prison to asylum.[247] As the cycle unfolded, prison doctors would diagnosis an inmate's unruly behavior as insanity and arrange for a transfer to an asylum. The asylum doctors would evaluate the patient, offer some treatment, and eventually certify a cure which sent the inmate back to jail. As the years went by, such prisoners passed time after time through the revolving door between jail and hospital. Of course, the prisoner was not a passive participant and either through real or feigned mental illness propelled the process along. The doctor's faith, eroded by conniving inmates, probably leaned towards downplaying the gravity of most ailments. Eventually the physician's healthy skepticism gave way to cynicism and indifference.

William Barr was just twenty years old when a ham fisted robbery led to a ten year stint at Sing Sing Prison. About three years of the sentence passed uneventfully, eventually interrupted by an attack of insanity which a prison doctor labeled as mania. The doctor completed the appropriate paperwork and Barr was transferred to an asylum. The asylum doctors who treated the inmate apparently kept no written records but vividly recalled his stay. Barr was not a favorite of the asylum doctors who described him as violent, impulsive, and immoral. In spite of their convictions that Barr was sane, the asylum doctors nonetheless provided treatment for two years. This lengthy period of treatment, for a patient with no mental illness, ended with Barr's return to prison.

About nine months passed before the prison doctor, citing a combination of mania and melancholia, again referred Barr back to the asylum. The admitting doctors at the asylum were not pleased. They remembered Barr as undisciplined, irritable, mean, impulsive and most definitely not insane. Mania and melancholia presented alternating pictures of exuberance and despondency. Asylum doctors understood that during the manic phase of emotional excitation the behavior commonly gravitated towards violence. Yet their intense dislike of Barr might have biased their medical opinions. Following Barr's readmission the asylum doctors put

---

247 Carlos F. MacDonald, "Feigned insanity, homicide, suicide," *American Journal of Insanity* 35, no. 3 (1879): 411-32.

the staff on notice, ordering extra vigilance in an effort to uncover the presumed malingerer. After nine days the doctors again certified Barr free from insanity and back to prison he went.

Just a few more months passed before Barr lived up to his doctor's description of "an ugly customer".[248] A prison detail, including Barr, received a temporary reprieve from confinement in order to clear snow surrounding the jail. Barr took his freedom as an opportunity to flirt with passing females, which earned a rebuke from a guard. Over the next few minutes the two sparred with each other. The inmate brought the dispute to a vicious conclusion by bashing the guard's skull with a shovel. Barr's behavior changed drastically following this dramatic event. Over the next few weeks he spoke incoherently in a loud and boisterous fashion, complaining that the devil was tormenting him. On one particularly violent occasion, while acting like a raving maniac, he tore his cell apart. Naturally, Barr's attorney invoked the insanity defense at the murder trial.

The trial court asked Dr. Gray to assemble a sanity commission. After agreeing to the request, Gray enlisted two other asylum doctors. The operation of the sanity commission resembled a judicial hearing. The commission members obtained sworn testimony from witnesses, produced a written record of the proceedings, received testimony from the defendant, secured Barr's prison records, and concluded the affair with a written opinion. As might be expected, the doctors found Barr sane. Curiously, the Commission's conclusion was admitted only as an advisory statement, having no practical impact on the trial. In fact, in a rebuff to the eminent physicians' conclusions, the defense attorney preceded with the insanity defense anyway.

Eight physicians found time in their busy schedules to testify at the trial. Two of the four medical witnesses for the defense were the same doctors who sent Barr from the prison to the asylum. With some minor diagnostic disagreements, all four defense doctors agreed that the prisoner was insane, suffering from mania. Of course, the four prosecution witnesses disputed their colleagues' liberal interpretation of Barr's criminal behavior. Throughout the medical testimony, the defendant put on quite a spectacle, apparently unable to control his random, nonsensical outbursts. Many court room observers sympathized with Barr, thoroughly convinced that he was hopelessly insane.

---

248 Ibid., 415.

The jury found Barr guilty of non-premeditated murder and demanded a life sentence. The condemned prisoner responded with several subsequent botched escape attempts which only aggravated the prison authorities. As a result, Barr was even more securely confined eliminating any hope of escape. Apparently, the guards were less concerned with Barr's escaping through death. He hanged himself, once again raising questions about his sanity. With Barr's voice now permanently silent, and whispers of incompetence raising concerns about the prosecution's medical witnesses, it was time for the doctors to circle the wagons and fend off public criticism.

The case of William Barr was rushed into print in one of the leading medical journals. Carlos MacDonald, one of the asylum superintendents who testified at the trial, authored the defensive article. MacDonald insisted that Barr's suicide was a sane act, no evidence of depression or mania interfering with his conclusion. Perhaps sensing the weakness of his argument, MacDonald invoked the names of Isaac Ray and John Gray as fellow authorities who insisted that suicide was commonly committed without a whiff of mental illness. MacDonald's high wire act attempting to distance himself from any responsibility for Barr's suicide was not convincing. The asylum doctor clearly believed Barr was an evil miscreant, faking all prior episodes of mental illness, and deserved punishment instead of treatment. Unfortunately, as MacDonald probably well understood, the Abraham Man never wrote a script ending in death.

The case of William Barr illustrated the thorny position asylum superintendents straddled with suicide. It was an uncomfortable position the doctors struggled to overcome. After climbing to the top of psychological medicine, and planting the flag claiming sole ownership, it took a mighty effort from the asylum doctors to convince the public that suicide was not the product of mental illness. After all, the same doctors endlessly emphasized the subtleties of mental illness that only their brilliance could illuminate. Many lay people, shaking their head in disbelief when hearing of a suicide, frequently assigned the senseless act to an irrational mind. The asylum superintendents appreciated the risk of suicide, an outcome they could never fully control and the subsequent blame they could not escape. Nonetheless, a good deal of ink was spilled attempting to normalize suicide.

Asylum doctors under the tutelage of John Gray placed a diagnostic premium on discovering physical signs associated with mental illness. Acute mania, for example, invariably produced an elevated heart rate, fever, sweating, wild looking eyes, restless movement, and a dry tongue.

The presence or absence of these conditions served as objective tests of insanity. In many cases the doctor's conviction of a genuine mental disorder relied on changes in the pulse or perspiration. The association between physical signs and mental symptoms was not as firm as many doctors supposed. In spite of that tenuous relationship, one of the main reasons doctors insisted on physical proof of insanity was in an effort to defeat the Abraham Man.[249]

John Gaffney spent a good deal of time playing cards in a local saloon. The combination of alcohol and gambling unfortunately turned into an incendiary mix, an outcome that consumed Gaffney. A smoldering dispute with a fellow player erupted in violence, brought to a quick resolution by Gaffney with a bullet. Gaffney's trial moved swiftly, his head no doubt spinning with the rapidly moving events, and ended with a conviction. The jury demanded the death sentence and Gaffney's appointment with the gallows was quickly scheduled. His attorney made feeble attempts to postpone or reverse the sentence to no avail.

Having exhausted all legal means of rescuing himself Gaffney made an appeal with a greater chance of success. Word leaked out from the Buffalo, New York jail that the prisoner would speak with the press. Gaffney's words had barely left his mouth before excited members of the local newspaper descended on the convicted felon. With a mixture of contrition and confession, Gaffney deftly played on the sympathies of the reporters. The article seemed to be part of an elaborate ruse designed to herald the appearance of the Abraham Man.

A few days before the grim reaper would claim Gaffney a group of priests met with the condemned man. The priests were shocked by Gaffney's blasphemous, profane abuse. Surely a man soon to meet his Maker would show a bit of reflection, perhaps even praying for an eternal mercy. Gaffney would have none of this, instead exhibiting a mindless agitation that left the priests fearing for their safety. One of the priests pointedly asked Gaffney if he understood that death was near. The prisoner took no notice as he continued his irrational loquaciousness. The alarming change in Gaffney's conduct, when combined with his celebrity status, forced his jailers to seek a medical assessment.

Not one, but five local physicians examined Gaffney. In the main they all agreed that Gaffney might be insane and requested additional time for further observations. The physicians' opinions varied a bit. One physi-

---

249 Edward N. Brush, "Feigned insanity," *American Journal of Insanity* 35, no. 4 (1879): 534-42.

cian was impressed by the physical signs of insanity and the prisoner's perseverations. A second physician admitted the possibility of feigning but countered his own suspicions by noting the actor's apparent artistry. Yet another doctor, playing detective, hid just out of sight of the prisoner. He was close enough to hear Gaffney's disjointed discourse and left the surreptitious encounter convinced that the prisoner suffered from acute mania. The weight of five medical doctors opining insanity persuaded the Governor of New York to call upon his reliable friend, Dr. John Gray.

Dr. Gray and a colleague, Dr. Oakley Vanderpoel, examined Gaffney on three successive occasions before declaring the whole matter a fraud. On one visit, Gray spent hours listening to the mad ravings of the presumed lunatic. The fatigue of such a long performance taxed Gaffney's skills. Sensing the weakness, Gray started peppering the inmate with a volley of questions. During the doctor's verbal assault Gaffney slipped and answered a question. Gray pounced and accused Gaffney of faking. As might be expected, the prisoner responded by trying to physically attack the accuser. Gaffney's apparent misstep left Gray suspicious and surmising sanity.

Dr. Vanderpoel conducted a physical examination of the accused looking for objective signs of insanity. Gaffney's pulse was regular and then increased with a slight bit of exertion. His muscle tone showed no evidence of wasting. The doctor monitored Gaffney's skin temperature, sort of like a crude lie detector. The pair of examiners would purposely stress the patient but failed to detect a persistent rise in the skin temperature, which they considered a common feature of insanity. Vanderpoel closely observed Gaffney's face and again failed to detect the characteristic asymmetrical facial movements commonly believed associated with insanity. Gaffney's eyes reacted normally to changes in the light and lacked the vacant, sometimes hostile, intense gaze of the insane.[250]

The doctors sent the Governor a short response, "After a satisfactory examination of Gaffney, we found him sane — a case of feigned insanity."[251] Although sorely disappointed by the outcome, Gaffney revealed, "...well Doctor, I hope you do not blame me for trying to save myself. If I could

---

250 "John Gaffney: His simulated insanity testimony of Dr. Vanderpoel," *New York Times*, Feb. 14.
251 "Gaffney, the wife-murderer, feigning insanity," *New York Times*, Feb. 11, 1873.

live I would lead a better life."[252] Gaffney never got the chance to reform, required now to keep his date with the hangman.

Some actors failed in their deceit by not knowing the disease state too well, crumbling when confronted, or being overly dramatic. Reuben Clapp avoided these pitfalls, aided perhaps by a previous admission to a state lunatic asylum. In any event, federal authorities arrested Clapp for passing counterfeit money, leaving the former asylum patient in a small jail cell. A few days later a loud raucous commotion alarmed the jailers. Rushing to the source, the guards discovered Clapp dancing about in the nude. Two doctors examined the frenzied inmate and left without making a firm diagnosis. Over the next four days Clapp kept up an incessant babble, appearing confused and disorganized. The doctors found no physical signs of mania, his pulse being fairly regular. Clepp destroyed his cell, turning the space into a pig sty. Despite five days without sleep and a continuous display of erratic behavior, the doctors were unmoved in their suspicions that Clepp was malingering. To settle the matter, the doctors and the jail authorities concocted a rather harsh scheme. The inmate was reduced to the most meager food rations and his cell left filthy. After several days of starvation conditions, Clepp broke down and asked for more food. The doctors considered this prima facie evidence of deceit along with the prisoner's promise to settle down.[253]

The Abraham Man excelled when taking the stage as an epileptic. Suddenness of onset and short duration made this an easy role. In most cases, doctors made the diagnosis entirely based on the subject's history. Doctors rarely had the good fortune to witness a real seizure. In fact, seizures observed in prisons, military settings, and the criminal justice systems were often phony. A criminal's successful portrayal of epilepsy was tantamount to grabbing hold of the brass ring, inasmuch as all bad behavior attributed to the seizure was usually a complete bar to prosecution.

John Ordronaux recognized the ease of simulating a seizure and the difficulty disproving the deceptive drama. The doctor offered some guidance in an effort to help distinguish true from false seizures. According to Ordronaux, the first step in separating the genuine seizure from the phony fit depended on a clear grasp of what real convulsions looked like. An authentic convulsion could occur anywhere without regard for per-

---

252 Edward N. Brush, "Feigned insanity," *American Journal of Insanity* 35, no. 4 (1879): 534-42.

253 "A prisoner's pretense: He shams insanity for ten days," *New York times*, Jul. 21, 1878.

sonal safety. In the midst of a fit, a true epileptic may injure themselves while the faker will studiously avoid harm. An individual suffering a true seizure will lose consciousness and be insensible to their surroundings. They will not feel pain or hear loud noises. The pupils are fixed during a real seizure while a light shone on the eye of the faker will show the pupils contract. Real seizures have "a red, bloated contorted face, foaming at the mouth and" they might bite their tongue. When the seizure is over the victim, "wears a vacant stupid look...complains of headache and fatigue..." These are difficult, but certainly not impossible, features to feign.

The artful dodger was a literary figure created by Charles Dickens in his famous book, Oliver Twist. Dickens's tells the story of a group of young thieves carefully schooled in their craft by Fagin, a sort of cunning, criminal headmaster. Fagin would teach the boys useful jobs such as pick pocketing and provide a safe harbor to divvy up the spoils. The characters in Oliver Twist, although fictitious, were quite believable. James Clegg was born in England about five years after Dickens finished Oliver Twist. He eventually immigrated to America but his early years in England seemed like a perfect copy of Fagin's school for wayward youths.[254]

James Clegg was a roguish young lad who quickly strayed from his parent's home in England. Despite efforts to instill Christian virtues in their son, he quickly set about defeating the education. At the tender age of nine Clegg launched his criminal career by stealing money from his father's store. Evidencing a shrewdness that would have impressed a skilled robber, the young Clegg avoided detection by throwing the blame elsewhere. He continued to practice and perfect pilfering. Around the age of sixteen Clegg left home, and with a young girl by his side, set about taking care of her by stealing even more frequently. His mother intervened and had her son arrested. Following a short incarceration Clegg remained with his mother, but bored by the dull home life, fled to London.

The move to London led to a chance encounter which forever changed Clegg's life. While aimlessly strolling the streets late one night Clegg noticed, "a crowd of people around a man in a fit. I went among them, and robbed two strangers of their watches. A young thief that seen me get them came up and wanted his share...He then introduced me to the gang of thieves he was working with..."[255] The Fagin-like leader of the band of thieves was known simply as McCarty. The Abraham Man must have personally trained McCarty to be a dummy chucker. A dummy chucker

---

254 Carlos F. MacDonald, "Feigned epilepsy," *American Journal of Insanity*, 37, no. 1 (1880): 1-22.

255 Ibid., 7.

was a colloquial term applied to a person faking a fit. While the dummy chucker entertained onlookers with a seizure, his confederates picked the pockets of the distracted dupes.

Clegg relished the role as McCarty's understudy and in short order became an accomplished dummy chucker. The standby role gave way to a permanent position when the teacher was arrested. Clegg started having seizures on a fairly regular basis, and while his fellow thieves worked the crowd, the dummy chucker himself was tenderly transported for medical care. The charade continued unabated until one unfortunate day when a bungled theft ensnared the dummy chucker. Removed at once to jail, Clegg now found himself awaiting trial. The prospect of a lengthy period of incarceration did not appeal to the thief and through discussions with his attorney a novel legal strategy was employed. Clegg chucked a dummy while in the courtroom, an act which immediately brought the proceedings to a halt. A doctor was hastily summoned, and after a medical evaluation, pronounced the offender a hopeless case of epilepsy. The judge, perhaps not desiring another dramatic display, dropped the charges and dismissed the defendant. Clegg reveled in the outcome and once back on the street trumpeted the release as irrefutable evidence of his technical competence. As a result, Clegg's stock soared as his brand of dummy chucking fattened his profits.

Like any good business, the dummy chucker always looked for new opportunities. Clegg took his franchise into churches and funerals, both venues populated by pious, particularly unsuspecting pigeons, which were plucked bare. Perhaps the ease of the operation, along with an abundance of greed, lulled the crooks into taking bigger risks. Clegg, once again joining forces with McCarty, agreed to chuck a dummy as a diversion for a bank robbery. The unlucky McCarty was captured and again sent to prison. Clegg escaped but a few months later was convicted of fencing fellow thieves' ill-gotten stuff.

Clegg showed a different side when he assaulted a guard in prison. Facing the prospect of another conviction, the dummy chucker returned to feigning fits. The drama netted the convict a lighter sentence after medical doctors testified that Clegg's epilepsy hindered his ability to control aggressive behavior. Over the next few years, the dummy chucker pitched a fit whenever prisoner labors grew too onerous. Not all doctors were gullible and occasionally Clegg encountered a skeptic. These situations subjected the actor to tests "such as having a lance shoved under my nails and stuff put into my eyes..."[256] In every instance the doctor, maybe still suspicious, eventually yielded and labeled Clegg's seizures genuine.

Other inmates started emulating Clegg, hoping for the same benefits. The rash of seizures deepened the suspicions of prison authorities who successfully punished some of the less capable actors. The imitators probably forced Clegg to adapt by achieving new heights in dissimulation. Clegg rewrote the drama apparently recognizing that his act was stale. Early one morning, the dummy chucker launched his most ambitious play. Perched precariously on a ledge inside the prison Clegg suffered a fit and a thirty foot fall. Whether he miscalculated the distance is unknown but the fall caused serious injuries. The act succeeded and prison officials never again challenged Clegg's claim of epilepsy

After Clegg served his prison term he fled to America, lining his pockets for the last time with stolen money from England. Clegg disembarked in New York and soon introduced his new countrymen to the fine art of dummy chucking. Faking fits in this fashion, for purposes of pinching bystanders, was an instant hit among the criminal class. The story unfolded in a familiar way, the dummy chucker fooled the crowd while unsuspecting onlookers paid for the performance with their watches and wallets. Doctors would examine Clegg and sorrowfully diagnose epilepsy. Clegg one again proved himself an adept dummy chucker but a poor thief when a botched robbery landed the immigrant in prison. After a faked seizure, prison authorities transferred Clegg to the Asylum for Insane Criminals in Auburn, New York.

Carlos MacDonald, the Superintendent at the Asylum for Insane Criminals in Auburn took a special interest in James Clegg. While initially debating the legitimate nature of the seizures, the doctor eventually convinced himself that the whole affair was a fraud. MacDonald described Clegg's first seizure at Auburn, "I found him on the floor, his face distorted and livid; frothy saliva, tinged with blood, was oozing from his mouth; his body was apparently violently convulsed..."[257] The physical signs of a seizure such as dilated pupils and rapid breathing enhanced the performance but MacDonald retained his skepticism. With little to back up his claim, MacDonald accused Clegg of feigning a seizure. A few days later another seizure brought a similar condemnation.

The mere force of MacDonald's allegation of fraud supposedly brought forth a confession from Clegg. The dummy chucker, who had

---

256 Ibid., 11.
257 Ibid., 15.

fooled people for years, now apparently wilted after a few verbal challenges. MacDonald, claiming victory over his quarry, promptly returned
Clegg back to prison. The asylum doctor offered a few tips that helped
unmask Clegg, including his status as a prisoner, the "confession" of faking fits, and "the thumbs were not closed within the palms..." Facts that
did not fit the faking, like the dilated eyes, were dismissed.

James Clegg surely feigned fits for profit. It also seems likely that
Clegg suffered real seizures. His body carried the scars of serious injuries,
a seemingly unnecessary prop. Scores of doctors previously diagnosed
epilepsy. Part of MacDonald's fervor in finding feigning can be traced
to the asylum's credibility. The nascent field of medical psychology, institutional care, public funding and expert witness testimony relied on
accurate detection of malingering. Failure to identify the Abraham Man
corroded the asylum doctors' claim of professional competence.

The actor bore some risk for a bad performance. John Murray was a
denizen of the underworld and plied his thieving craft in the environs
surrounding New York City. The hapless burglar was arrested and rather quickly brought before the bar of justice. It seems most unlikely that
Murray and Clegg ever crossed paths but the former took a page from
the latter. In a pirouette of high drama, Murray fell to the court room
floor with an agonizing seizure. The display could not have come at a
more inopportune time. Two doctors immediately rushed to the aid of
the prostrate victim, and conducting a hasty examination, promptly declared the seizure a fraud. Counsel for the defense, no doubt mortified by
the doctors' announcement, probably imagined the case lost. If so, that
was indeed the outcome. The jury, perhaps piqued by the phony play,
convicted the felon without even leaving the room.[258]

Sometimes the actor was so bad that critics, in the form of medical
witnesses, were unnecessary. John Donnelly stole a horse and wagon
but kept his treasures for only a short time. He was quickly arrested but
probably believed that his recent escape from an asylum would prevent
punishment. After making this announcement Donnelly demonstrated
insanity. "He glared around, rolled his eyes, and demanded justice in a
tone loud enough to be heard all through the building." The prosecutor,
nonplussed by the show, accused Donnelly of fabricating insanity. No
doctor testified, instead the prosecutor simply stated that it was common knowledge that Donnelly was a shrewd horse trader. The affecta-
tions conveniently appeared only when the long arm of the law grabbed

---

258 "Insanity feigned in court," *New York Times*, Nov. 1, 1876.

the horse thief. Donnelly's performance earned him the scorn of the court and five years in prison.[259]

The Abraham Man relentlessly broadened the boundaries of legal insanity. An expansive definition of insanity simplified the play and helped ensure success. Without a doubt, the most generous excuse equated inebriation with insanity. A fashionable philosophy advocated, "In all cases of inebriate criminals there is mental defect and incapacity to reason sanely or control their acts. An inebriate who does criminal acts cannot be of sound mind. A criminal who is an inebriate is not sane. No inebriate is fully sane and no criminal can be of sound mind long".[260] Exculpating a drunk's bad behavior sounded preposterous to most late nineteenth century Americans but in reality the concept merely expanded the notion of moral insanity. It was a dangerous development which, if widely sanctioned by the courts, threatened to erode the very foundation of justice. After all, the Abraham Man could easily, and enjoyably, simulate alcoholism. The Superintendent of the Buffalo State Asylum recognized the threat and used the case of Peter Otto as a prop to ridicule proponents of inebriate insanity.

No one enjoyed a spot of whiskey more than Peter Otto. When not imbibing, Otto was a pleasant man, pious by nature and a rather reliable worker. During one bout with the bottle he met his future wife, and in a drunken stupor, married her. A few months after the ceremony, Otto was more than a little surprised when his wife gave birth to a child. This bred brewing doubt about his wife's previously professed chastity. The fireworks started in earnest when the newlyweds moved in with his mother.

In the beginning all went well with the triad but over time the arguments grew more heated between the son and his wife. It seemed to Otto that his mother always sided with his wife. Otto's drinking increased in some direct relationship to the troubles in the marriage. His wife also indulged in the intoxicating beverages which only fueled the acrimonious arguments between the pair. On one occasion the fight turned physical and Otto assaulted his better half. She promptly had him arrested and the querulous husband spent the next six months in jail.

Otto returned home after the brief confinement, contrite and affectionate for a few days. His renewed love affair with alcohol soon displaced his wife and the hot-temper again seared his wife. The main irritant at this time was his mother's refusal to cede her ownership in

259 "A horse-thief feigns insanity," *New York Times*, Aug. 5, 1875.

260 J. B. Andrews, "The case of Peter Louis Otto," American *Journal of Insanity* 45, (1888): 220.

the house to him. Naturally, Otto expected to inherit the house but he desired the property sooner. His mother, in quiet cahoots with his wife, deemed him unfit to own the house because of his reckless alcohol related behavior. Otto suspected his wife was undermining his efforts and grew increasingly angry.

Otto's anger turned malevolent. In late November, he pawned a prized watch for a small pistol. He was unfamiliar with the operation of the handgun and a few days later sought instruction from the pawn shop's owner. Otto now had the means to murder his wife and a few days later the opportunity arose. His wife awoke in a particularly foul mood and refused to make Otto's breakfast. He resorted to a liquid repast, no doubt fuming at his wife's intransigence. About mid-morning Otto's wife was outside tending to the laundry when he summoned her back inside. A few moments later five shots rang out and Otto's wife lay dead. The murderer fled the scene and made his way to the store where he worked. Otto was visibly intoxicated when he was arrested at the store. After consultation with his attorney, Otto asserted a defense based on alcoholic insanity. Dr. Judson Andrews, the Superintendent of the Buffalo State Asylum, evaluated Otto's mental state.

Dr. Andrews interviewed Otto once a week on three successive occasions. During the first visit, Otto faithfully rendered all details of his early life and could dwell pensively on the bitter marriage. He could not, or would not, describe any details of the murder. In fact, Otto stoutly denied his wife was dead and believed his present incarceration was a conspiracy to deprive him of his mother's house. Andrews probably left the first encounter in a state of judgmental equipoise, neither believing nor disbelieving the story. The subsequent visits helped Andrews clarify the matter.

The second visit with the prisoner was notable for the growing magnitude of memory loss. Otto claimed not to recognize Andrews, denied the former suspicions of his wife's infidelity, and pointedly reminded the doctor about his poor memory. For the first time Otto admitted hearing auditory hallucinations, disembodied voices near his cell making vague accusations. At the third and final visit, Otto's apparent condition had deteriorated. Once again, Otto claimed not to recognize Dr. Andrews, but this time the forgetfulness extended to events recently discussed. The prisoner answered most questions by simply stating, "I can't remember."[261]

---

261 Ibid., 213.

Andrews knitted the three interviews together and concluded that Otto was faking. There were too many factual inconsistencies and too much insistence on memory problems. The poor memory was quite self-serving, mostly encompassing potentially incriminating details of the murder. The fact that Otto's symptoms worsened as the trial approached also hinted at malingering. Dr. Andrews eventually testified that Otto was sane. Otto was convicted of murder and sentenced to death. The condemned murderer sought relief through the appellate courts but this failed. In a last desperate bid to avoid the hangman's noose, Otto appealed to the Governor of New York. Otto persistently claimed that he suffered from a severe emotional disorder, again creatively asserting inebriate insanity. Despite any misgivings the Governor might have privately harbored, he nonetheless appointed two physicians to examine the prisoner. The doctors found no evidence of mental illness. With all avenues of clemency exhausted, Otto was hanged.

The Abraham Man strengthened his acting credentials during the Civil War. Following the war, the emerging medical legal interest in emotional disorders guaranteed new venues for increasingly sophisticated simulations. Doctors responded by sharpening their diagnostic skills in an effort to defeat this troublesome trend.

CHAPTER 8: TROUBLESOME TREND

In less sophisticated times it seemed easier to unmask the malingerer. A combination of poor acting and healthy skepticism made it more difficult to convince a jury. The Abraham Man adapted by adopting ever more clever disguises.

The imprecise definition of insanity contributed to its ambiguous legal application and exploitation by the Abraham Man. Monomania was a common type of insanity diagnosed by physicians in the nineteenth century, a broad label that covered virtually any form of seemingly compulsive behavior. Aside from this general definition, in a troubling trend that gained momentum, it seemed that any habitual behavior, particularly if paired with a criminal act, could qualify as a monomania.

Charles B. Huntingdon was born in 1822. His father was a cabinet maker who lived a respectable life and raised his son accordingly. All was not well though. Charles was a lackluster student, and despite the father's vigorous application of corporeal punishment, failed to improve. In fact, he seemed totally indifferent to discipline. He was a curious boy who enjoyed dissecting toys and other instruments around the home in an effort to understand their inner workings. At the age of twenty-one he left home and traveled to New York City. He soon gained employment in a furniture store. His ambitions shortly led him to join efforts with another young man. The pair opened a furniture store with a great flourish and little else. Their lack of business experience led to bankruptcy, leaving Charles' credit in shambles. The chastened son briefly returned home but the allure of the big city again beckoned. Without a shred of practical education, Charles assumed the role of an investment broker. Nothing came of this venture but the ever hopeful Charles simply shifted gears, launching one failed scheme after another. With each unsuccessful enterprise his indebtedness grew. Charles even took a run at setting up a bank, the phony management eventually leading to a criminal indictment. Nonplussed by the conviction, Charles dreamed up another idea. He would print impressive looking stock certificates and sell the documents to investors in a new bank. This too crumbled and Charles' towering mountain of debt eclipsed any hope of financial recovery. Along the way, he perfected the practice of inventing imaginary business partners and bank managers, and signing their fictitious names to scores of documents. His luck ran out late in 1856 when a series of bank notes, rather uncharacteristically clumsily forged, led to his arrest.[262]

Huntingdon was quickly released from jail after posting bail. His trial for forgery began late in December and continued over Christmas. The facts overwhelmingly suggested the defendant's guilt. The prosecution presented all the witnesses necessary to expose the fraud. Except for the creative genius of Huntingdon's defense, this case would have passed quietly without much fanfare. The defense counsel repackaged the facts of the case, openly admitting his client's criminal duplicity, and then stunned the court by asserting the insanity defense. The defense lawyer recognized a pattern in Huntingdon's repetitious behavior. In spite of failure after failure, his client pursued one scheme after another. All involved some degree of chicanery with phony documents, phantom pursuits, and persuasive rhetoric. Well known and shrewd investors lost fortunes. Only one explanation could account for this behavior - a monomania for forgery.[263]

The prosecution's clever arguments breathed new life into a case at risk of quickly becoming another humdrum case. Local newspapers were losing interest in the story line but this curious twist guaranteed the public's interest. So the reporters returned to the court room and listened to the defense. Mr. Brady, the defense attorney, spent several minutes explaining why the insanity defense was appropriate. According to the seasoned lawyer, Huntingdon perpetually pursued failed ventures without recognizing the inherent peril. Even while in prison awaiting the trial, Huntingdon adopted a devil-may-care attitude which totally perplexed

---

262 "Trial of Charles B. Huntingdon for forgery," *New York Daily Times*, Dec. 20, 1856.

263 "Extraordinary phase of the Huntingdon trial," *New York Daily Times*, Dec. 20, 1856.

the attorney. The only explanation that accounted for Huntingdon's al-most jovial behavior was insanity. Brady coupled his client's characteristic nonchalance with his feckless schemes in arriving at the monomania. Another compelling bit of sophistry cooked into the insanity defense was Huntingdon's artlessness. It was easy to uncover his schemes and Huntingdon never tried to escape. Brady invited the jury to study the defendant's life history and observe a pattern of senseless schemes, endlessly perpetrated with no hope of success. Huntingdon was a monomaniac driven by an irrational compulsion. The attorney summarized the case by noting, "Where the peculiarities of the mind, however, deprive the subject of the power to distinguish right from wrong in the commission of any particular act in its nature criminal, and when the impulse to commit the act is irresistible and uncontrollable, no matter what amount of cunning may accompany the act, and no matter what motive may have actuated the individual, his hand is guided by a power which he cannot resist, and the act is not his own."[264]

Drs. Gillman and Parker examined Huntingdon and endorsed the diagnosis of a moral insanity. Their testimony was soundly ridiculed by a leading newspaper, which in turn prompted Huntingdon's attorney to publicly chastise the editor. In the court room the audience tilted towards Huntingdon and, after a rousing closing argument by the defense, a spontaneous round of applause confirmed the bias.

The prosecutor took the final opportunity to sway the jury by revisiting and rebutting key defense arguments. Instead of seeing a life dominated by eccentricity, the prosecutor cut to the chaste and labeled the endless schemes as the work of a master criminal. It seemed odd to the attorney that the defendant could amass one half million dollars in his short stint on Wall Street, wallow in luxury, and still claim insanity. Family and friends never suspected insanity. In spite of this, the prosecutor claimed, the two medical experts opined insanity. The doctors based their diagnosis entirely on Huntingdon's word. As might be expected, the prosecutor scoffed at the doctors' naiveté. After all, the defendant was a forger, educated in the nuances of fraud and a proud disciple of the Abraham Man. As the prosecutor argued, if Huntingdon could fool some of the brightest and shrewdest businessmen on Wall Street it was child's play to dupe two doctors. It never seemed to dawn on these doctors that Huntingdon could feign insanity.

---

264 "The trial of Charles B. Huntingdon for forgery," *New York Daily Times*, Dec. 20, 1856.

At the conclusion of the attorneys' closing statements the trial judge took center stage. The judge's instructions to the jury began with a re-markable commentary on the vast scope of Huntingdon's fraud. Moving on, the trial judge summarized key points in the trial and reminded the jury it was the State's responsibility to prove Huntingdon's guilt beyond a reasonable doubt. Following the instructions, the jury deliberated for four hours. The defense's initial success was seen in the jury's first bal-lot, when nine jurors supported conviction, two supported the insanity defense, and one lone juror cast his ballot for acquittal. The fractured fact-finders resumed their discussions and eventually reined in the three dissenting votes. Huntingdon was found guilty.[265]

The trial of Charles B. Huntingdon for forgery captivated the pub-lic's attention. The man's swagger, accumulation of riches, penchant for race horses, and even faster women was a sure fire formula of money and sex. The newspapers' circulation surely swelled during the fourteen day trial. The introduction of medical testimony offered a unique twist. Two learned doctors took the stand and imperiously transformed a dedicated criminal's life into insanity. One of the doctors ludicrously testified that the defendant was insane from childhood, and even if he committed a murder in the courtroom, could not be held responsible. The doctors' tes-timony insulted the jury's common sense and marked yet another inaus-picious introduction of medical testimony in a high profile legal case. The doctors failed to see the Abraham Man, clearly visible to the medically untrained eyes of the lay jurors.

In the years before the Civil War the notion that any singular piece of odd or deviant behavior was a mental aberration, exhibited by an oth-erwise normal person, took root and assumed the monomania moniker. It was an infectious trend, easily spread, and socially destructive. If the behavior ran counter to social norms, or was frankly criminal, it seemed that a growing legion of doctors, lawyers, charlatans, and quacks stood ready to exonerate the victim.

A prosperous Philadelphia man, Napoleon Bancroft, sought the do-mestic services of a young woman. After a bit of searching, Bancroft employed a young German girl. At first, she seemed the perfect au pair, cheerful, attentive to Bancroft's children, and efficient with the chores. After a few weeks the family noticed small items missing and expensive clothing deliberately torn. When questioned, the domestic servant stut-tered and stammered and reluctantly pinned the blame on Bancroft's

---

265 Ibid.

four-year-old son. The little boy was dutifully punished, repeatedly, since the thefts continued. He doubtlessly protested in a pitiful manner but to no avail. The mischief accelerated one day when the live-in caregiver breathlessly reported a fire in the house. The panic stricken father doused the blaze but four more fires mysteriously erupted over the next few hours. A friend of the family happened upon the scene, and while helping extinguish the flames, grew suspicious of the young woman. Naturally when confronted she blamed the young boy. The family friend persisted in his accusations, finally convincing the fire chief to investigate. A scorching interrogation forced a partial confession from the girl. In the court room she fully admitted causing the fires and thefts. For some unknown reason, instead of punishing the miscreant, she was sent to a phrenologist. Perhaps the notion that a young woman could be both criminally mischievous and an arsonist defied common concepts of feminine behavior. In any event, an obliging phrenologist carefully examined her skull, convinced she was a perfect specimen of a monomania compelled to commit crime.[266]

The early growth of medical expert witness testimony got off to a rocky start. The public seemed unimpressed with the testimony, even if it was novel and a bit titillating. Part of the public's discomfort arose from a deep distrust of efforts to evade the just punishment expected for criminal behavior. Perhaps in other cases, obtuse medical testimony insulted the jurors' common sense. Many doctors came to the witness stand and conjured up madness out of the wispiest fragments of a defendant's life. When challenged, the medical witness might patiently, pompously, or indignantly explain that detecting the subtleties of insanity required the skill of a trained observer. Never mind that family and friends were oblivious to the malady. The net result of medical testimony was as an ever increasing trend towards labeling criminal behavior as insanity. The public's cynicism grew along with the development of medical jurisprudence. Lurking in the shadows of many cases was the Abraham Man. The failure of medical witnesses to consider malingering hobbled their credibility.

Monomania was a fashionable term affixed to any indecorous behavior. Awarding the title was not the exclusive province of medicine. Newspaper reporters would write vivid tales documenting all types of apparently idiosyncratic behaviors, inexorably dragging the reader to

---

266 "Singular and extraordinary case of arson," *Chicago Press and Tribune*, Nov. 15, 1859.

monomania. Such stories offered the public amusing anecdotes but the reporter's conclusions were shallow and only served to trivialize mental illness. The label seemed to serve many purposes, such as providing a superficial, uncritical explanation of behavior, discrediting an opponent through a pejorative declaration, and exonerating the misdeeds of right-minded people who engaged in wrong-headed conduct.

The Reverend John C. Town was somewhat of a ne'er-do-well, floating between phrenology, preaching, and pseudo investing. His passion was praying in a loud voice, almost as if the volume would reach the heavens. For several months, Town practiced his faith at the Daily Union Prayer Meeting in Chicago. The congregation quickly grew tired of Town's boisterous invocations, some of which the more pious members believed bordered on the blasphemous, and so they petitioned for his removal. Town ignored their pleas and threats, leading the distressed congregation to forcibly remove him. The itinerant soul now found himself charged with disorderly conduct. The judge hearing the case was unmoved by the zealot's lengthy monologue and fined Town three dollars. "The defendant left the Court in high glee, clapping his hands and grinning sardonically..." The short story ended by concluding the obvious, Town was a monomaniac.[267]

Occasionally, when not fawning over a sensational trial or filling the front page with a curious bit of behavior, newspapers took the opposite tack and lamented the growth of medical jurisprudence. Editors who adroitly manipulated lurid tales that sold the tabloids would periodically ignite a self-fueled controversy. "The doctors and lawyers are every year adding new and curious chapters to the treatises on medical jurisprudence. The number of cases in which insanity is put forward as a justification for crime is increasing so rapidly, both here and in England, that the moral as well as legal responsibility of individuals for their acts, and above all, for their criminal acts, bids fair to disappear altogether."[268]

The stimulus prompting this newspaper's ire was a doctor's testimony in a criminal trial. Apparently the defendant suffered from an old head injury which led the medical witness to connect the ancient medical history with his alleged crime. The doctor testified that a closed head injury commonly resulted in a change in personality, often characterized by irritability, headaches, and memory lapses. The slightest provocation, such as the consumption of alcohol or simply a sleepless night, could tip the

---

267 "A troublesome monomania," *Chicago Tribune,* Jul. 24, 1865.
268 "The brains of criminals," *New York Times,* Jun. 4, 1864.

person into an uncontrollable frenzy. Perhaps the well-meaning medical witness intended to contain his statements to the case at hand but a newspaper's editorial seized the implications. In true breathless fashion, the editorial comments hyperventilated that a knock about the head was so common among criminals that "we shall have to abandon all attempts to punish crime." Beyond the hyperbole, the editorial raised a legitimate, but obliquely addressed anxiety, about authentic arguments. Anyone could assert a past head injury, manufacture a few subjective symptoms, receive medical endorsement, and quite possibly escape punishment.[269] Doctors inadvertently facilitated the Abraham Man's fraudulent behavior. By reducing insanity to a long forgotten and unproven injury, criminals along with their willing medical and legal accomplices, could medicalize any misconduct as insanity.

The public's schizophrenic response to medical testimony sometimes shifted when social-political forces favored compassion over conviction. In these situations, usually involving a female's criminal transgression, a sympathetic picture painted the woman a victim of momentary insanity. The woman's legal defense strategy inverted the disdain typically reserved for a perpetrator. Through the process, the true victim was vilified and the women's conduct cast as virtuous, although tainted by a touch of understandable madness. Once again, medical professionals added the needed legitimacy to advance the legal argument.

Elizabeth Beatty succumbed to the romantic advances of a young man simply referred to as McCormick. Their torrid relationship left Beatty pregnant. Over the next nine months it seems reasonable to imagine a mixture of affection, ardor, altercations, and mounting acrimony. Eventually it became evident that McCormick had no intention of restoring the woman's virtue through marriage. The child was born outside the sanctity of marriage. Beatty's unrequited shame soon gave way to vengeance. She had her former lover arrested for abandonment. The judge fixed a date for the trial at the arraignment. As both parties in the contest were leaving the court room, Beatty produced a hidden hand gun and fatally shot McCormick. Naturally, a number of individuals witnessed the murder, handing the prosecution a presumably prima facie case. The prosecutor's common sense calculation did not convince the jury. Beatty's attorney stoked the jury's emotions, portraying the young girl as an irrationally distraught victim of debauchery. The notion of madness not murder or mania not malevolence suited the juror's morality. After de-

---

269 Ibid.

liberating for a few hours, the jury foreman declared Elizabeth Beatty insane. Since the temporary emotional insanity lapsed with her paramour's death, Beatty was unconditionally released by the court.[270]

Ellen Burke might have followed in the footsteps of Elizabeth Beatty if not for the interference of concerned family members. Several family members petitioned a county court to declare Burke insane. The impetus for this claim arose from Burke's passionate infatuation with Mr. McCarty. Apparently, the woman's romantic worship was not reciprocated, a fact obvious to family members when McCarty left the city unannounced. Even after returning to the city McCarty made no attempt to contact Ellen. Nonetheless, the jilted woman clung to sentimental fantasies of a romantic reunion. In one instance, suspecting infidelity from her former beau, she secretly followed him to a bawdy house. At this point, Ellen might have converted her love to hate and traveled down the path of vengeance. She never got the chance. Instead, family members interpreted her unrealistic preoccupation with McCarty as a dreamy delusion deserving removal to an asylum. The family members could identify no instance of unusual behavior in Ellen's life. A doctor discovered no evidence of insanity, just some minor eccentricities which did not warrant the humiliation of an asylum visit. The court agreed.[271]

Doctors rescuing fair damsels from distress reached a pinnacle with the Harris Trial. The crime once again captivated the attention of newspaper reporters who dutifully attended to every detail. The evidence in the case seemed inarguable but that was before the defense secured the professional services of the Superintendent of the US Government Insane Asylum. According to the straight forward description provided by the prosecution, Mary Harris was a scorned woman seeking revenge. In December, 1864 she traveled halfway across America, accompanied throughout the journey with her trusty pistol. She arrived in Washington, DC and made her way to the Treasury Department. Harris asked for Judson Burroughs by name and then partially concealed herself in the hallway awaiting his arrival. Burroughs strolled down the hallway completely unaware of the looming tragedy. Harris waited until Burroughs was just a few feet away and shot him. To make sure she killed him Harris fired a second time. She then coolly strode past the victim lying on the floor and made her way nearly outside before she was apprehended.[272]

---

270 "A girl acquitted for shooting her seducer," *Chicago Tribune*, Sep. 20, 1863.
271 "Love and insanity," *Chicago Tribune*, June. 4, 1864.
272 "Washington news: Progress of the trial of Miss Harris," *New York Times*, Jul. 19, 1865.

Mary Harris was arrested and taken to a local jail. A day after the murder the Nation's Capital was all abuzz with rumors and speculations. As might be expected, the victim of the crime was cast as a cad. With a bias reflecting the mores of the day, Burroughs was variously depicted as a wandering womanizer or bigamous spouse. Harris did little to dispel the percolating presumptions surrounding Burroughs. On the other hand, she did sense the importance of shaping the media and quickly granted a reporter's interview request.

The reporter's prose captured the essence of Miss Harris, and at the same time betrayed a sympathetic tone. The defendant was weary and a bit agitated when she met the reporter. The first few hours of confinement took a heavy toll on the young woman. The keen eye of the trained newspaper man saw a woman "of good figure, rather slight; has a well formed head; dark hazel eyes; fine hair, which seemed in the light in which we saw it to be black; cut short, and worn in curls; is graceful in her manners, naturally intelligent..." This pretty woman in a tight spot made a good first impression.[273]

Mary Harris was a nineteen-year-old girl sitting forlornly in jail. The reporter asked a series of probing questions which the young defendant obligingly answered. Harris first recalled her poor Irish family and the tribulations growing up in Iowa. At the age of twelve she first met the much older Judson Burroughs. As the years passed by Mary noted that Burroughs's affection took a more romantic turn, or so she fancied. Eventually her suitor left Iowa, and over the next few months the only communication between the two was through a few letters. Mary pressed the evanescent relationship, convinced that Judson had proposed marriage before leaving Iowa. Her story to the reporter took an unusual turn at this point. About a year before the murder, Mary received an unsigned letter asking her to meet the mystery writer at a house of ill repute in Chicago. She mulled the matter over and finally decided to accept the invitation. She traveled to the big city but upon her arrival at the bordello could not locate the mysterious letter writer. She presumed, without a shred of evidence, that Burroughs penned the letter. In any event, another similarly unsigned letter beckoned the young woman back to Chicago. Again her efforts went unrewarded. By now, Mary was frustrated and angry at Burroughs. She sought the help of an attorney and a detective, with the apparent aim of suing Burroughs for a contractual

---

273 "The Washington tragedy: An interview with Miss Harris, her statement of her relations with the deceased," *Washington Chronicle*, Feb. 2, 1865.

breech of his marriage proposal. At some point during Mary's pursuit of Judson a whiff of scandal surfaced. The young woman and her family vigorously denied whispered rumors of an illicit affair. With her reputation now sullied, Mary desperately sought to restore her virtue. The rejected woman made plans to confront her former beau when she learned that Judson had married shortly after leaving Iowa and subsequently moved to Washington, DC.[274]

The reporter took copious notes as Mary continued her story. A few months before the murder, Mary recalled purchasing a pistol. She explained that friends felt her frequent travels placed her at risk and a pistol was a prudent insurance policy. After buying the pistol Mary read the accompanying directions and somehow managed to load the weapon. After this, the hand gun was packed among her baggage and forgotten. Armed with a heaping dose of righteous indignation, and a loaded pistol, Mary made her way to Washington, DC. She entered the Treasury building with her face veiled, located her target, and "I suddenly felt lifted up; my arm was extended as stiff as iron, and I saw him fall; I knew nothing more until I was called back as I was leaving the building."[275]

The reporter, in an effort to promote a fair and balanced account, also interviewed Dr. Burroughs, the brother of the deceased. Dr. Burroughs, the President of a Baptist Seminary, told a decidedly different tale. In his version of the affair, Dr. Burroughs adamantly noted that his younger brother never proposed marriage, attempted unsuccessfully to sever all contacts, provided notice of his eventual marriage, and even arranged a meeting between his wife and Mary. Judson was an honorable man, a true gentleman, and a devout Baptist.[276]

Nearly six months passed before the trial began. During that time both sides prepared their respective cases by interviewing witnesses, obtaining depositions, and plotting strategies. District Attorney E.C. Carrington and his assistant, Nathaniel Wilson, represented the prosecution. The defendant assembled a panel of four eager attorneys including Joseph Bradley, D.W. Voorhees, Judge Mason, and W.Y. Fendall. Judge Wylie kept the lawyers in line. Jury selection occupied the lawyers for the first few days. The large audience focused their attention on the young defendant. Her first court room appearance captivated everyone, including the male reporters. "The prisoner was tastefully attired in a

---

274 Ibid.
275 Ibid.
276 Ibid.

black silk dress, and a tight fitting coat or basque of the same material, trimmed with braid and beads; a black bonnet trimmed with straw, and wore a black veil which almost completely concealed her features. Her hair was worn in ringlets."[277]

The prosecutors presented what they believed to be incontrovertible evidence of guilt over the first few days of the trial. Betting on the jury's common sense, and the legal concept of res ipsa loquitur, the prosecution confidently concluded their case quickly. That was a serious miscalculation by the prosecution attorneys who only had to wonder what four defense lawyers might conjure up. Their curiosity was satisfied when the defense proposed the insanity defense. This improbable argument certainly ran counter to the court room persona presented by the demure, feminine, and fashionable Miss Harris. Instead of a broken heart, the defense insisted that Miss Harris suffered from a broken mind. Apparently the abrupt termination of a disputed five year relationship unhinged the young woman, leaving her no choice but to plan a murder, travel a thousand miles, disguise herself, and then in an irrational moment kill her former beau. In an effort to prove the passion the two shared, Miss Harris, without a sliver of embarrassment, gave her attorneys nearly a hundred love letters. The defense attorneys read many of the romantic letters to the jury.[278]

The letters that passed between the two star crossed lovers were eloquent, amorous, and sentimental. By themselves, the letters merely documented a romantic relationship. It took the eminence of an asylum superintendent to read insanity between the lines of the passionate prose. Charles H. Nichols, the Superintendent of the US Government Hospital for the Insane, came to the rescue of the woman after identifying several incidents of insanity. Of course, each moment of mental instability was tied to some tribulation in her love life, placing the blame squarely on Burroughs. Nichols patiently explained to the jury how Miss Harris suffered from insane violence. He formed his opinion after two visits with Miss Harris in her jail cell. Although Nichols initially suspected some fabrications, Miss Harris apparently swept these concerns aside with her charming sincerity and fetching features. Nichols gathered more pertinent information about Harris including evidence of a mildly nervous disposition, a concentration of that anxiety during her monthly menstrual period, a history of diarrhea, and a suspicious turn of mind. After Bur-

---

277 "The trial of Miss Mary Harris: Impaneling of the jury," *New York Times*, Jul. 9, 1865.

278 "The Harris trial," *New York Times*, Jul. 11, 1865.

roughs left Iowa one witness claimed Harris became depressed, sleepless, and mildly anorexic. The doctor took his various observations and insights, swirled them about, and came up with a mixture he called paroxysmal mania. According to Nichols, the combination of these symptoms twisted the girl's mind. When slighted by her lover Harris amplified the perceived insult by becoming agitated and homicidal. During these angry moments Nichols testified that the young woman became irrational. The prosecutor probably expressed disbelief in the doctor's medical gymnastics but Nichols persisted. Nichols admitted that the paroxysms could last from minutes to days, conveniently covering the cross county crime. The possibility that Harris purchased a pistol seeking vengeance for her betrayal did not faze the medical witness. Nichols categorically dismissed any possible prosecution theory that would hold Harris criminally responsible. It mattered not to the doctor whether Harris acted out of cool deliberation, disguise, or deceit. Nichols doggedly maintained that all behaviors surrounding the murder, no matter how distant or rational, emanated from an insane mind. The fact that Harris made no effort to disguise her murderous motives, to escape, and spoke sorrowfully of the murder further buttressed the doctor's convictions. Of course, the prosecution disputed this naïve interpretation. With all of its inconsistencies, the testimony of the Superintendent of the US Government Hospital for the Insane must have powerfully resonated with the jury.[279]

Dr. Nichols tiptoed around the presumed etiology of insanity in this young woman. He satisfied himself that Harris suffered from recurrent bouts of painful menstruation, otherwise known as dysmenorrhea, and felt no compunction to take the matter further. Dr. H. May harbored less reserve and directly dealt with the subject. May was unwilling to ascribe insanity to dysmenorrhea but only because he had never seen such a case before. Instead, May believed the woman suffered from hysteria. According to this witness, hysteria developed when a dysfunctional uterus produced a secondary disease state in the brain. The victim of hysteria suffered from depression and irritability. During a bout of hysteria the woman was impressionable and impulsive. May calculated that the woman's insanity arose from hysteria, exaggerated when Burroughs abruptly abandoned Harris. Adding a flourish to his testimony, May reminded the jury that few things can unsettle a woman's mind more than a broken heart.[280]

---

279 "Washington news: Continuation of the trial of Miss Harris," *New York Times*, Jul. 14, 1865.

280 "More testimony in the case of Miss Harris," *New York Times*, Jul. 16, 1865.

The case was looking rather bleak for the prosecution. A parade of medical witnesses solemnly swore that Miss Harris suffered from periodic insanity, aggravated by an abnormal menstrual cycle. In hopes of denting the defense momentum, the prosecution countered with two medical witnesses. Dr. William P. Johnson testified for the prosecution and naturally took a different view of Miss Harris. Johnson dwelled on the dysmenorrhea, acknowledging the emotional toll, but insisted that insanity did not result from the painful condition. Doctor Noble Young worked at the jail where the charming defendant passed her time. At no time did the jail doctor observe irrational behavior. He did confirm the defendant's retreat to bed, plagued by three days of painful menstruation.[281]

The prosecution sprinted towards the finish line with a stirring closing argument. Mr. Wilson chose his words carefully but began his summation by noting the distinguished coterie of attorneys and doctors forming a moat around the helpless young woman. In words dripping with ridicule, Wilson commented that the "prisoner, although obscure and poor, has been able to summon to her assistance an array of counsel representing every phase of professional eminence and excellence..." Wilson explained the matter no further, leaving the jury to speculate why these men abandoned their usual clients, the rich and famous. The prosecutor then led the jury back to the basic facts. "The prisoner at the bar...armed with a pistol...sets out on a journey of one thousand miles in search of a man she hates... She goes to the Treasury Department ... when he appears ... she fires ... cocks her pistol and fires a second time."[282]

Perhaps at this point, the prosecutor turned towards the jury and admonished them. "A young woman who fancies herself, or, if you please, has been slighted, aggrieved or injured, is with her own hand to execute the offender, and to receive the approval of those who are sworn ministers of the law."[283] The prosecutor reminded the jury of their social responsibility in punishing such odious and obvious misconduct. To do otherwise would unravel the moral threads of justice. As he proceeded with the summation, Mr. Wilson implored the jury to use common sense and not be swayed by high sounding words from men of medicine. In particular, Wilson ridiculed the concept of paroxysmal insanity, which lasted just long enough to cover the crime and extinguish mental responsibility. With the insane fit now resolved there was no need for confine-

---

281 Ibid.

282 "Washington news: Progress of the trial of Miss Harris," *New York Times*, Jul. 19, 1865.

283 Ibid.

ment in an asylum, or so the defense suggested. Ms. Harris would literally get away with murder, if the jury accepted the desperate defense ploy. The prosecution dismissed talk of dysmenorrhea and insanity and instead invoked the time honored notion, "Heaven has no rage like love turned to hatred, nor hell a fury, like a woman scorned."[284] Mr. Wilson ticked off the components of the woman's behavior which, when assembled by the prosecution, neatly fit the pattern of a repudiated love. In an effort to deflect the defendant's feminine charms, the prosecution relentlessly reminded the jury that this attractive and demure woman nurtured a hatred that led to a cold blooded murder. The prosecution concluded their lengthy summation. It was now the defense attorneys turn.

The defense attorneys elected Mr. Voorhees to close their case. Voorhees delivered an impassioned speech reminding the jury of the insults, innuendo, and ignominy suffered by Miss Harris. Learned men of science carefully examined the young woman and concluded, without hesitation, that Harris was insane when she pulled the pistol's trigger – twice. The closing argument by Voorhees was powerful and when he resumed his chair at the conclusion of the remarks a hush descended on the court room. The trial judge broke the silence by discharging the jury. Not more than ten minutes passed before the jury returned and declared Miss Harris not guilty of murder. The audience's pent up emotions exploded with loud cheers and women weeping. Mary Harris fainted.[285]

The not guilty verdict reverberated across the country, particularly the role played by the insanity defense. A sense of injustice crept into most discussions with some newspaper editors struggling to make sense of the verdict. As one editorial lamented, "any young and moderately pretty woman, may, upon her unsupported allegation that her victim has wronged her, either by seduction under promise of marriage or promise of marriage without marriage," could commit any crime of violence with impunity. Hyperbole aside, special rules seemed to apply to women accused of murder. A group of contemporary observers tried to make sense of the Harris verdict by noting that the death penalty was the court's only punishment option in this case. In an effort to avoid the spectacle of hanging a woman the jury accepted the insanity defense. The insanity

---

284 William Congreve, "The mourning bride," In *Masterpieces of the English drama*, edited by F. Schelling (New York: American Book Company, 1912), 416.

285 "Close of the great trial: Very curious proceedings," *New York Times*, Jul. 20, 1865.

plea was the perfect choice since it was sanctioned by science. An esteemed asylum superintendent added the necessary credibility.[286]

The diagnosis of kleptomania signaled the arrival of another troublesome trend, that of converting larceny to lunacy. Before a medical label was attached, most people regarded this behavior as shoplifting. A number of apparently singular attributes, including an almost exclusive prevalence among women, captured the attention of some doctors. It seemed incomprehensible that a young attractive woman, often dwelling among the upper classes, would stoop to stealing. The notion of theft, often rooted in images of popular phrenology, could not countenance anyone other than a desperate male brute committing larceny. When a rich woman fumbled a five finger discount a reliable contingent of medical doctors came to the rescue. The doctors dissected the criminal act, applied the alternate label of kleptomania, and confidently equated the malady with madness. The explanation often convinced otherwise skeptical jurors, many of whom may simply have accepted the medical excuse as a way to keep a young woman out of jail. The net result was a steep increase in cases of kleptomania.

In some cases, unscrupulous women counted on the special treatment afforded the fairer sex. A mother and daughter team, perhaps lingering too long over a pretty dress, were arrested while pilfering a large bolt of calico cloth. The mother had rather ingeniously fashioned a bag beneath her dress, into which she secretly placed the stolen items. A quick search of the mother's lodgings revealed a house chock full of misbegotten garments. Instead of shuffling the culprits off to jail, the authorities first diverted the pair for a medical examination. The die was cast.[287]

The obvious, and for many people odious, use of kleptomania as an excuse to avoid punishment for pilfering bred a new brand of social cynicism. It seemed that this diagnosis applied almost exclusively to well-off women. As one editorial dryly noted, "It would certainly seem if, in the present enlightened state of medical science, the best physicians cannot themselves positively tell the sane from the demented, that at least the plea of kleptomania should no longer be admitted in the courts as an excuse for crime; for, as matters now stand, great injustice must certainly be often done, and the weight of that injustice always falls on those whose poverty makes in them a crime what in the rich is only an allow-

---

286 "Trials for murder," *Chicago Tribune*, Jul. 24, 1865.
287 "Kleptomania," *Hartford Daily Courant*, Aug. 15, 1868.

able eccentricity."[288] The attributes of the Abraham Man were adopted by women.

Kleptomania, along with pyromania and dipsomania, constituted specimens of the disputed class of moral mania. Moral mania was a convenient insanity that excused gross lapses in proper social behavior. Naturally, the ill-informed public cast a wary eye on medical doctors who explained shoplifting, arson, and public drunkenness as special examples of insanity. In most cases the doctors testified that the signs of insanity accompanying these conditions were subtle, thus defying the lay public's ability to identify the malady. Detection of kleptomania, and the other moral manias, required a skillful observer. Fortunately, not all doctors accepted the notion of moral mania. Dr. Gray, the Superintendent of the Utica, New York Insane Asylum, vigorously opposed moral mania. The famous physician's religious sensibilities were insulted. A pugnacious Gray defined kleptomania as "a word used to express thieving; I don't believe in it; I don't believe in any of the so called "moral insanities." I believe they are crimes."[289]

Gray was not alone in deriding kleptomania. Newspapers periodically reported the chance encounter between a "fashionable lady" and a store merchant. With a keen eye for the pretty pilferer, the shopkeepers sometimes ensnared a well-heeled young woman. Of course the woman would protest the accusation but when faced with a possible arrest her memory returned along with the stolen goods. These stories helped local editors lampoon kleptomania. "Common people are frequently arrested for stealing; but polite, fashionable ladies are sometimes caught taking that which does not belong to them. This is called "kleptomania" ... [T]hey take a few articles which they covet but cannot induce husbands or papas to procure for them."[290]

On some occasions the benevolent treatment of female thieves ended in tragedy. Mary Gatewood enjoyed a fairly prosperous life until her husband died. His death catapulted Mary and her son into a deep abyss of poverty. Eventually the desperate situation forced the beleaguered widow to relinquish custody of her son. To make ends meet, the attractive woman turned to shoplifting. Her first efforts were cautious, stealing only trivial items. As she gained confidence, more costly items disappeared from store shelves. As it happens, Mary was rather ham fisted

---

288 "Kleptomania: Some curious facts thereanent," *New York Times*, Jan. 3, 1869.
289 "The trial nearing an end; Objections to the defense covering old ground," *New York Times*, Jan. 4, 1882.
290 "Kleptomania," *Milwaukee Sentinel*, Apr. 10, 1866.

which resulted in numerous arrests. The kind-hearted police listened sympathetically to Mary's travails, and without fail, released her. On one occasion her shoplifting resulted in a brief stay at an asylum, ostensibly to cure her kleptomania. As might be imagined, soon after release from the asylum Mary resumed her former ways. By now the local merchants had convinced the police to look beyond Mary's unfortunate financial plight and take action. After a particularly expensive piece of cloth went missing, local detectives confronted Mary. She essentially admitted the theft. The detectives asked Mary to accompany them to the police station. She demurred, saying she needed a few minutes to get ready. The police patiently waited outside the restroom until a "gurgling noise" piqued their curiosity. Mary did not respond when they knocked, and the police naturally reacted by breaking down the door. The ill-fated kleptomaniac lay dead on the floor, a victim of a self-inflicted laceration across the throat.[291] Years of compassion and thoughtless labeling probably overlooked a deep depression.

According to some experts, one of the telling signs of kleptomania could be discovered through a careful examination of the person's hands. Shoplifters, otherwise medically known in some cases as kleptomaniacs, had a "broad palm, broad, square fingers, whose clasp leaves upon your own an unpleasant adhesiveness, a clammy sort of stickiness...denoting not only a propensity to take hold of things, but a very strong disinclination to let go of them..."[292] The anatomic description of kleptomania seemed to be an extension of phrenology, as applied to a person's hand. Whether it made sense or not, the pseudoscience of physiognomy cast a necessary aura of medical credibility as the conversion from larceny to lunacy evolved. In a further effort to sever the link between stealing and punishment, the advocates of kleptomania pointed to cross generational case studies proving that the malady was inherited. It seemed that some families bred thieves, hinting at a genetic etiology which totally absolved the kleptomaniac from any subsequent responsibility. Of course the familial transmission was highly selective, favoring mostly rich, attractive women.

Anne Hopkins was an attractive twenty-five-year-old woman who liked shopping but apparently abhorred purchasing the products. This troublesome trend came to an abrupt conclusion when a conscientious

---

291 "Remarkable case of kleptomania," *Bangor Daily Whig and Courier*, Dec. 7, 1868.

292 "An involuntary thief: Indication of kleptomania," *Milwaukee Sentinel* Apr. 9, 1869.

clerk caught Miss Hopkins secreting a small piece of fashionable lace in her purse. The clerk alerted a nearby floor walker who detained the woman while the clerk fetched the police. As might be imagined, when confronted with the suspicions, Miss Hopkins indignantly denied the clerk's declaration. The police officer settled the dispute by searching the woman's purse. Unfortunately, the pretty piece of lace put the lie to Miss Hopkins's protestations. In a most ignominious moment, she was arrested and escorted to the local jail.

A further search of Miss Hopkins's large purse revealed a set of forks, an odd item to carry about. The forks still had a store-identifying label which led the police to query that merchant. This investigation once again substantiated shoplifting. With the damning evidence beginning to pile up, and her feminine fascinations failing, the cornered women gambled on one last ploy. Miss Hopkins politely requested that Professor Crittendam, apparently a teacher she favored, be summoned to police headquarters. The police complied and soon the good Professor was listening incredulously as the shoplifting story unfolded. In the meantime, the police contacted the young woman's family. The father, a well-regarded member of the community, was dumbfounded. A search of Anne's room revealed a treasure trove of jewelry and clothing, all of which the young woman apparently had stolen.

Professor Crittendam saved Miss Hopkins. At his insistence, a hastily arranged bail hearing resulted in her exit from jail. A trial date was set, but through further unspecified interventions, the matter was settled quietly out of court. The newspaper provided the unstated legal justification by declaring Miss Hopkins "a genuine case" of kleptomania.[293]

Not everyone was enthralled with kleptomania. Certainly the true victims, the merchants, decried a social system which allowed the bulk of shoplifters to escape punishment. The merchants tried combating the petty thievery in a number of ways, none of which were particularly effective. In some cases the merchants accepted a sort of rolling restitution. Well placed men, hoping to avoid the publicity of their wives' arrest, would work out a deal with some merchants whereby all the women's ill-gotten gains would simply be charged by the store keeper. This happy arrangement allowed the woman to bypass the long lines at the checkout counter, the husband avoided public embarrassment, and the merchant suffered no monetary losses.

---

293 "Kleptomania: A genuine case," *St. Louis Daily Globe-Democrat*, Mar. 4, 1878.

Some store keepers adopted a less liberal and certainly more aggres-sive stance towards female shoplifters. For the most part these store keepers believed that kleptomania was nothing more than a clever ruse exploited by lawyers and supported by ill-informed doctors so fashion-able women could escape punishment. These merchants prosecuted ev-ery instance of shoplifting and refused to accept out of court settlements. Somehow shoplifters learned of these tactics and subsequently skirted these stores. This gave rise to a compelling argument. Those stores which adopted strict prosecution policies almost never suffered at the hands of a kleptomaniac. The store owners reasoned that this proved that klepto-mania was not the result of an irrational, uncontrollable emotional insan-ity but instead suggested that the female perpetrators quickly deduced the risks of detection and operated accordingly.

Dr. Charles H. Hughes, a former Superintendent of the Insane Asy-lum at Fulton, Missouri, agreed with the merchants. Hughes objected to his colleague's equating a solitary symptom with a mental disorder. In his view, stealing could only rise to the level of insanity when the per-son exhibited other symptoms, such as hallucinations or delusions. Such theoretical discussions, despite the soundness of Dr. Hughes's reason-ing, rarely swayed the course of prosecutions. It was expensive to pros-ecute petty thefts, often politically unpalatable, and all too frequently cast the merchant as an ogre. For these reasons, the notion that the "class of people who have escaped so long under the pretense of kleptomania had better wake up, with the advance of reason and common sense, to a realization of the fact that it won't be very long until the fashionable kleptomaniac will lie down in the same gray stone cell with the petty thief and the common robber," was a wistful thought.[294]

The parade of monomanias seemed inexhaustible. A creative con man, taking acting lessons from the Abraham Man, could bend any deviance into some semblance of insanity. For example, although never as widely deployed in the courtroom as kleptomania, pyromania still enjoyed some success in excusing otherwise brash cases of fire setting. Pyromania basically relied on the tried and true formula that an inexplicable act, particularly one subject to periodic expression, suggested insanity. The inexplicable portion of the definition was generally reserved for moral lapses among certain groups, such as women, the rich, and the educated, where such displays of behavior shocked the public's sensibilities. In

---

294 "You mustn't steel; For the kleptomania scheme is about "played out," *St. Louis Daily Globe-Democrat*, Sep. 7, 1879.

most cases of incendiarism, the male culprits were juvenile offenders or hired arsonists, neither of which garnered much public sympathy. Even though arson was a huge problem, and even when the fires killed innocent people, the newspapers almost never undertook their signature breathless sensationalism.[295] The lack of drama, along with the scruffy miscreants, added to the medical legal disinterest in pyromania. None the less, some artful dodgers tried.

Hugh Miller stood plaintively before Judge Hurd, indicted for torching two houses. Miller apparently kept up with the popular literature fanning the infatuation with insanity. "About six years ago I was arrested on a charge similar to my present. What I did at that time was prompted by some hidden desire in my mind which was uncontrollable."[296] The forlorn felon continued his monologue, lamely dismissing the dangers of arson while casting himself as the victim of an invisible mental demon. Miller wisely steered clear of any spiritual references such as "the devil made me do it," opting instead for a scientific story. In pleading for treatment, and not punishment for his incendiary past, Miller desperately sought a villain. After pondering the matter for a moment, the defendant seriously proposed, "I believe today that the excessive smoking of cigarettes was the starting point in my mental downfall".[297] Perhaps in Miller's mind the similarities in lighting up a cigarette and someone's property provided proof of an unhealthy mental fascination with flames. The defendant's alleged fixation about fire seemed to meet the definition of a monomania, specifically pyromania. Miller might have succeeded if his claim was accompanied by the testimony of a medical expert. Unfortunately, he faced the judge alone. The dubious magistrate dismissed Miller's excuse, countering with twenty years of incarceration.

One of the most troublesome trends in the early development of medical legal practice involved dipsomania. Christoph Wilhelm Hufeland added the term dipsomania to the medical lexicon in the early years of the nineteenth century. Hufeland was a well-respected German Physician who authored influential works on the clinical practice of medicine.[298] The word dipsomania was a far more flattering, and obscure, moniker than drunkenness. Hufeland, and those he persuaded, reserved the diagnosis of dipsomania for periodic, uncontrollable bouts of binge

---

295 "Incendiarism," *New York Times*, Sep. 5, 1870.
296 "Blames the cigarettes," *Atchison Daily Globe* (Kansas), Apr. 14, 1897.
297 Ibid.
298 M. V. Magnan, "Clinical lectures on dipsomania," *Alienist and Neurologist* 5, (1884): 691-7.

drinking. The episodic bursts of bolus drinking fit well with the general theme of mania, a mental condition known for its periodic states of frenzied behavior. Intermittent and unpredictable behaviors also fit well with popular notions of epilepsy, a physical brain disorder underlying many examples of erratic behavior, possibly including repeated bouts of alcohol intoxication. The concept of dipsomania was a laudable early effort to destigmatize alcoholism. By offering a scientific explanation for periodic intoxication, doctors challenged the traditional homily demonizing drunkenness as a moral weakness.

Dipsomania is a word lost in time. During the nineteenth century the diagnosis was widely recognized, even though controversial, by most physicians. If physicians had confined dipsomania to the hospitals it might have survived into modern times. Problems arose when the diagnosis started creeping into the courtroom. The role of alcohol and the law was complicated but certain basic tenants guided the adjudication of criminal matters. For the most part, the law considered intoxication a voluntary vice. The indulgent use of alcohol dulled the drinker's senses, slowed his reflexes, impaired his judgment, and heightened the possibility of bad behavior. All of these responses were predictable and fully within the realm of common knowledge. As a consequence, an "alcohol made me do it" legal defense rarely swayed suspicious juries. In some cases of habitual inebriation, dementia or even insanity ensued, conditions which could lead to a successful mental defense. While complete exoneration was rare, nineteenth century jurisprudence adopted a more liberal attitude when considering alcohol as a factor mitigating punishment. Juries typically focused on the defendant's deliberation, planning, and malice when considering the type of punishment. Alcohol might promote more spontaneous behavior, limiting the planning, deliberation, and malice that collectively added weight to a defendant's sentence.[299]

Dipsomania was a dangerous diagnosis. In fact, the Abraham Man could not have been more pleased. Dipsomania turned the conventional view of drunkenness upside down. Throughout the course of human history, doctors, philosophers, and theologians morally condemned drunkenness. All this stood to change in the nineteenth century when clever lawyers, determined defendants, and discerning doctors joined forces to advance the medical concept of dipsomania. The habitual drunk was converted from reprobate to reputable. Dipsomania signaled an uncon-

---

299   Alfred S. Taylor, *Medical jurisprudence* (Philadelphia: Blanchard and Lea, 1856), 742-3.

trollable urge to drink, leaving the victim firmly in the grip of an unyield-ing compulsion. Individuals engaging in unseemly behavior could now assert a legal defense claiming dipsomania caused their misconduct. Ma-lingerers, no doubt, reveled in the possibilities of getting drunk, commit-ting a crime, and charging the whole affair to dipsomania.

In an effort to distinguish ordinary drunkenness from dipsomania, leading medical doctors proposed all sorts of rules. In keeping with gen-eral theories of the time, doctors believed that dipsomania ran in fami-lies, suggesting a hereditary transmission. This sort of thinking added a physical basis to the disorder while relieving the victim of moral respon-sibility for their over indulgence. In contrast to habitual drunkenness, the dipsomaniac cycled through periods of sobriety alternating with intemperance. Admittedly the interval between the two states could be quite short, justifying a sort of rapid cycling dipsomania which blurred the line with habitual drunkenness. The dipsomaniac struggled with the bottle, at times succumbing to depression. The habitual drunk on the other hand showed no internal strife, accepting his lot without thought.

Dipsomania seemed to preferentially afflict the intellectual class, striking at the rich and educated. In one example, a successful Pennsyl-vania physician killed his wife and a personal friend. His murderous ram-page sprang from a deep seated belief in his wife's infidelity. The doctor assembled a cracker-jack team of defense lawyers and medical experts. At the trial, his lawyers leaned heavily on the insanity defense, hinting but never openly stating, the doctor's compulsion to drink. Dipsomania lurked in the background, probably an effort to protect the doctor's tat-tered reputation. Instead of the public's expected conviction for first de-gree murder, the jury convicted the doctor on a lesser charge.[300]

As might be expected, the restrictive definition of dipsomania chafed some authors who sought a more liberal interpretation of the disorder. As one doctor noted, "dipsomania is regarded as a form of insanity; and if it is further understood that the inebriety is merely a symptom of a seri-ous mental disease and for which he is no way responsible, then the law should hold him guiltless of crime as if the act had been perpetrated by an individual suffering from any form of insanity..."[301]

The mindless pursuit of alcohol, and the abandonment of fam-ily, friends, reputation, and employment, seemed irrational. Despite the pleas of loved ones or the various punishments suffered, the dipsomaniac

---

300 Charles K. Mills, "Some forms of insanity due to alcohol, especially in their medicolegal relations," *Quarterly Journal of Inebriety* 28, no. 4 (1905): 228-9.
301 "Inebriety and crime," *The Quarterly Journal of Inebriety* 26, no. 2 (1904):137-45.

relentlessly and recklessly returned to alcohol. In time, the term dip-somania extended beyond alcoholism, and enveloped other substances such as opium. The key feature uniting alcohol and drug abuse under the label dipsomania was the all-consuming preoccupation with intoxica-tion. It seemed inevitable that the asylum experience, with its massive structure and devoted staff, would extend its therapeutic management to the treatment of dipsomania. The immoral self-indulgence of the ha-bitual drunkard gave way to dipsomania, an hereditary mental disorder which destroyed reason and resolution.

The contagion of excuse making was incredibly infectious. Any man-ner of deviant or criminal behavior attracted a slew of pundits. News-paper editorials routinely flogged the deceptions practiced, to the detri-ment of social justice, by duplicitous doctors and lawyers. "For a number of years past, it has been possible to secure medical experts, who would prove a man sane or insane as powerful interest might dictate...It is quite possible that an insane man might have a "shuffling gait," "clammy hands," "restless eyes," and that his tongue might occasionally point to the right instead of the left; but these peculiarities are not invariable concomitants of cranial disorder, were people generally compelled to submit to such vigorous tests as to their sanity, the majority of the race would be prov-en..." insane.[302] A similar castigation noted, "It is the most astounding fact in the whole history of the administration of criminal jurisprudence, that within the past few years, nurtured by the vagaries and senseless theo-ries of medical men on the subject, and supported by the testimony of so-called experts, offers insanity as his defense, assured that he will have the assistance of medical authors and experts. And, as a consequence, we have had just as many different kinds of insanity as we had crimes."[303]

In some respects the public's repugnance with the excesses of medical legal excuse making served two purposes. It eventually put the brakes on a runaway process that threatened the moral basis of the judicial system. Left unchecked, the fate of felons would be decided by doctors. The use of a jury was under assault, as experts in mental subtleties claimed a su-perior authority. With the extension of each liberal medical explanation, the threshold for asserting mental non-responsibility dropped. This fa-vored the Abraham Man who flourished when ambiguity reigned. Vague definitions of mental illness, sometimes reeking of social bias, favored fraud. Only a combination of strictly applied medical legal definitions

302 "Insanity experts," *Frank Leslie's Illustrated Newspaper*, Aug. 23, 1884.
303 "Insanity as a defense for crime," *Los Angeles Times*, May 27, 1883.

of mental responsibility, better diagnostic assessments, elimination of charlatans and quacks from the courtroom, and a sober reassessment of the role of the medical expert could keep the system from careening over a cliff of irrelevance and ridicule. It was against this back drop that the criminal trial of the century took place in America.

CHAPTER 9: GRAND FINALE

A final act brought all the players together for one last momentous scene. Drs. Gray and Hammond, along with many of their esteemed colleagues, squared off in the medical legal bout of the century. As usual, the Abraham Man lurked in the shadows, always ready to fool the famous physicians. The stage for the grand finale was steadily built throughout the greater part of the nineteenth century as the medical profession's scientific sophistication steadily increased. The profession's diagnostic acumen and therapeutic proficiency elevated the status of doctors. Like all pioneers, the more intrepid members of the profession explored new frontiers. Most doctors preferred the familiar terrain of organic pathology, shunning the mysterious and metaphysical world of mental disorders. A famous few forsook the traditional path trod by most doctors, instead building reputations as insanity experts.

Not surprisingly, as doctors ventured forth into the scientifically uncharted world of mental maladies, they began the journey with their prized possessions. To guide their steps, the doctors relied on the illumination provided by their knowledge of the human body, their keen powers of observation, and a physician's positivism. As a testament to their powers of persuasion, large asylums soon dotted the American landscape. The asylums served several purposes. The great edifices stood as monuments proclaiming a new era in the scientific treatment of insanity. Asylums also conveniently isolated the insane, removing from public view the scary spectacle of the wandering, unpredictable madman. Society seemed safer.

Some of the doctors specializing in the treatment of insanity soon became celebrities. The doctors' popularity grew, partly as a result of ravenous egos fed by an insatiable public curiosity about mental illness. Newspapers and magazines featured stories on all aspects of human behavior, ranging from the salubrious to the salacious. All manner of experts, such as spiritualists, theologians, quacks, and charlatans competed with physicians in gracing the pages of the print media. Human nature being what it is, rivalries among the groups soon developed with each casting aspersions on the others' credibility.

The legal profession seized the possibilities. Defense counsel in particular increasingly exploited the testimony of insanity experts. Previously open and shut cases for the prosecution now became contestable affairs. Unfortunately, a number of inequities crept into the system. It was not a matter of chance that the first great surge of legal interest in medical testimony accompanied determined efforts to undermine a person's last will and testament. Of course, initially only rich estates benefitted. As will after will fell to ever more specious arguments, a few sage observers fretted as the orderly process of transferring wealth spiraled out of control.

A similar pattern arose in criminal courts, where increasingly aggressive use of psychological defenses threatened the public's faith in the fair administration of justice. At first the public seemed enamored, or perhaps titillated, by medical testimony that seemingly explained unusual or bizarre behavior. With important criminal cases, newspapers offered an almost verbatim record of a doctor's musings. The reader could bask in the expert's eloquence, perhaps even favorably influenced by the rhetoric. The aura of conviction typically faded with the next edition, when another persuasive physician brusquely repudiated the previous testimony. The battle of experts, a reflection of the vigorous to and fro characteristic of America's adversarial legal system, did little to bolster the credibility of medical testimony. With equal amounts of passion, sententious experts staked out diametrically different positions. The science of human behavior was inexact and skilled lawyers took advantage of the ambiguity. Psychological medicine was elastic; it could be bent and twisted to accommodate virtually any legal pleading.

Insanity's incertitude was the Abraham Man's playground. Many medical practitioners understood the imperative need for the accurate and reliable detection of malingering. Doctors used the asylums as a sort of behavioral laboratory, making detailed observations of their patients through which they understood insanity. For the most part, these patients were indigent and suffered from the more severe forms of mental illness. Efforts to generalize clinical findings from this subgroup often foundered on the shoals of common sense. The court room witnessed many wrecks when dueling insanity experts, seeking a tactical advantage, stretched the concept of mental non-responsibility too far. In some cases, for example, well regarded experts proclaimed that any prior episode of insanity, even in the face of a full recovery, left the individual morally blameless for perpetuity. Naturally, only an insanity expert could detect the subtle residual evidence of a decade's old nervous breakdown. Far from instilling a sense of professionalism, such proclamations seemed pretentious.

An increasingly watered down definition of insanity, to avoid the consequences of bad behavior, made malingering much easier. There were several factors that favored stretching the limits. In some situations the insanity defense served supposedly humanitarian purposes. Punishing a woman for pilfering seemed, to some, unfair. A cohort of doctors, championing kleptomania, performed acts of medical legerdemain, transforming shoplifting from a crime to mental illness. Newspapers published the particulars and soon a boom in kleptomania threatened merchants. Artful female thieves learned the script and when arrested, no doubt coquettishly cried about their "affliction." Unfortunately, this ruse uniformly failed among the down-and-out.

Another factor eroding public confidence with the insanity defense was spiritualists, quacks, and charlatans all of whom battled for recognition in the court room. In many cases, egalitarian judges admitted their testimony. The shape of a person's head or a spiritual medium's incantations entered legal records as evidence for or against mental responsibility. All of this made for good reading, helping explain the front page treatment accorded such testimony by newspapers. The stories were entertaining but a sense of skepticism undermined the witnesses' credibility.

Towards the end of the nineteenth century the public's infatuation with psychological medicine was waning. Newspaper editors openly lampooned the inconsistent opinions of insanity experts. The spectacle of learned doctors pontificating about the vagaries of mental illness did not inspire confidence. Despite their eloquence and experience, asylum doctors could not reliably detect the Abraham Man. In matters of great import, such as a murder trial, the implications of missing malingering came at the cost of fair verdicts. It was against this backdrop of a deepening distrust with the insanity defense that Charles Guiteau shocked America.

Charles J. Guiteau was an inconsequential gadfly who finally commanded attention with the events of 2 July 1881. After an irresolute life, marked by a string of personal failures, Guiteau achieved the recognition he craved by shooting President James A. Garfield. The brazen act, coming less than two decades after the assassination of President Abraham Lincoln, left America stunned. The principal conspirators in the first presidential assassination faced swift justice, either by hanging or lengthy prison sentences. John Wilkes Booth, cornered by the military at Garrett's Farmhouse in Port Royal, Virginia, died from a gunshot wound after refusing to surrender. Booth's diary contained an entry, ostensibly providing one motivation for the murder when he wrote, "God simply made me the instrument..." of Lincoln's punishment.[304] Although Booth implied divine inspiration for the assassination, much as Guiteau would, political retribution seemed a more imperative motivation. Despite the heinous nature of the indefensible crime, suggestions of insanity never gained any serious traction in subsequent discussions of Booth's behavior. Lewis Powell, one of Booth's conspirators, made a feeble attempt to mount an insanity defense but that effort ultimately failed and he was hanged. With the passage of a mere sixteen years, and another presidential assassination, both Charles Guiteau and the insanity defense went on trial.

Guiteau was a curious character. As he passed through life, his acquaintances invariably split along two lines, some seeing a scoundrel and others a psychotic. The principal characteristic dividing peoples' opinion of Guiteau was his obdurate sense of self importance. Those who dismissed Guiteau as a scoundrel interpreted the boundless conceit as an act, willfully and skillfully perpetrated to further his criminal ambitions. For others, the egotism bordered on megalomania, tapping into a popular notion that excessive, exuberant and endless enthusiasm signaled insanity. It was this self-conceit that inevitably brought Guiteau into conflict with nearly everyone he bumped into.

Guiteau lived a life of fraud. Whether in the service of an antisocial scheme or the product of a near delusional sense of self-importance, he always portrayed himself as a man of means, politically connected and successful. In fact, nothing could have been further from the truth. When he arrived in New York he rented a room on Broadway, a shabby affair, but conveniently adjacent to a well-known law firm. The adjacency al-

---

304 Samuel Alexander Mudd, Netie Mudd, Thomas Ewing, and Edward Spangler, *The life of Dr. Samuel A. Mudd* (New York: Neale Publishing Company, 1906), 240.

lowed Guiteau the opportunity to bamboozle clients. Guiteau furthered the illusion of prosperity by living in fashionable sections of the city. He mingled with the other boarders, often using the social intercourse as an occasion to impress them with his supposed circle of political and business associates. Guiteau succeeded only in alienating his fellow residents. Even more troubling, at least for the landlords, was Guiteau's habit of skipping out when the rent was due. He managed to stay a few steps ahead of irate landlords for a while but around 1874 was finally arrested and hauled into court.[305]

Eliza Simpson recalled her first encounter with Guiteau. "He was a low-sized man, of slight build, with light hair and complexion, a wiry mustache, and a bit of a goatee. He was faultlessly attired, and, rising when I entered the parlor, he drew from his pocket a large pasteboard card, perhaps five inches in length and three in breadth, on which was presented "Charles J. Guiteau, Attorney and Counselor at Law..."[306] The ostentatious presentation gave no hint of what would follow. Initially, the new boarder paid his rent on time but after a few weeks he fell behind. Simpson demanded payment, Guiteau agreed, and gave the landlord a check. He left soon afterwards fully aware of the fact that the check was worthless. The intrepid landlord tracked him down but relented on the payment when she discovered the pitiful plight of her former renter. Guiteau then bounced from one lodging establishment to another, generally for about a week each, before leaving under cover of darkness to avoid paying the bill.

Charles Guiteau was born in Freeport, Illinois in 1839. His father was a cashier at a local bank, a staid occupation which earned the family a steady income and a respectable place in the community. Mr. and Mrs. Guiteau had three sons, including Charles, and one daughter. Charles was a problem child, forever dreaming and scheming, and accomplishing little else. His parents eventually came to the conclusion that Charles was a bit daft, and hoping to reverse the trend, even arranged some sort of mental treatment during his youth. Around the age of twenty-five Charles left home, still preoccupied with fame and glory but lacking the resolve to realize his goal.[307]

Frances Guiteau, the assassin's sister, spoke sympathetically about Charles. While acknowledging her brother's eccentricities, she rational-

---

305 Ibid.
306 Ibid.
307 "The assassin: Guiteau long ago disowned by his father-Habits and peculiarities," *New York Times*, Jul. 4, 1881.

ized his irresolute life as a byproduct of childbirth. "Before he was born his mother was sick with brain-fever. His mind seemed to be affected by this hereditary trouble. All through his childhood he was flighty." In remembering their younger days together, Frances always believed Charles would become insane. At one point, the worried family asked John Rice, their longtime friend and doctor, to evaluate Charles' mental state. Rice believed that the Guiteau's youngest son was indeed mentally imbalanced, a progressive condition that would ultimately leave Charles an "imbecile." Frances recoiled at the thought of placing Charles in an insane asylum. Her stated reason was his harmless nature. Charles avoided the usual vices such as alcohol and tobacco, was never threatening, and leaned towards a life as a clergyman. Perhaps the family hoped that Charles' ecclesiastical enthusiasm would straighten his warped mind. Unfortunately, just the opposite occurred as Charles twisted his theology to match his grandiose thinking.[308]

A cousin of the presidential assassin, a veterinarian living in Battle Creek, Michigan, unreservedly declared Charles Guiteau insane. Guiteau traveled to Battle Creek in the late 1870s and delivered a series of sermons during which he fantastically claimed himself the equal of Jesus Christ. These rousing public revelations apparently transported the lay evangelizer into an altered state of consciousness. Spiritual visions, far from convincing his audience, left them uneasy and doubting the speaker's sanity. A sense of despondency accompanied the sermons, so much so, that his cousin worried about Guiteau committing suicide.[309] Guiteau popped up in Buffalo in the same general time period, a sort of itinerant preacher, presenting a lecture on the coming of Christ. His appearance left an indelible mark on the mind of A.J. Bigelow. Bigelow ran a small printing shop which Guiteau patronized, desiring advertising circulars to promote his public lecture. Guiteau introduced himself as "a lawyer, theologian, and politician," a presentation accompanied, no doubt, by an impressive flourish. The only mark Guiteau left behind was that of a "religious fanatic with a mania for meddling in politics." As was his custom, Guiteau did his best to avoid paying for the printer's work.[310]

The roving ministry beckoned the lay preacher. Guiteau apparently spent the better part of 1878 traversing the country. At one point he was in Davenport, Iowa drumming up business for a public talk about Chris-

---

308 "Guiteau's life and habits," *New York Times*, Jul. 5, 1881.
309 "Guiteau's insanity," *New York Times*, Jul. 13, 1881.
310 "The assassin: Guiteau long ago disowned by his father," *New York Times*, Jul. 4, 1881.

tianity. His powers of elocution excited no interest leaving him without an audience. That same year he showed up in Hartford, Connecticut, somehow finagling a seat on the stage alongside a pair of well-known evangelists.[311]

Guiteau spent a great deal of energy erecting an illusion of prestige and power. In most cases the only person persuaded by the charade was Guiteau. For his efforts, he was shunned, ridiculed, or dismissed as a crank. Some of his more fantastic, clearly grandiose ideas were presented with such fervor that his audiences listened politely before quietly declaring Guiteau a raving lunatic. Carter Harrison, a former mayor of Chicago, recalled a visit from Guiteau in 1876. According to the mayor, Guiteau was peddling a marvelous new building material, similar to cement but infinitely stronger and able to resist the ravages of time. The inventor was willing to part with the formula in exchange for its use in building a vast national memorial. As the incredulous mayor recalled, "It was to reach beyond the tops of the highest mountains, and not only was it intended to surpass the pyramids in immensity, but was to rival them in endurance..." Harrison concluded that only a feverish mind could seriously propose such a grandiose plan. Guiteau pressed on, possibly driven by a delusional conviction. He presented Harrison expertly detailed drawings of the proposal, which clearly represented a substantial investment in time and thought. The mayor listened out of courtesy, suggested he would study the plan, and bid Guiteau adieu hoping never to hear from the lunatic again. Over the next few months Guiteau made periodic inquiries but receiving no satisfaction, demanded Harrison return the project drawings. Harrison complied, doubtless relieved with Guiteau's exit.[312]

As might be expected, the wanton attack on President Garfield unleashed a throng of newspaper reporters eager to uncover the tiniest tidbit about the assassin. These journalists tracked down just about anyone with personal knowledge of Guiteau, an intense effort undertaken in the days immediately following the shooting. Americans, by and large appalled by the attack, were at the same time intensely curious to learn more about the man who shot their president. Some of the best descriptions came from family members.

---

311 "Guiteau's life and habits," *New York Times*, Jul. 5, 1881.
312 "The assassin: Guiteau long ago disowned by his father," *New York Times*, Jul. 4, 1881.

An intrepid reporter found John Guiteau, a brother of the assassin, working for a large life insurance company in Boston.[313] From the interview the reporter learned that John firmly believed his younger brother was insane and he illustrated the point by recalling certain events. According to John, the family looked forward to Charles completing his college studies and assuming a respectable position in life. The youngest son did poorly in school and soon dropped out. Charles wandered aimlessly for a while but then joined the Oneida Community.

Guiteau's interest in the Oneida Community waxed and waned. He spent about five years with the commune followed by an acrimonious parting. Part of Guiteau's dissatisfaction might have stemmed from his unpopularity. Even though complex marriage was sanctioned, the women of the commune avoided Guiteau. He left the commune a few years after the Civil War ended.

After leaving Oneida, Guiteau joined his brother in Chicago and began studying the law. Somehow, perhaps through patronage, Guiteau was permitted to practice law. He set up a small practice devoted to bill collections but his indifferent work ethic led to financial ruin. Even at this point in his life, John Guiteau detected an ominous trait in his brother, "it being almost a mania with him to gain notoriety in any conceivable way."[314]

By 1875 the older brother clearly saw a further deterioration in Charles. Guiteau, having failed as a lawyer, was now turning his increasingly warped thinking towards odd beliefs about the second coming of Christ. He wrote a treatise on the subject, proclaiming direct inspiration from God. After this venture, Charles cooked up a scheme to buy the Chicago Tribune Newspaper. With nary a farthing to his name, he approached a banker seeking a loan to make the purchase. In exchange for the loan, Guiteau promised to make the bank president the next state governor. As might be expected, he left the bank with hubris intact but no money.[315]

To many casual observers Guiteau was simply a rascal. Reporters had no trouble uncovering a legion of merchants, landlords, and restaurateurs that were stiffed by the man. A group of disgruntled shopkeepers disparagingly recalled an incident where they hired Guiteau to collect a debt. Apparently, Guiteau played both parties, on the one hand demand-

---

313 "Who and what the assassin is," *New York Times*, Jul. 4, 1881.
314 "Who and what the assassin is," *New York Times*, Jul. 4, 1881.
315 Ibid.

ing full payment from the debtor while complaining to the merchants that only a fraction of the bill could be recouped. The merchants agreed to settle the debt for a nominal sum but Guiteau already had the full amount and simply disappeared. The incensed merchants took steps to disbar the lying lawyer.[316]

The behavior of Guiteau swung like a pendulum, at times seeming more distinctly antisocial and then swinging back towards the more eccentric, if not insane. Even with the seeming oscillations, his behavior seemed to move in a fairly discernible range, much like a pendulum swings within the confines of a clock case. Guiteau's high handed behavior that left so many businessmen high and dry, for the most part, furthered his boundless immodesty. The man cultivated an image of importance and prosperity, not derived through ability but achieved through either artifice or mental aberration. In other words, was Guiteau a polished Abraham Man, a master mountebank, or a monomaniac driven by a delusion of grandeur?

In an ominous portent, Guiteau sent a letter to James Garfield shortly after the president assumed the office. The sheer audacity of the missive, coming from an unknown author, surely sparked a momentary chuckle. In any event, the letter was consigned to the loony bin. Following the attack on Garfield, reporters uncovered the letter and read the characteristic chutzpah of Guiteau. "I, Charles Guiteau, hereby make application for the Austrian Mission. Being about to marry a wealthy and accomplished heiress of this city, we think that together we might represent this Nation with dignity and grace. On the principle of "first come, first served," I have faith that you will give this application favorable consideration."[317] The author took the extra step of writing the note on paper bearing the hallmark of a fine hotel, no doubt one still smarting from the deadbeat's stealthy departure. In any event, the President ignored the request and Guiteau, as usual, smarted from the snub.

A darker side of Guiteau blossomed in the months before the assassination. Whereas before family and acquaintances described an eccentric but innocuous individual, a number of reports surfaced describing Guiteau's smoldering temper sometimes giving way to menacing threats of violence. In one example, an attorney in Milwaukee angrily asked Guiteau to leave his office. Although the particulars were not reported, the response was. Guiteau roundly criticized the attorney's behavior and

---

316 "Tracing Guiteau's history," *New York Times*, Jul. 6, 1881.
317 "Guiteau's impudence," *New York Times*, Jul. 7, 1881.

openly threatened to kill a dozen lawyers. The remark was probably dismissed as an expression of Guiteau's resentment but similar episodes around the same time, at least in retrospect, suggested a more pernicious process. A merchant ran afoul of Guiteau when he refused to sell an expensive suit without some money up front. It seems likely that Guiteau's reputation preceded him. On the other hand, Guiteau's angry response that the shop keeper, "carry a pistol and watch his chances," seemed out of character for a person habitually described as harmless.[318]

Annie Bunn married Charles Guiteau in 1869. At the time, Guiteau was living with his brother and studying the law. Annie moved to Chicago around 1865 when she was eighteen years old, putting her skill as a telegraph operator to work. After two years sending messages by wire, she left that position and took a job as a librarian with the Women's Christian Association. It was here that Annie met her future husband. Apparently, the pair got along famously with Annie particularly impressed by her suitor's piety. John Guiteau offered to buy the newlyweds a small, furnished house but the younger brother recoiled at the offer of benevolence. Instead, the husband and wife moved into an expensive hotel, which neither could afford. Annie slowly saw the pattern develop. Her husband would run up a bill and then furtively decamp, relocating to new lodgings. Eventually, the couple separated, ostensibly so Annie could find a job. Annie's childhood guardian, Lydia Needles, recalled her first encounter with Charles Guiteau. At this point, Lydia knew the relationship was crumbling between the husband and wife. Perhaps colored by Annie's woeful letters, Lydia's mental impression of Charles was a less than charitable thought that, "You're nothing but a big lump of pomposity." In any event, by casting vague aspersions of infidelity, Annie sought and received a divorce.[319] During the evidentiary phase of the subsequent divorce, Annie secured the testimony of Clara Jennings, "a loose woman," who confirmed the adultery.[320]

The divorce was finalized in 1874. Annie moved to Colorado and remarried. Shortly after the assassination, a local newspaper reporter tracked Annie down. As the reporter discovered, the court granted the divorce citing adultery and ordered Guiteau to pay alimony. In addition, the court prevented Guiteau from remarrying without Annie's permission. Many months passed and, of course, Guiteau never paid a dime in

318 "Guiteau's revengeful disposition," *New York Times*, Jul. 9, 1881.
319 "The assassin's married life; Annie Bunn's unhappy union," *New York Times*, Jul. 7, 1881.
320 "Mrs. Guiteau's divorce," *New York Times*, Jul. 29, 1881.

alimony. Then out of nowhere, Annie received a letter from her former husband asking permission to remarry. Wise to her ex-husband's wily ways, she first demanded the long overdue alimony. Guiteau responded that his betrothed was rich and right after their union was sanctified, he would send the money. Annie ignored the reply.[321]

By all accounts, Charles Guiteau's assassination of President James Garfield was a premeditated event. He arrived in Washington, DC on March 6, 1881, and displaying his trademark antics, hopped from one hotel to another. About two months later, Guiteau made up his mind to kill the President. He then set about purchasing a handgun but with funds always elusive he borrowed money from an acquaintance on the pretext of paying his rent. Guiteau examined two pistols at O'Meara's store in Washington, DC, seeking to buy the largest caliber and flashiest looking weapon. With an eye towards history, and personal fame always driving the man, Guiteau wanted a handgun that would be an attractive museum piece. As always, Guiteau's pretensions exceeded his means, so he settled for the less ornate, ten dollar, handgun.[322]

The President's first brush with death occurred on June 12, 1881. Guiteau was idly seated in a park in Washington when Garfield made his appearance. Guiteau followed the President to church, and after carefully surveying the scene at the church, concluded that he could not shoot the President without injuring innocent bystanders. He returned later and again examined the church, this time satisfied that a window offered an opportunity to shoot the President. Guiteau might have made that attempt but he learned from the newspaper that the President would not attend church on the chosen day. Instead, Garfield's wife was planning a vacation in New Jersey. Armed with his pistol, Guiteau lay in wait at the Baltimore and Potomac Railroad. The President's party arrived as advertised on June 18, 1881. Guiteau readied himself but at the last moment decided not to shoot the President. His reason for demurring was the sickly condition of President Garfield's wife.[323]

Guiteau remained steadfast in his goal of shooting Garfield. On July 1st, Guiteau spied the President leaving the White House in the company of Secretary of State James G. Blaine. Guiteau followed the pair on foot until they entered Blaine's home and then patiently waited for an opportunity to shoot Garfield. Once again, fate intervened leaving no chance

---

321 "Guiteau's divorced wife," *New York Times*, Jul. 10, 1881.
322 "Guiteau's murderous plans," *New York Times*, Jul. 15, 1881.
323 Ibid.

for Guiteau to get off a clean shot. The persistent assassin rose early on July 2nd and made his way to the Baltimore and Potomac Railroad station, having carefully learned of the President's travel plans. While waiting at the station Guiteau hired a carriage to take him to the jail. The President made his appearance and the assassin struck. Guiteau fired two quick shots in succession and the President fell to the ground gravely injured.[324]

Guiteau made no effort to elude capture. In fact, scarcely an hour passed before the assassin was occupying a cell in Washington's District Jail. Upon arrival Guiteau was, "neatly attired in a suit of blue, and wore a drab hat, pulled down over his eyes, giving him the appearance of an ugly character." One of the officers escorting the man to his cell remembered Guiteau from an earlier encounter. A few weeks earlier Guiteau tried to visit the jail but was denied admittance by this guard. As more information surfaced, it became apparent that Guiteau actually made several attempts to enter the jail. In any event, Guiteau remained fairly nonchalant as the arrest and incarceration unfolded.[325] Perhaps Guiteau believed his actions were justified. In the usual way with him, two interpretations surfaced. Some people believed the shooting a calculated political act while others saw a deeply disturbed man driven by insane impulses. At the time of his arrest, Guiteau produced a letter written to General William Tecumseh Sherman. The short note read,

> I have just shot the President. I shot him several times as I wished him to go as easily as possible. His death was a political necessity.
>
> I am lawyer, theologian, and politician. I am a Stalwart of the Stalwarts. I was with General Grant and the rest of our men, in New York during the canvass. I am going to Jail. Please order out your troops, and take possession of the jail at once.
>
> Very respectfully,
> Charles Guiteau.

The imperious concluding statement seemed odd, particularly when Sherman disavowed any familiarity with the author.[326]

Guiteau's claim of being a "Stalwart of Stalwarts" was a political statement. Stalwarts were a vocal division within the Republican Party seeking a third term for President Grant. At the nominating convention

---

324 Ibid.
325 "Guiteau in jail; The assassin saved from the mob and locked in a cell," *New York Times*, Jul. 3, 1881.
326 Douglas Linder, *Charles Guiteau (Garfield Assassination) Trial*, (Mar. 23, 2010), http://www.law.umkc.edu/faculty/projects/ftrials/guiteau/guiteaunotetosherman.html.

the Stalwarts failed in their bid, with James Garfield receiving the nod. In an effort to placate the Stalwarts, the nominating body selected the more conservative Chester Arthur as the Vice-President. Guiteau counted himself among the Stalwarts and believed that by elevating Arthur to the Presidency he would unite a badly divided Republican Party.[327]

Guiteau relished the national attention. Just a few days after the shooting, he consented to a set of probing questions by his brother-in-law George Scoville. Scoville was an attorney who later represented Guiteau during the criminal trial. On this occasion though, Scoville was a distressed family member seeking answers. The district attorney, also in attendance, listened closely. Scoville pointedly asked Guiteau why he shot Garfield. In response, Guiteau stated, "It came to me first as a revelation from God, while I was in bed one evening six weeks ago." He then explained how the shooting would unite the Republican Party. No argument could dissuade Guiteau's belief that he had acted in accordance with God's will and with the public's approval. Even more remarkable were his thoughts on the possibility of punishment. "They can't punish me. There can't be murder without a murderous intent, and I have never had any more intent to kill him than I had to kill you. I only meant to shoot him for the good of the country.... I have nothing against Mr. Garfield. I have just as friendly a feeling for him to-day as you have, and there can't be murder in such a case as that."[328]

The question of Guiteau's sanity became the central focus of public discourse. The enormity of the crime seemed to darkly color the debate with conspiracy theories dominating the early days. Guiteau helped dispel the myth of co-conspirators, proudly claiming sole credit for the crime. As details of the assassin's behavior began to emerge much of the sentiment coalesced around a narrative describing an odd, egotistical, scoundrel. The press, while perhaps accepting the premise that Guiteau was a peculiar person, in most cases extended no further sympathy. "The insanity plea will, of course, be set up in his defense, but it will need stronger evidence than has yet been produced to convince any average jury that it is well founded."[329] Another factor weighing against Guiteau was the six week span spent stalking the President. "On the contrary, the length of time during which he appears to have entertained a purpose to

---

327   Malcom Townsend, *Handbook of United States political history for readers and students* (Boston: Lothrop, Lee and Shepard Company, 1905), 188.

328   "A talk with the assassin," *New York Times*, Jul. 5, 1881.

329   "Is Guiteau insane?," *Frank Leslie's Illustrated Newspaper* (New York), Jul. 30, 1881.

assassinate the President, including the purchase of a pistol, the dangerous character of it, his persistent and tranquil pursuit of the President,
his preparations for flight, and his leaving behind papers that might become the basis of a plea of insanity, all seemed to indicate a sound mind."[330]

Throughout the month of September, 1881 the Federal Government
made steady progress in bringing Guiteau to trial. The defendant had
less success securing legal counsel, leaving the assassin miffed at the lack
of expected support. He made an appeal to his brother-in-law, George
Scoville, who vacillated until prodded by his wife. Guiteau was America's bête noir, and anyone arguing otherwise could expect a similar
vilification. The court appointed Leigh Robinson to help Scoville. Long
before the trial began Scoville signaled his intent to pursue the insanity
defense.[331] Guiteau's defense confronted a group of five attorneys led by
the chief prosecutor, Wayne MacVeagh. The other attorneys included
George Corkhill, E.B. Smith, Elihu Root, John Porter, and Walter Davidge. Walter Cox served as the presiding judge. In prosecuting the
crime, MacVeagh had access to several eye witnesses, the autopsy results,
and copious notes documenting Guiteau's jailhouse interviews.[332]

The arraignment took place on the 14th of October, 1881. Guiteau's appearance produced a momentary commotion. "His black clothing being
rather faded, while his shirt was of a cheap striped material. He wore
neither collar nor cuffs, and there was no sign of any attempt at a toilet.
His hair was cropped close; so, too was his moustache...The removal of
his hat revealed deep wrinkles in his forehead..." The prisoner pled not
guilty to the indictment and then sat quietly for the remainder of the
proceedings.[333]

From the outset Scoville struggled against the odds. The case was
deeply unpopular and Guiteau's cavalier behavior did not help. Criminal
defense lawyers would not risk their reputation on the high profile case.
Guiteau's attorney was inexperienced and lacked the financial where-
with-all to mount a robust defense. To make matters worse some of the
witnesses Scoville mentioned at the arraignment took umbrage at his request. A.E. MacDonald, the Superintendent of the New York City Insane
Asylum, protested the demand on his expertise. "As I have had no communication with you, directly or indirectly, I am at a loss to understand
the use of my name..." Scoville answered MacDonald's letter with an

330 "The conspiracy story exploded," *New York Times*, Jul. 5, 1881.
331 "Guiteau's approaching trial," *New York Times*, Sep. 30, 1881.
332 "Preparing to try Guiteau," *New York Times*, Sep. 29, 1881.
333 "Arraignment of Guiteau," *Frank Leslie's Illustrated Newspaper*, Nov. 5, 1881.

apology of sorts. The beleaguered attorney lamented the little time left to prepare a defense, the lack of money to pay an expert, and the reluctance of many doctors to support Guiteau. His only option was to compel medical testimony through a summons. MacDonald was not pleased.[334]

The trial finally started on the 14th of November which offered Guiteau's brother-in-law an extra week of preparation. Most of the public attention focused on the sanity of the accused since pretty much everyone, including Scoville, conceded his role in the assault. In an effort partly to educate and perhaps also to shape public opinion, newspapers reminded readers that, "The question is not at all whether GUITEAU is sane, but whether he was responsible for his act." At the conclusion of the trial the judge would instruct the jurors to consider all the evidence and determine if Guiteau had a mental disorder, could discriminate between right and wrong, and knew he was violating the law when he shot the President.[335]

The prosecution had the resources and the witnesses necessary to lay out the assassination in methodical detail. Most of the government's case was already in the newspapers so not many revelations surfaced. Guiteau, as always, managed to take center stage and provided the entertainment portion of the trial. The man adopted an entirely different attitude from that displayed during the arraignment. At the arraignment Guiteau looked disheveled and dazed, responding quietly to the proceedings. As soon as the trial started Guiteau perked up, became aggressive, belligerent, boisterous, and openly rebellious. By the fifth day of the trial Scoville was fed up with Guiteau's antics. In a remarkable admission of his own incompetence, Scoville pleaded with the trial judge to restrain his client. The attorney deemed himself powerless to control his client. As might be expected Guiteau jumped to his feet and screamed, "You are no criminal lawyer, and I have no confidence in your capacity. I propose to get two or three of the first-class lawyers in America to manage my case." Guiteau's pointed but accurate criticism of Scoville brought Judge Walter Cox into the fray. The judge admonished the prisoner and threatened to remove him.[336] This entire exchange escalated between the threesome but Guiteau's tirade raised troubling issues.

The presiding judge heard Guiteau's complaint about his attorney's inexperience. The court dismissed the prisoner's request. At the same

---

334 "Troubles of Guiteau's counsel," *New York Times*, Jul. 6, 1881.
335 "Guiteau's trial," *New York Times*, Nov. 14, 1881.
336 "Guiteau's dastardly act," *New York Times*, Nov. 19, 1881.

time, the court attempted, without much success, to prevent Guiteau from representing himself. The prisoner's irrepressible behavior, constantly disruptive to the court room decorum, could have raised concerns about Guiteau's mental competency. Competency is an essential component of a fair criminal trial, requiring a defendant possess the capacity to understand the charges, conduct or contribute to his defense, and understand the reasons for punishment.[337] The trial judge, based on observations of the defendant's demeanor, could have ordered a mental inquiry to determine Guiteau's mental competency. That did not occur.

Guiteau's insanity defense began in earnest with his attorney patiently explaining the law to the jury. Scoville must have understood the jury's deep skepticism about the insanity defense. Nonetheless, the attorney pushed forward, advancing a very liberal definition of the defense by arguing that any lifetime evidence of insanity left the individual forever tainted. He cited various legal opinions which supported this argument. Scoville also knew that the insanity defense was in serious jeopardy for another reason. The specter of the Abraham Man haunted the trial. To deflect this challenge, Scoville devoted a considerable amount of time to the subject. "It would appear from the evidence that the defendant did not know anything about insanity, and never visited an insane asylum, and had never given the subject any thought or attention...It was absolutely impossible for a man who never knew anything about it to feign insanity so as to deceive an expert."[338]

Scoville's professed faith in the doctors' unfailing accuracy in detecting the Abraham Man probably did little to convince the jury. The defendant's court room behavior did not help. For the most part, the impression left on court room observers seemed to run the gamut from those who believed Guiteau was faking insanity to those who saw a rakish troublemaker or a buffoon. In any event, after addressing the issue of malingering, Scoville turned his attention to Guiteau's life history. The attorney's goal was twofold. He first stressed the hereditary nature of insanity in Guiteau's family and then chronicled the defendant's idiosyncratic behavior from childhood. Scoville traced insanity among many members of the family, stretching back nearly a hundred years in time in an effort to document a familial trait. Guiteau listened intently to the story, becoming more animated and disruptive when the narrator took up the accused's life. Many of these interruptions provoked laughter in

337   Isaac Ray, *A treatise on the medical jurisprudence of insanity* (Boston: Charles C. Little and James Brown, 1871), 142.
338   "Guiteau's insanity plea," *New York Times*, Nov. 23, 1881.

the court room, which only seemed to goad more badinage from Guiteau. For example, Scoville attempted to portray his client as a listless drifter, constitutionally incapable of focusing his weak mind on any activity for a prolonged period. During one of these excursions, Guiteau piped up, "I had the brains enough, but I had theology on my mind. That is the reason I did not get on in the law business. There is no money in theology, and that is the reason I did not get rich. I am out of the business now, though" The spontaneous remark elicited howls of laughter in the court room and no rebuke from the trial judge.[339]

The court made feeble efforts to suppress Guiteau's incessant chatter. The man kept up a running conversation, in many cases rebutting Scoville's statements immediately following their utterance. At one point, he even complimented the prosecution. Editorial opinions seemed much harsher than the trial judge. In one example, an editorial suggested that, "if he cannot be otherwise kept quiet during the progress of the trial, the case ought to be adjourned for a brief period and Guiteau committed to solitary confinement in a dark dungeon on bread and water diet."[340]

Guiteau's exasperated attorney surprised his client by reading letters he wrote to his father. Guiteau first complained that the letters were read out of sequence followed by accusations that Scoville was misrepresenting the contents. "I say that the Deity inspired the act, and he will take care of it. You need not try to make out that I am a fool, because you cannot do that; I repudiate your theory on that point." Almost on cue, Scoville took the opportunity to amplify Guiteau's preoccupation with religion and the manner in which it morphed into a delusional conviction to remove the President. "He was impelled by an irresistible impulse to do that thing..."[341]

The parade of defense witnesses followed Scoville's opening statements. Dr. John A. Rice personally examined the defendant on numerous occasions in 1876. He came to the conclusion that Guiteau was insane. The doctor based this opinion on Guiteau's family history of insanity, the defendant's grandiose behavior, hyper religiosity, and proclivity to violence. Rice suggested the family place Guiteau in an insane asylum. The family ignored this sage advice.[342]

Another set of witnesses described a lecture Guiteau gave in Boston. The billing for the event exhorted potential attendees, "Do not fail to hear

---

339 Ibid.
340 "A threat to gag Guiteau," *New York Times*, Nov. 26, 1881.
341 "Testimony for Guiteau," *New York Times*, Nov. 24, 1881.
342 Ibid.

the Hon. Charles J. Guiteau, the little giant from the West. He will show that two-thirds of the race are going down to perdition." When Guiteau entered the lecture hall he could scarcely contain his anger at the nearly empty room. He fumbled through his papers and then delivered a rambling talk. The befuddled audience could make no sense of what Guiteau said. Then, in an obvious pique of rage, the speaker suddenly left the lectern. The small crowd, stunned by Guiteau's brusque withdrawal, milled around awhile and eventually dismissed the man as insane.[343]

The most anticipated event of the trial took place towards the end of November, 1881. It was the moment for Charles Guiteau to testify.

The court room was packed. A number of doctors listened intently as Guiteau testified. It was not uncommon for doctors to base their opinions solely on court room evidence. Of course this was problematic since the doctors did not control the legal process and could not ask medically relevant questions. Nonetheless, many doctors felt no constraint in later testifying about a defendant's sanity after hearing these slanted presentations.

Scoville asked Guiteau about his childhood. The assassin remembered virtually nothing about his mother who died when he was seven years old. His memory was much sharper when discussing his father. The first great dispute occurred when the father remarried. Guiteau was incensed that he was not consulted. Guiteau described his father as a religious fanatic who constantly pressured his son to join John Noyes' Oneida Community. As might be expected, the son resisted and insisted on getting an education that would lead to a productive profession. Casting his father's wishes aside, Guiteau traveled alone to Ann Arbor, Michigan. He enrolled in a school and tried in vain to study. All the while, his father kept up a relentless campaign to get his son to Oneida. In deference to his father, Guiteau finally acceded and took up the study of the religious tenants espoused by Noyes. He spent long hours, late into the night, pouring over the material. Guiteau then took the next step in bending to his father's pressure and joined the Oneida Community in 1860. In reflecting on his experience, the defendant could summon up only contempt for Noyes by recalling that "The whole theory was to enable Noyes to sleep with young girls."[344]

Guiteau described the Oneida Community as a cult, warping his mind forever. Noyes was the undisputed master, apparently proclaiming

343 Ibid.
344 "The assassin testifies," *New York Times*, Nov. 30, 1881.

an influence greater than any other known Christian prophet. Clearly, Guiteau came under his spell. He spent five years in the commune until finally breaking free in 1865. His departure was short lived. Guiteau traveled to New York City, hatching a plan to start a religious newspaper. Although geographically separated from the Oneida Community, Guiteau's feverish mind gave him no peace. Noyes inculcated his brethren with eternal damnation if they left the commune. Unable to break free of the sect's creed, Guiteau returned to Oneida seeking salvation. After a brief sojourn the defendant finally fled Oneida for good. It seems clear that Guiteau left the commune as a transformed man.[345]

The doctors observing Guiteau testify saw a nervous man who at times became quite excited. He would gesticulate with a violent passion at times and later laugh at some amusing anecdotes. There seemed little doubt that Guiteau was a devout, and odd, student of the Bible. The man spent four fervent years visiting libraries and perfecting his theory on the Second Coming of Christ. Guiteau's infatuation with Sankey and Moody, a famous pair of evangelists, led to even more emotional investment in the idiosyncratic theory, as evidenced by his determination to educate the public through a series of lectures. From the witness stand, the defendant explained his thinking. "I went to work and wrote my lecture. The idea of that lecture is, briefly, this, that the second coming of Christ occurred on the destruction of Jerusalem, in the clouds directly over Jerusalem; that it was an event in the spiritual world, and that the destruction of Jerusalem was the outward sign of His coming. I hold that for all these 18 centuries, the Churches have been in error supposing the second coming of Christ to be in the future."[346] Guiteau launched his speaking tour soon after he wrote the lecture. He traveled from city to city and in each location met small, skeptical audiences. He resolutely expected God to provide the means to accomplish the task. He recalled many instances when quiet supplications furnished a roof over his head or led a train conductor to ignore the expected ticket.

The month of November, 1881 was coming to a close as Guiteau again ascended to the witness chair. Among those sitting at the defense counsel's table was Dr. Charles. Nichols. A larger group of medical experts crowded around the prosecution lawyers. Guiteau revisited his wandering years after he left the Oneida Community. The man traveled the width and breadth of America lecturing about Heaven and Hell to empty

---

345 Ibid.
346 "The assassin testifies," *New York Times,*

audiences. In spite of his devout faith he grew dispirited at his empty and destitute life. It was as this point, in early 1880 that Guiteau's interests shifted towards politics. He wrote speeches which as usual were ignored. He also pressed his case for a political appointment to the Paris Consulship.[347]

Guiteau perpetually misread social cues. For example, he would send a memo to President Garfield which a secretary would read and then reply that the Chief Executive was unable to see Guiteau "that day." Guiteau, forever seeing events through a self-centered, grandiose filter interpreted "that day" not as a polite and permanent dismissal but instead as a momentary delay awaiting a free spot in the President's schedule. As a result he persisted in his efforts to meet with Garfield. Naturally this came to naught. Guiteau eventually gave up, with his mental energies now consumed by concerns about the perilous state of the Republican Party. "I kept reading the newspapers and kept being worried and perplexed, and in a great state of mind about the future of the country...I saw this Nation was going to wreck." While in this frame of mind, Guiteau recalled lying in bed when the idea of killing Garfield first occurred. "Before I went to sleep the impression came on my mind like a flash that if the President were out of the way the difficulty would be solved."[348]

From that time forward Guiteau prayed fervently for divine intervention. Guiteau received no reply, a silence he interpreted as affirmation of God's desire to kill Garfield. The witness recalled the details with passion, often speaking rapidly, gesturing wildly, and striking the railing for emphasis. The prosecution challenged Guiteau's piety eliciting even more animated behavior from the witness. In spite of a withering cross examination Guiteau never deviated from his story. "I felt the Deity would take care of me. I never entertained the idea of murder in the whole matter." As an instrument of God's will on earth, Guiteau adamantly believed himself blameless.[349]

The medical experts observed Guiteau closely. He seemed oddly oblivious to his plight, fully satisfied the Deity would protect him. His court room theatrics, seemingly inspired by a mixture of petulance, grandiosity, and paranoia, left room for multiple interpretations. The least flattering concluded that, "The miserable wretch who is supposed to be

347 "Guiteau's "inspiration"," *New York Times*, Dec. 1, 1881.
348 Ibid.
349 "Guiteau's story finished," *New York Times*, Dec. 3, 1881.

on trial for murder is permitted to turn the daily proceedings into the broadest farce by his simulation...of madness..."[350]

Throughout the trial the Abraham Man stood in the way, mocking and ridiculing the doctors' pretensions. The public, increasingly weary of an elastic insanity that seemed to excuse any wrongdoing, seemed to snap in Guiteau's case. Newspaper editorials flagrantly dismissed Guiteau as "shamming mad" while extolling the unerring ability of medical doctors to detect the fraudulent portrayal of insanity. "Few undertakings are more hopeless than the attempt to deceive competent, scientific observers counterfeiting insanity."[351]

In the months preceding Guiteau's attack on President Garfield a more typical newspaper article attacked the incompetence of doctors and bemoaned the ballooning numbers of insanity acquittals. The Abraham Man was never more successful. Guiteau evoked very little public sympathy. His rowdy court room behavior, apparent lack of remorse, association with the controversial Oneida Community, and hefty hauteur alienated nearly everyone in America. Guiteau's irritation at the prosecution's repetitive cross-examination was interpreted as a criminal's cunning attempt to avoid entrapment. Of course, Guiteau was not required to testify but insisted, partly from lack of faith in his defense counsel and partly from a lifelong need to be in the spotlight, no matter how damaging. It seemed that every advantage afforded other criminals was harshly dismissed in Guiteau's case.

Despite the uniformly negative press coverage and general social disdain for the accused, a total of twenty-four medical experts expressed their opinion. The leading luminaries in America, along with a supporting cast of lesser known experts, staked out positions on both sides of the great Guiteau insanity debate. The doctors for the prosecution testified against a much smaller group for the defense. The witnesses for the defense included Charles Nichols, Charles Folsom, James McBride, Golding, Walter Channing, Theodore Fisher, and James Kiernan. The prosecution's medical experts included, Allan Hamilton, Janin Strong, S.M. Shaw, Orpheus Evarts, Alexander.E. MacDonald, Randolph Barksdale, John Callender, Walter Kempster, and John Gray. With only a few exceptions all were asylum doctors and many were superintendents of their respective institutions. The exceptions included Noble Young who was the jail physician and an oculist named Dr. Loring who testified for

---

350 "The Guiteau trial at Washington is fast becoming a hideous burlesque," *Frank Leslie's Illustrated Newspaper*, Dec. 10, 1881.

351 "Shamming insanity," *New York Times*, Dec. 5, 1881.

the prosecution. The defense witnesses only responded to hypothetical questions posed by the defense counsel. Only one physician, Edward C. Spitzka, unequivocally believed Guiteau insane.[352]

Mr. Scoville launched the insanity defense on the 5th of December, 1881 by calling Dr. James Kiernan as the first medical expert witness for the defense. As usual, Guiteau chattered throughout the day's testimony, alternately chastising Scoville, instructing the presiding judge on points of law, and interrogating the witnesses. After a momentary delay, occasioned by one of Guiteau's interlocutory comments, Scoville deposed the witness. The witness briefly described his qualifications. Kiernan was not an asylum superintendent but devoted much of his clinical practice to mental illness. Scoville then asked the witness to comment on a very detailed hypothetical question. "Assuming it to be a fact that there was a strong hereditary taint of insanity in the blood of the prisoner at the bar; also, that at about the age of 35 years his own mind was so much deranged that he was a fit subject to be sent to an insane asylum; also, that at different times after that date during the next succeeding five years he manifested such decided symptoms of insanity, without simulation, that many different persons conversing with him, and observing his conduct, believed him to be insane; also, that in or about the month of June, 1881, at or about the expiration of said term of five years, he became demented by the idea that he was inspired of God to remove by death the President of the United States; also, that he acted on what he believed to be such inspiration, and on what he believed to be in accordance with the Divine will in the preparation for and in the accomplishment of such a purpose: also, that he committed the act of shooting the President under what he believed to be a Divine command, which he was not at liberty to disobey, and which belief made out a conviction which controlled his conscience and overpowered his will as to that act, so that he could not resist the mental pressure upon him; also, that immediately after the shooting he appeared calm and as if relieved by the performance of a great duty; also, that there was no other adequate motive for the act than the conviction that he was executing the Divine will for the good of his country—assuming all of these propositions to be true, state whether, In your opinion, the prisoner was sane or insane at the time of shooting President Garfield?"[353] Dr. Kiernan responded to the question without hesitation by declaring Guiteau insane.

---

352   Francis Wharton, *Wharton and Stille's medical jurisprudence*, Vol. 1 (Philadelphia: Kay and Brother, 1882), 553.
353   "Guiteau's mental state," *New York Times*, Dec. 6, 1881.

Mr. Davidge cross examined the witness, first challenging Kiernan's agnosticism and lack of asylum experience before moving on to substantive matters. Kiernan stood fast as the prosecutor sought to undermine his testimony. This first medical witness at Guiteau's trial believed the accused suffered from an inherited insanity. Guiteau agreed, openly declaring his father badly "cracked," particularly about religion. At another point, Guiteau clarified how God communicated with him. "The Lord injects an inspiration into my brain and leaves me to work it out in my own way — that Is the way I get my inspiration. God does not employ fools to do His work; He gets the best brains He can find."[354] Of course, Guiteau believed God had made a wise choice.

The prosecution continued to question Kiernan and finally drew blood. In response to one of Davidge's questions, the witness confidently stated that one in five people would eventually become insane. Guiteau quipped, "That would take you in, Judge." The howls of laughter in the court room led to further bantering between the attorneys. After the levity subsided, Kiernan resumed his testimony discussing moral insanity.[355]

Charles Nichols, the Superintendent of the Bloomingdale Asylum in New York, testified next. Nichols was well known in Washington, DC, having previously served as the Superintendent of the US Government Hospital for the Insane. Scoville repeated the hypothetical question previously asked of Dr. Kiernan and in return received the same reply. That simple exchange concluded Nichol's contribution to Guiteau's defense.[356]

Dr. Charles Folsom followed Nichols. Folsom lectured on mental disorders at Harvard University. He specialized in treating insanity and briefly worked at an asylum. Once again Scoville repeated the same hypothetical question to the witness, who dutifully declared Guiteau insane. Dr. Samuel Worcester turned out to be a troublesome witness who quarreled with Scoville. The two engaged in a brief argument which Scoville terminated by asking the witness to leave. Dr. William Golding, the current Superintendent of the US Government Hospital for the Insane, followed that embarrassing setback. The more compliant Golding, after hearing the now repetitive hypothetical question from Scoville, declared Guiteau insane. Dr. Walter Channing testified next. Channing claimed experience as a staff physician at several asylums. He too considered Guiteau insane. The last doctor of the day to testify for the defense was

---

354 Ibid.
355 Ibid.
356 Ibid.

Theodore Fisher. Fisher was the Superintendent of the Boston Lunatic Asylum. Like Worcester, he chafed at the restraints imposed by Scoville's hypothetical question before agreeing that Guiteau was insane.[357]

Scoville severely restricted the medical witness's testimony. The attorney might have feared the consequences of a withering cross examination, hoping perhaps to minimize the damage by limiting the doctors' court room role to simply answering a hypothetical question. It did not seem to go well. Two of the medical doctors openly criticized the hypothetical question which suggested that Scoville poorly prepared his witnesses. It was all over in a matter of hours. It was now the prosecution's turn.

The prosecution began the rebuttal of the insanity defense by calling close associates of the accused's family who repudiated the history of mental illness in Guiteau's father. Perhaps the most influential witness was Benjamin Buckley who served as the family's physician for many years. Buckley could recall no instance of insanity in Guiteau's father, instead describing the man as an honorable and moral citizen. The prisoner objected to this characterization by noting that his father carefully hid his idiosyncratic behavior from public view. Scoville roughed the witness up a bit by asking some pointed questions about the patriarch's obsession with the Oneida Community. Buckley knew nothing of the matter, possibly dulling his credibility.[358]

The Reverend R.S. MacArthur, a pastor at the Calvary Baptist Church in New York, was a more effective witness. MacArthur first met Guiteau and his wife in 1872. He soon learned that Guiteau was down on his luck and desperately trying to revive his fortunes. The pastor introduced his new parishioner to men of prominence, paving the way for profitable prospects. Guiteau upended the whole affair when he was arrested for immoral behavior. In a desperate attempt to get out of jail, the prisoner beseeched MacArthur for bail. The Reverend refused and soon thereafter took steps to remove Guiteau from the Church. MacArthur based his petition to excommunicate the prisoner after learning of Guiteau's frequent adultery. During MacArthur's testimony, Guiteau repeatedly interrupted with a mixture of protestations and confessions. The prosecution summarized MacArthur's comments by declaring, "what the defense calls insanity is nothing more than devilish depravity." The

---

357 Ibid.
358 "Guiteau's insanity plea; Witnesses who regard the family as perfectly sane," *New York Times*, Dec. 8, 1881.

court room erupted in laughter and applause, once again illustrating the court's meager control.[359]

Of all the medical witnesses, Edward C. Spitzka made the most compelling argument supporting the insanity defense. In fact, Spitzka was lambasting the government's case in medical journals long before he set foot in the court room. "The manner in which the Guiteau case is being prosecuted furnishes a striking illustration of the defects of our expert system." In another article Spitzka wrote, "There is not a scintilla of doubt in my mind ..." that Guiteau was insane. The doctor reached the same conclusion after he conducted a careful examination of the prisoner. To guard against malingering, the doctor assumed the false name of Professor Brown. He left the interview convinced of Guiteau's insanity and testified to that affect. "He has got the insane manner as well marked as I have ever seen it in an asylum." Spitzka also commented on Guiteau's odd smile, boundless egotism, and irresolute life as indications of a congenital abnormality of the brain.[360]

The prosecution was stung by Spitzka's testimony and responded with a lengthy, punishing cross examination. Three attorneys attacked his testimony, barely tilting the doctor's equilibrium. In an early effort to rattle the witness, Corkhill, one of the three attorneys grilling Spitzka, asked the doctor if he believed in God. Spitzka refused to answer the question even after the presiding judge intervened. The witness defiantly stated, "It is to my point of view an impertinent question in a country that guarantees civil and religious liberty." Corkhill retreated to more comfortable ground after this rebuke and questioned the doctor's ability to detect malingering. Again, the prosecutor made little headway as Spitzka countered with numerous examples of simulation he uncovered. Unfazed by the witnesses' poise, Corkhill tried to score points by attacking Spitzka's published comments criticizing "the expert system." Spitzka responded that, "The habit of calling experts witnesses for a side and not for the court" encouraged doctor shopping. In other words, the attorney would formulate his legal strategy and then secure expert witnesses who supported that position. "And as there are in our profession men who are weak and bad, you may get such men to sell their opinions in cases where the United States Treasury is behind them." Try as they might, the prosecution could not flummox, outflank, or discredit this remarkable man.

359 "Guiteau's bad character," *New York Times*, Dec. 9, 1881.
360 Frederick A. Fenning, "The trial of Guiteau," *American Journal of Insanity* 90, no. 1 (1933): 127-39.

Editorial pages excoriated Spitzka. The doctor was clearly out of step with the public sentiment. "He had never, he admitted, been professor in any medical school, and had never had charge of an insane asylum...The low and seedy 'experts' who lend themselves to such a scheme for hire for the sake of notoriety, are scarcely less worthy of execration than the brute in whose behalf they testify."[361]

Dr. Fordyce Barker was the prosecution's witness. Barker had unambiguous opinions about insanity, even though the focus of his medical practice was obstetrical. He devoted a portion of his time to the study of mental disorders and gave a few medical school lectures on the subject. His decisive stance on insanity, while delivered with a crisp self-confidence, bordered on the imperious. Barker's proclamations included, "There is no such disease known to medical science as hereditary insanity." In addition, the witness claimed that delusions did not necessarily suggest insanity. On the subject of moral insanity, Barker dismissed the diagnosis as, "a term loosely used to excuse or palliate conduct which is, on any other theory, indefensible." On cross examination the witness was forced to admit that insane persons may act in an immoral fashion, but even so, Barker weakly carved out an exception for Guiteau. Barker's strong opinions apparently came more from personal convictions than from observations of the accused. When Scoville asked Barker if he examined Guiteau, the doctor disdainfully replied, "I had no personal desire to do it."

Dr. Wilson Noble had frequent opportunity to observe the prisoner in his role as the jail doctor. Noble was not a specialist in mental disorders but nonetheless asserted that Guiteau was sane. In fact, the jail doctor believed the prisoner was quite shrewd, at times demanding, but totally rational. As the doctor's testimony unfolded, Guiteau's sister attempted to interrogate the witness. An angry exchange followed between the prisoner and his sister. At no point did the presiding judge intervene.[362] A similar, even more abusive scene, erupted when the prosecution called Guiteau's former wife as a witness. Throughout the examination, the prisoner attacked both attorneys for raising questions about his failed marriage, reserving his most venomous assault for Scoville. "What is the use of going into that, Scoville: you are a consummate jackass. I would

361 "Another very remarkable "expert" was produced last week by the defense in the Guiteau trial," *Frank Leslie's Illustrated Newspaper*, Dec. 31, 1881.
362 "Upsetting the defense," *New York Times*, Dec. 16, 1881.

rather have a 10-year old boy to try this case than you." Once again the presiding judge let the prisoner dominate the court room.[363]

Francis Loring was an eye doctor. He examined Guiteau on two separate occasions. After carefully studying the prisoner's eyes, Loring could not identify any irregularities that might suggest brain disease. The next medical witness, Dr. Allan McLane, had several years of clinical experience treating the insane. This doctor looked for the physical stigmata of insanity and spent three sessions with Guiteau searching for any clues. He carefully measured Guiteau's head, and in spite of finding a prominent bump, declared the prisoner's skull fully symmetric. The prisoner's tongue deviated to the left but again the doctor dismissed this finding as insignificant. Since Guiteau's teeth were perfectly uniform, his skin supple, and his pulse strong McLane concluded that the prisoner was sane. The doctor deviated only slightly from his dissertation on the physical diagnosis of insanity. He admitted that Guiteau was eccentric, an opinion based on Guiteau's court room behavior. On the other hand, McLane suggested that Guiteau "was playing a part." As might be expected, the prisoner disagreed.

To practically everyone, except himself, Guiteau was a pariah. The assassin seemingly maintained a curious "la belle indifference" to his legal jeopardy, which stood at the core of some inexplicable behaviors. Taking the man at his word, the calm indifference arose from a deeply religious conviction that his fate was in God's Hands. Other observers interpreted his behavior as evidence of malevolent malfeasance, skillfully manipulating the trial with an ingenious impersonation of the Abraham Man. Clearly, Guiteau was in charge and relished the spotlight. Guiteau's vainglorious disposition was an insatiable and indisputable hallmark of the assassin. So, when a pair of sculptors, Clark Mills and his son Theodore approached Guiteau in prison, requesting to immortalize the assassin in plaster, he readily agreed. A momentary dust up threatened to scuttle the project when Guiteau objected to removing his beard. The artists explained that by removing the facial hair the plaster cast would be perfect, capturing his image impeccably, and preserving his likeness for eternity. Guiteau relented, with his narcissism sufficiently soothed, and quietly allowed the artists to apply the suffocating plaster.[364]

The sculpture of Guiteau's head allowed the artists to precisely map the assassin's skull. During Theodore Mills "examination of the prisoner

---

363 "Proving Guiteau sane," *New York Times*, Dec. 17, 1881.
364 "Making a cast of Guiteau's head," *New York Times*, Dec. 19, 1881.

he found that the faculties on the left side of the head appeared to be normal and well developed, but the right side was almost flat, as though diseased. The front of the head was also found to be one inch shorter than behind, and it is altogether the most curiously shaped head he has ever seen." Mr. Scoville, understanding the importance of this observation, naturally considered introducing this evidence to bolster the insanity defense.[365]

In the days just before Christmas, 1881, the prosecution continued to hammer away at Guiteau's insanity defense. Determined doctors strode to the witness stand and dispassionately destructed the insanity defense. In one example, Dr. Mclane Hamilton, tediously dwelled on the assassin's use of the word inspiration, a term Guiteau used to explain how God inserted the idea to kill President Garfield into his mind. Hamilton's apparent task for the prosecution was to ensure the jury did not equate an inspiration with a delusion. A delusion was more commonly associated with insanity, hence the need to separate the two terms. Instead of applying his own medical lexicon based on a careful examination of the prisoner, Hamilton descended into a spiritual and philosophical prattle. Guiteau, ever irritable and ready to pounce, lashed out at Scoville's cross-examination of the witness. "You had better drop this, gentlemen, and put Clark Mills on the stand. He is a better man for you. Dry that thing up. Clark Mills took a bust of my face. He thought that someone hereafter would be interested in it. He thought I was a great man. He was the man that did Jackson, opposite the White House. He thinks I am a greater man than Jackson, though Jackson has been President, and I haven't been President yet. Mills wanted to immortalize his name by getting it on my bust; so I took off my beard for his benefit. He is a great deal better man for you than this one. He said that one side of my head was badly deficient."[366]

Guiteau was still simmering when Dr. Worcester testified. The doctor, who previously was a defense witness, had abruptly cut his testimony short after objecting to Scoville's hypothetical question. He returned as a witness for the prosecution, now insisting that Guiteau was sane. Scoville peppered the flip-flopping physician with questions while at the same time fending off the defendant. Guiteau was getting ever more agitated and loudly and persistently proclaimed that the prosecution had paid Worcester $500 to change his mind. The witness ignored Guiteau,

---

365 Guiteau and his counsel," *New York Times*, Dec. 21, 1881.
366 "Guiteau's trial resumed," *New York Times*, Dec. 22, 1881.

who instead took his wrath out on Scoville. In a remarkable fit, one coun-
tenanced by the court, the prisoner exploded, "Get out of the case, you
consummate idiot. You have got no more brains for this kind of work
than a fool. You compromise my case in every move you take."[367]

Guiteau seemed to have a decent grasp of the legal issues involved in
his trial. In fact, he frequently reminded the court that he was assisting
Scoville. When the medical witnesses descended into some mind numbing discussion of religion or detailed descriptions of real insane persons,
the defendant would penetrate the fog by asking what the asylum doctors had to say about his mental state on the day of the shooting. The
doctors usually ignored the prisoner's pointed queries.

In yet another example of twisted testimony, Dr. Selden H. Talcott,
an asylum superintendent, declared it impossible to be insane during a
crime but recover their senses afterwards. At a later moment the witness
also testified that a person could be completely sane even if they were
compelled by mental illness to commit a crime. For Talcott, all of the
ambiguities of insanity evaporated when discussing Guiteau. The prisoner caustically commented, "I do not care two snaps about the expert
testimony. If 500 men were to come into court and swear that I was sane
on the 2d of July I would not care a snap about it. They do not know anything about how far my free agency was destroyed. That is the issue here.
The Lord knows it, and has taken care of it."[368]

The trial paused for Christmas. Guiteau celebrated the holiday by
publishing a greeting to the American People. Guiteau's letter was a mixture of personal and apocryphal revelations. From his jail cell the author
recalled past Christmases, wrote of lifelong loneliness, the mental injury
incurred from six years in the Oneida Community, and how he saved the
country by shooting Garfield. Elements of grandiose thinking permeated
the text. "The last war cost the Nation a million of men and a billion of
money. The Lord wanted to prevent a repetition of this desolation, and
inspired me to execute his will. Why did he inspire me in preference to
someone else? Because I had the brains and nerve, probably, to do the
work. The Lord does not employ incompetent persons to serve Him. He
uses the best material He can find ... I, of all the world, was the only man
who had authority from the Deity to do it... This irresistible pressure to
remove the President was on me for 30 days, and it never left me when
awake. It haunted me day and night ... It was the most insane, foolhardy

---

367 Ibid.
368 "The great murder trial," *New York Times*, Dec. 24, 1881.

act possible, and no one but a madman could have done it. But the pressure was so enormous that I would have done it if I had died the next moment ... I have no doubt as to my spiritual destiny. I have always been a lover of the Lord, and whether I live one year or thirty, I am His. As a matter of fact, I presume I shall live to be President."[369]

Guiteau cheerily greeted the court room after the Christmas break. Storm clouds were gathering though with the prosecution bound and determined to silence the prisoner. Newspaper editorials strongly endorsed a tough approach.[370] Just before that thunder clap, the prosecution presented another medical witness. Dr. Alexander E. MacDonald, the venerable Superintendent of the New York City Asylum for the Insane, who did his level best to support the prosecution. His tedious and tendentious testimony raised the age old question of how many angels can dance on the head of a pin. The doctor followed the template of prior prosecution witnesses in taking particular aim at Guiteau's use of the word inspiration. The effort was to minimize, trivialize, and distance the term inspiration from a delusion. MacDonald, perhaps in an effort to bolster the distinction, further split delusions into two convenient categories, one insane and the other sane. So, even if the jury believed Guiteau was delusional they now had an expert claiming a new species of sane delusions which presumably arose among normal people. An even more amazing admission made by the expert followed. MacDonald insisted that insanity was not hereditary. Of course this testimony hit the defense's evidence of mental illness in Guiteau's family. The doctor continued his assault on Guiteau's story by significantly stating that a ten day course of insanity was the shortest he had ever encountered. MacDonald was forced to admit that monomaniacs could suffer a momentary lapse in sanity but Scoville failed to develop this point.[371]

MacDonald's most popular comments followed his accusation that Guiteau was faking. The court room erupted in applause and continued without rebuke by the presiding judge. The witness based this opinion on a two hour interview with the defendant and observations made in the courtroom. Even though MacDonald considered insanity a physical brain disorder which resulted in abnormal behavior, he conducted the sketchiest physical examination of the prisoner. The doctor's opinion of malingering grew principally from the contrast between the two hour

---

369 "Guiteau's Christmas greeting," *New York Times*, Dec. 28, 1881.
370 "Guiteau in the dock," *Frank Leslie's Illustrated Newspaper*, Jan. 14, 1882.
371 "Is Guiteau acting a part," *New York Times*, Dec. 28, 1881.

jail interview and Guiteau's behavior in court. MacDonald believed that the prisoner showed too much interest in the trial and only interrupted when witnesses hurt him. "I think that an insane person, showing such excitement and making such interruptions, would not have so much method or so much deliberation in the selection of the time and nature of these interruptions. They would be made simply when the impulse came upon him..." That assessment seemed to ignore the prisoner's rancorous treatment of Scoville, his frequent flattery of the prosecution and the probability that Guiteau was insane in the weeks before the shooting but afterwards resumed his baseline odd and eccentric behavior.[372]

Randolph Barksdale, the Superintendent of the Central Lunatic Asylum in Virginia and John Callendar, the Superintendent of the Tennessee Hospital for the Insane dutifully testified next. Both followed a similar pattern, accusing the defendant of feigning insanity, vigorously denying the diagnosis of moral insanity, and attacking the "horse doctor" Spitzka. The reference to a horse doctor was a demeaning attack on Spitzka, who before turning his attention to mental illness, was a veterinarian. Of course, the sallies against Spitzka were also an attempt to discredit a non-asylum doctor mustering the courage to testify about insanity.[373]

The prosecution's efforts to silence or intimidate Guiteau failed miserably. Guiteau kept up a steady barrage of banter from the dock. The uncowed prisoner listened as Dr. Walter Kempster, the Superintendent of the Northern Hospital for the Insane testified. Kemper was an associate editor of the American Journal of Insanity, a position which no doubt led to close cooperation with John Gray, the celebrated leader of the Utica, New York Insane Asylum. Kempster delivered reliable testimony for the prosecution. He found nothing unusual about the prisoner's skull, attacked the "horse doctor," and insisted Guiteau was an accomplished Abraham Man. The doctor stumbled with his unambiguous dismissal of moral insanity. Through a bit of clever research the defense attorney unearthed a document which seemed to show Kempster accepted the diagnosis, at odds with his testimony. The defense attorney "then read from the report certain extracts, one of them being as follows: "A young man was admitted during the preceding year, presenting the symptoms described by some writers under the head of 'Moral Insanity'..." The prosecution did their best to extricate their dangling witness, not by chal-

---

372 Ibid.
373 "The testimony and arguments," *New York Times*, Dec. 29, 1881.

lenging the doctor's apparent disingenuous testimony but instead by attacking the defense attorney.

Guiteau had little reason to rally. Even though he kept up a spirited resistance the tide was turning against him. In bringing the prosecution's case to a close, Porter admonished the court not to stray from the famous McNaughton definition of legal insanity requiring the defendant be unable to distinguish right from wrong. Guiteau's defense rested on a more liberal definition of insanity which excused criminal responsibility for an act when a mental disorder coerced the behavior through an irresistible impulse. This was not a novel legal theory. Judge Cox ruled on the prosecution's motion by deciding, "I feel sure that I am not transcending the privilege of the court when I say that there is no evidence in the case outside of his own declaration tending to prove irresistible impulse as a thing by itself and separate from the alleged delusion. Therefore, the case does not seem to me to present or call for any ruling on the hypothesis of an irresistible impulse to do what the accused knew to be wrong... In this case I think there is no testimony showing that it can exist by itself ... it would only confuse and perhaps mislead the jury to give them any instruction upon the subject of irresistible impulse..." The horse doctor would have disagreed.

If much of the prosecution's medical testimony rang the same bell it might have been due to the influence of John P. Gray. As the Government's chief medical advisor, the famous asylum superintendent's figure loomed large, albeit mostly hidden from public view. Naturally, many of the prosecution's medical experts traveled in the same social and professional circles as Gray. During the defenses' closing argument, Guiteau's attorney ripped the roster of medical experts who disagreed with each other, particularly on the important issue of malingering. For all of their assumed knowledge and unmatched professional skills, these insanity experts still could not identify the Abraham Man.[374] On the other hand, these same medical experts brooked no disagreement when asserting Guiteau's sanity. The doctors seemingly ignored the incongruence between the two positions.

Scoville's closing statement to the jury was a plea for fairness and a broadside blast on the prosecution. The attorney complained that "a conspiracy on the part of the District Attorney, Mr. Porter, Mr. Davidge, and the expert witnesses, Drs. Hamilton, MacDonald, Kempster, Gray, and Worcester, and the object of the conspiracy was to hang the defendant."

---

374 "An Argument for Guiteau," *New York Times*, Jan. 15, 1882.

He also complained that the press was biased, stoking hatred for the defendant. Scoville was particularly upset with Dr. Gray, "the big gun of the prosecution" who testified with such damaging pomposity.[375] Expanding his criticism of Gray, the attorney bitterly complained that "the prosecution had reserved until the close of the case, supposing that he would carry the jury by his grand, round, well-proportioned, overwhelming declarations." Moving on from Gray, the attorney called Dr. Kempster a liar for drawing a false picture of Guiteau's head and then, based on the phony artwork, proclaiming no abnormalities existed. After this rather uncharacteristically aggressive attack, Scoville shifted to more soothing tones exhorting the jury to fairly weigh the evidence.[376]

Throughout the latter part of the trial Guiteau insisted on having the last word with the jury. Judge Cox allowed the request, apparently reasoning that to do otherwise might strengthen Guiteau's claims of an unfair trial. The courtroom was packed when Guiteau addressed the jury. Over the next several hours, the prisoner reviewed a legal definition of insanity, thanked his attorney, and then read a previously published letter to the American public. Guiteau advised the jury, "If I fired it supposing myself the agent of the Deity I was insane and you must acquit. This is the law as given in the recent decision of the New York Court of Appeals. It revolutionizes the old rules, and is a grand step forward in the law of insanity. It is worthy of this age of railroads, electricity, and telephones..." His utterly undeflatable self-esteem came across as he announced, "Some of the best people of America think me the greatest man of this age, and this feeling is growing." After faintly thanking Scoville, while noting his manifest deficiencies, the defendant began reading his letter. His whole persona changed. It was as if Guiteau was on a stage with an admiring audience. He wept at times, gestured grandly to emphasize a point, lowered his voice for dramatic effect, and "read in a sing-song way which caused a laugh among the audience." The man was almost totally oblivious to his coming fate.[377]

It was snowing and growing dark when Judge Cox concluded the jury instructions. The members of the jury left the court room at 5:15 pm. Guiteau wanted to leave the crowded courtroom and was escorted out. Those left in the courtroom were now in almost total darkness, passing

---

375 "The defense of Guiteau," *Frank Leslie's Illustrated Newspaper,* Jan. 28, 1882.
376 "Scoville's speech ended," *New York Times,* Jan. 21, 1882.
377 "A happy day for Guiteau," *New York Times,* Jan. 22, 1882.

their time guessing the jury's verdict. They only had to wait fifty minutes before the jury foreman announced "Guilty as Indicted".[378]

With the jury's verdict rendered, the asylum experts probably expected the convicted assassin to dissolve into a cowardly puddle of emotion. After all, the braver doctors had publicly branded Guiteau a fraud. Their concept of the Abraham Man required the unmasking of a conniving cheat, revealing through the disclosure, the true nature of the craven act. Standing bare before the court, stripped of their charade by the masters of the mind, the testifying expert witnesses reveled in vindication when the ersatz lunatic confessed to the fraud and begged for mercy. Apparently Guiteau never read that script as he remained uncowed when Judge Cox sentenced the assassin to hang. With a mixture of rage and grandiosity, the convicted felon replied, "I am not afraid to die... I know where I stand on this business. I am here as God's man and don't you forget it. God Almighty will curse every man who has had anything to do with this act."[379] Not for a moment believing God would abandon him, Guiteau wrote another letter to the American Public seeking funds and demonstrating forbearance. He closed the appeal with a magnanimous flourish, "Some people think I am the greatest man of the age, and that my name will go into history as a patriot by the side of Washington and Grant."[380]

William Hammond did not testify at Guiteau's trial. He shared his thoughts on the case at a medical legal meeting a few weeks following the jury's verdict. Hammond, never a darling of the asylum superintendents, staked out a contrary position. It was the former Surgeon General's opinion that Guiteau suffered from reasoning mania. This species of insanity left the victim prone to extreme mood swings and fits of violence. Even though Hammond believed Guiteau was insane, he supported the death sentence.[381] At another medical meeting, Dr. Spitzka, the vile "horse doctor" ridiculed by the press and disciples of John Gray, continued a somewhat lonely crusade. Spitzka forcefully argued that post mortem examinations on insane individuals rarely identified any brain pathology. The asylum superintendents, some of whom like Gray condoned autopsies, begged to differ.[382]

---

378   "Guiteau found guilty," *New York Times*, Jan. 26, 1882.
379   "Guiteau to be hanged," *New York Times*, Feb. 5, 1882.
380   "More blasphemy from Guiteau," *New York Times*, Jan. 27, 1882.
381   "Reasoning mania," *New York Times*, Mar. 2, 1882.
382   "Insanity discussed," *New York Times*, May, 4, 1882.

As the time grew closer to the hanging the tone at some medical meetings changed. Recriminations and reservations replaced the typical rapport. The society president at one prominent medical group placed a motion before the membership seeking a stay of execution and the appointment of a new insanity commission to examine Guiteau. "He prefaced his propositions by saying that a large body of physicians in this country, probably a majority of experts, and a no less large and respectable body of lawyers, were convinced of the insanity of Guiteau and of the valuelessness of the expert evidence adduced on the trial."[383] Spitzka was in attendance and no doubt approved the resolution. The stinging nature of the proposal, implicitly condemning some powerful asylum superintendents, was too toxic and the motion was tabled.

Meanwhile, Guiteau was appealing the trial verdict. During his few remaining months as a mortal being, he continued a feverish pace pushing letters to the press along with his crowning achievement, the publication of "The Truth and the Removal." Guiteau presented his book, The Truth and the Removal, to the American public in the closing days of his life. In many respects, it was a dredged up compilation of religious lectures previously presented to empty assemblies. Guiteau subtitled his work as a "Companion to the Bible," an undying testament to the man's religious fervor. The first portion of the book focused on such weighty topics as, "A Reply to Attacks on the Bible, Some Reasons Why Persons are Going Down to Perdition, and the Predicted Fate of the Earth." The second part of the book set forth the author's "Synopsis of my Trial for Removing James A. Garfield." This portion of the book is remarkable only for the persistence of Guiteau's assertion that he acted in accordance with God's will. Guiteau took a broad swipe at the asylum superintendents by quoting an extensive editorial lambasting their medical testimony. "Those experts have had thousands of insane persons under their care. Many of these persons have committed homicides or other violent assaults... The insanity of no two of them showed itself in the same way. But they were all saying and doing things daily that were just as absurd and irrational as was the act of Guiteau... But when Guiteau does an absurd and irrational act they hold he is not insane, but simply 'wicked', 'depraved', under the control of his 'evil passions'... Even the witches were not hanged on such absurd testimony as this."[384]

---

383 "Appealing for Guiteau," New York Times, Jun. 8, 1882.
384 Charles Guiteau, The truth and the removal (n.p.: General Books, 2010), 135-6.

None of Guiteau's appeals succeeded. During his last twenty four hours, the press marveled at Guiteau's cool demeanor. The condemned man ate a hearty lunch and dinner, seemingly oblivious to his pending fate. The merchants of malingering who testified with such confidence at Guiteau's trial were probably mystified. How could such a sneak so calmly face oblivion? With his last breath, Guiteau never deviated from his profound and unshakeable belief that he had acted at God's request. Hours before he climbed the gibbet, Guiteau wrote his will. It was a simple affair requesting his book "The Truth and the Removal" not be forgotten and that his mortal remains not be used for "any mercenary purpose whatsoever".[385]

Guiteau was anxious that the hanging occur on time. He had occupied his last hours writing a poem and probably wanted a large audience at his final lecture. As the guards and the prisoner walked to the scaffold, "No man in the procession was calmer" than Guiteau. He quickly ascended the stairs as if Heaven was in reach. Shortly thereafter, addressing the mob at his feet, Guiteau spoke in a clear voice. "The following verses are intended to express my feelings at the moment of leaving the world."

> I am going to the Lordy, I am so glad,
> I am going to the Lordy, I am so glad,
> I am going to the Lordy,
> Glory hallelujah! Glory hallelujah!
> I am going to the Lordy.
> I love the Lordy with all my soul,
> Glory hallelujah!
> And that is the reason I am going to the Lord,
> Glory hallelujah! Glory hallelujah!
> I am going to the Lord.
> I saved my party and my land,
> Glory hallelujah!
> But they have murdered me for it,
> And that is the reason I am going to the Lordy,
> Glory hallelujah! Glory hallelujah!
> I am going to the Lordy!
> I wonder what I will do when I get to the Lordy,
> I guess that I will weep no more
> When I get to the Lordy!
> Glory hallelujah!

---

385 "Last will of Guiteau," *New York Times*, Jun. 30, 1882.

I wonder what I will see when I get to the Lordy,

I expect to see most glorious things,

Beyond all earthly conception

When I am with the Lordy!

Glory hallelujah! Glory hallelujah!

I am with the Lord.

The crowd cheered when Guiteau died. The press rejoiced, "The world rid of a wretched assassin" who "was conscienceless, garrulous, wicked, and blasphemous."[386]

Guiteau's body was scarcely cold before the doctors performed an autopsy, intent on proving that his brain showed no signs of disease. Insanity doctors not vindicated by a humbled felon sought reassurance in the dead man's brain. As might be expected, news reports of the autopsy glossed over and minimized some apparently minor abnormalities on the way to concluding decisively that Guiteau's brain was normal.[387]

The asylum doctors apparently sensed a growing backlash, perhaps both among colleagues and with the public, questioning their testimony at the trial. As an editor, Gray rushed to print an exhaustive review of the case in the *American Journal of Insanity*. Other articles soon appeared praising Gray. "We must offer our sincere congratulations to Dr. Gray upon the manner in which he has steered his way through the intricacies of this difficult case, and arrived at what we have already stated we believe to be the conclusion which is, all circumstances considered, in accordance with justice." Stripped of its hyperbole, Gray essentially believed that Guiteau "committed the act with the intention of pleading inspiration as a proof of insanity..."[388] Gray was not alone in this assessment as other asylum doctors chimed in. "The most competent witnesses testified to the opinion, founded upon observation, that Guiteau was playing a part during the trial..."[389]

Hammond continued to be a thorn in the side of the asylum superintendents. His endorsement of Guiteau's insanity elicited a hail of criticism in their medical journal. Leaping from the pages of a respected journal, an author mused, "we would suggest to Dr. Hammond that, as Guiteau is the most striking specimen of this kind of lunatic that has

386   "A great tragedy ended," *New York Times*, Jul. 1, 1882.

387   "Results of the autopsy," *New York Times*, Jul. 14, 1882.

388   "Case of Guiteau," *American Journal of Insanity* 39, no. 2 (1882): 199-207.

389   John Charles Bucknill, "The plea of insanity in the case of Charles Julius Guiteau," *American Journal of Insanity* 39, no. 2 (1882): 181-98.

yet been discovered, he should substitute for the cumbersome and inconvenient name that he has adopted, the unmistakable designation of "Guiteaumania".[390]

In the final analysis, the gathering of the best and brightest experts in mental illness produced a muddled record. One group of experts, populated by asylum doctors, unhesitatingly declared Guiteau the Abraham Man incarnate. Another group testified that Guiteau was insane but nonetheless responsible. Another much smaller group, derisively including a "horse doctor," believed Guiteau insane and not responsible.[391] Popular opinion and the lop-sided press coverage favored the position adopted by the asylum superintendents, who in turn, aggressively attacked the naysayers. In the end, only the Abraham Man won.

---

390   "Guiteaumania," *American Journal of Insanity* 39, no. 1 (1882): 62-8.
391   *Two hard cases*, Sketches from a physician's portfolio by W. W. Gooding, M.D., Vol. 1 (Philadelphia: Kay and Brother, 1882), 235-9.

BIBLIOGRAPHY

The alleged lunacy case. 1855. *New York Daily Times*, January 25.

Althaus, Julius. 1876. *Notes on the use of galvanism and faradism*. London: Longmans and Company.

American Association for the study and cure of inebriety. 1893. *The disease of inebriety from alcohol, opium, and other narcotic drugs*. New York: E. B. Treat Publisher.

Andrews, J. B. 1888. The case of Peter Louis Otto. *American Journal of Insanity* 45:220.

Armies. Philadelphia: J. B. Lippincott and Company.

Armstrong, Lebbeus. 1853. *The temperance reformation*. Second Ed. New York: Fowlers and Wells Publishers.

Another very remarkable "expert" was produced last week by the defense in the Guiteau trial. 1881. *Frank Leslie's Illustrated Newspaper*, December 31.

Appealing for Guiteau. 1882. *The New York Times*, June 8.

An argument for Guiteau. 1882. *The New York Times*, January 15.

The arraignment of Guiteau. 1881. Frank Leslie's Illustrated Newspaper, November 5.

The assassin testifies. 1881. *The New York Times*, November 30.

The assassin: Guiteau long ago disowned by his father—Habits and peculiarities. 1881. *The New York Times*, July 4.

The assassin's crazy ways; What the Hon. Emory A. Storrs knows about him. 1881. *The New York Times*, July 4.

The assassin's married life; Annie Bunn's unhappy union. 1881. *The New York Times*, July 7.

The assassination of President Lincoln and the trial of the conspirators. 1865. New York: Moore, Wilstach & Baldwin.

Atrocious murder at Germantown, near Philadelphia. 1867. *The New York Times*, May 27.

The attempt to kill Guiteau. 1881. *The New York Times*, September 13.

The Barmore will case; The surrogate refuses probate. 1875. *The New York Times*, December 31, 1875.

Barnes, Joseph K. 1879. *The medical and surgical history of the Civil War*. Washington, DC: United States Surgeon-General's Office, Government Printing Office.

A batch of conspirators; The plot to capture the Lewis estate. 1880. *New York Times*, February 1, 1880.

Bell, Alexander Graham. 1882. Upon the electrical experiments to determine the location of the bullet in the body of the late President Garfield. The Telegraphic Journal and Electrical Review XI (266):509-518.

———. 1882. Upon the electrical experiments to determine the location of the bullet in the body of the late President Garfield. The Telegraphic Journal and Electrical Review XI (265):491-493.

Blames the cigarettes. 1897. *The Atchison Daily Globe*, April 14.

Blandford, Fielding. 1894. *The treatment, medical and legal, of insane patients*. Fourth Ed. London: Oliver and Boyd, Tweeddale Court.

Blustein, Bonnie Ellen. 2002. Preserve your love for science: Life of William A. Hammond, American neurologist. Cambridge: Cambridge University Press.

Bourke, Roger. 1999. *The moon's my constant mistress': Robert Graves and the Elizabethans*. http://www.robertgraves.org/issues/18/9573_article_75.pdf (accessed May 21, 2009).

Bradford, Alexander W. 1854. *Report of cases argued and determined by the Surrogate's Court of the County of New York*, Vol. II. New York: John S. Voorhies, Law Bookseller and Publisher.

The brains of criminals. 1864. *New York Times*, June 4.

Bridges, Frederick. 1861. *Phrenology made practical*. London: George Philip and Son.

Brigham, Amariah. 1835. Observations on the influence of religion upon the health and physical welfare of mankind. Boston: Marsh, Capen, and Lyon.

Brush, Edward N. 1879. Feigned insanity. *American Journal of Insanity* 35 (4):534-542.

Bucknill, John Charles. 1882. The plea of insanity in the case of Charles Julius Guiteau. American Journal of Insanity 39 (2):181-198.

Bucknill, John Charles and Daniel Hack Tuke. 1879. *A manual of psychological medicine*. Fourth ed. London: J & A Churchill.

Buzzard, Thomas. 1869. A medico-legal case of injury to the nervous system. *American Journal of Insanity* 25 (4):514-518.

C, TS. 1871. The McFarland trial. *American Journal of Insanity* 27 (3):265-277.

Carnegie, Andrew. 2004. *Success and how to attain it*. New York: Cosimo.

Case of Guiteau. 1882. American Journal of Insanity 39 (2):199-207.

Case of Mrs. Elizabeth Heggie. 1868. *American Journal of Insanity* 25 (1):1-51.

Case of Perrine D. Matteson, indicted for murder in the first degree, plea, insanity. 1875. *American Journal of Insanity* 31 (3):336-344.

Chapman, GT. 1867. Sketches of the alumni of Dartmouth College: From the first graduation in 1771 to the present time, with a brief history of the institution Cambridge, MA: Riverside Press.

A claimant for millions; New developments in the contested will case of Joseph J. Lewis a strange and romantic story. 1877. *New York Times*, October 12, 1877.

Clemens, Samuel. 1919. The curious republic of Gondour, and other whimsical sketches. New York: Boni and Liveright.

Close of the great trial: Very curious proceedings. 1865. *New York Times*, July 20.

Congreve, William. 1912. The mourning bride. In *Masterpieces of the English drama*, edited by F. Schelling. New York: American Book Company.

The conspiracy story exploded. 1881. *The New York Times*, July 5.

The contested Leslie will. 1880. *New York Times*, September 9, 1880.

The "crank" question. 1882. *The New York Times*, January 4.

The Cruger will case. 1874. *The New York Times*, June 6, 1874.

The Cruger will case; The contested instrument not admitted to probate. 1875. *The New York Times*, July 3, 1875.

Davey, James George. 1864. Phrenology. *The social science review.* 2:81-83.

Davis, Charles E. 1893. Three years in the Army: The story of the Thirteenth Massachusetts Volunteers from July 16, 1861 to August 1, 1864. Boston: Estes and Lauriat.

Death of Dr. John P. Gray. 1886. *The New York Times*, November 30.

Deaths. 1908. New York State Journal of Medicine 8 (3):168.

The defense of Guiteau. 1882. Frank Leslie's Illustrated Newspaper, January 28.

Deutsch, Albert. 1945. *The mentally ill in America.* New York: Columbia University Press.

Diller, Theodore. 1912. *Franklin's contributions to medicine.* Brooklyn, NY: Albert T. Huntington.

Donovan, Cornelius. 1870. *A handbook of phrenology.* London: Longmans, Green, Reader, and Dyer.

Dr. Wm. A. Hammond on calomel and antimony. 1875. The Medical Eclectic, Devoted to Reformed Medicine, General Science and Literature 2:71.

Druitt, Robert. 1867. *The principles and practice of modern surgery.* Philadelphia: Henry C. Lea.

Duke, Thomas Samuel. 1910. *Celebrated criminal cases of America.* San Francisco: James H. Barry Company.

The Duncan estate. A large property and a singular will. 1873. *The New Times*, November 7, 1873.

Dunglison, Richard J., MD. 1873. *A Dictionary of Medical Science.* Philadelphia: Henry C. Lea.

Du Potet. 1838. Account of mesmerism. *London Medical Gazette.* 1:291.

Earle, Pliny M.D. 1857. *Medical opinion in the Parish will case.* New York: John F. Trow, Printer.

Early, Jubal. 1912. Jubal Early: Autobiographical sketch and narrative of the War Between the States. Philadelphia: J. B. Lippincott Company.

Echeverria, M.G. 1873. Criminal responsibility of epileptics, as illustrated by the case of David Montgomery. *American Journal of Insanity* 29 (3):341-425.

Esdaile, James. 1850. *Hypnosis in medicine and surgery.* New York: Julian Press.

'Execution' of John Hadcock. 1854. *New York Daily Times*, February 27.

An expert on insanity; More of Tilden that of Vanderbilt. 1879. *New York Times*, February 27, 1879.

Extraordinary case of needle mania. 1857. *New York Daily Times*, March 2.

Extraordinary phase of the Huntingdon trial. 1856. *New York Daily Times*, December 20.

Feigned insanity - Case of Joseph Waltz. 1874. *American Journal of Insanity* 31 (1):50-72.

Fenning, Frederick A. 1933. The trial of Guiteau. American Journal of Insanity 90 (1):127-139.

The fight for a million; A dead father's secrets exposed. 1877. *New York Times*, November 17, 1877.

Finney, Charles G. 1856. Moral insanity. *The Oberlin Evangelist*, September 10.

Flannery, Michael. 2004. *Civil War pharmacy.* Binghamton, NY: Haworth Press, Inc.

Flint, Austin. 1868. A treatise on the principles and practice of medicine. Philadelphia: Henry C. Lea.

Flourens, Pierre. 1846. *Phrenology examined.* Philadelphia: Hogan and Thompson.

Folsom, Charles. 1877. *Diseases of the mind in the treatment of insanity.* Boston: A. Williams and Co. Publishers.

The Fox sisters. 1889. *Journal of the Society for Psychical Research* (LVII), http://books.google.com/books?id=OGcAAAAAMAAJ&pg=PA16&dq=fox+sisters&lr=&as_brr=1#v=onepage&q=fox%20sisters&f=false.

Frank Leslie's will sustained. 1880. *Frank Leslie's Illustrated Newspaper*, December 18, 1880.

Frank Leslie's will; The contest opened before the surrogate. 1880. *New York Times*, February 15, 1880.

Frank Leslie's will; To be contested by his sons Harry and Alfred. 1880. *New York Times*, January 27, 1880.

Franklin, Benjamin. 1859. *Memoirs of Benjamin Franklin.* New York: Derby and Jackson.

The free love question; The Richardson-McFarland case before the woman's suffrage association-startling opinions and resolutions. 1869. *The New York Times*, December 9.

Gaffney, the wife-murderer, feigning insanity. 1873. *The New York Times*, February 11.

Getting out of the Army. 1886. *Chicago Daily Tribune*, September 26.

Gillett, Mary C. 1987. The Army medical department 1818-1865: Center of military history, United States Army, Washington, DC. Washington, DC: U. S. Government Printing Office.

A girl acquitted for shooting her seducer. 1863. *Chicago Tribune*, September 20.

Gray, John P. 1875. Responsibility of the insane: Homicide in insanity. *American Journal of Insanity* 32 (2):153-183.

―――. 1875. Responsibility of the insane: Homicide in insanity. *American Journal of Insanity* 32 (1):1-57.

―――. 1878. Suicide. *American Journal of Insanity* 35 (1):37-73.

The great murder trial. 1881. *The New York Times*, December 24.

A great tragedy ended. 1882. *The New York Times*, July 1.

Grissom, Eugene. 1877. Mechanical protection for the violent insane. *American Journal of Insanity* 34 (1):27-58.

———. 1878. True and false experts. *American Journal of Insanity* 35 (1):1-36.

Guiteau and his counsel. 1881. *The New York Times*, December 21.

Guiteau, Charles. 2010. The Truth and the Removal: General Books.

Guiteau found guilty. 1882. *The New York Times*, January 26.

Guiteau in jail; The assassin saved from the mob and locked in a cell. 1881. *The New York Times*, July 3.

Guiteau in New York. 1881. *The New York Times*, July 3.

Guiteau in the dock. 1882. Frank Leslie's Illustrated Newspaper, January 14.

Guiteau taken to court. 1881. *The New York Times*, October 15.

Guiteau to be hanged. 1882. *The New York Times*, February 5.

The Guiteau trial at Washington is fast becoming a hideous burlesque. 1881. Frank Leslie's Illustrated Newspaper, December 10.

Guiteaumania. 1882. American Journal of Insanity 39 (1):62-68.

Guiteau's "inspiration". 1881. *The New York Times*, December 1.

Guiteau's approaching trial. 1881. *The New York Times*, September 30.

Guiteau's bad character. 1881. *The New York Times*, December 9.

Guiteau's Christmas greeting. 1881. *The New York Times*, December 28.

Guiteau's dastardly act. 1881. *The New York Times*, November 19.

Guiteau's divorced wife. 1881. *The New York Times*, July 10.

Guiteau's impudence. 1881. *The New York Times*, July 7.

Guiteau's insanity. 1881. *The New York Times*, July 13.

Guiteau's insanity plea. 1881. *The New York Times*, November 23.

Guiteau's insanity plea; Witnesses who regard the family as perfectly sane. 1881. *The New York Times*, December 8.

Guiteau's life and habits. 1881. *The New York Times*, July 5.

Guiteau's mental state. 1881. *The New York Times*, December 6.

Guiteau's murderous plans. 1881. *The New York Times*, July 15.

Guiteau's prison. 1881. Frank Leslie's Illustrated Newspaper, September 17.

Guiteau's revengeful disposition. 1881. *The New York Times*, July 9.

Guiteau's story finished. 1881. *The New York Times*, December 3.

Guiteau's treatment in jail. 1881. *The New York Times*, July 21.

Guiteau's trial. 1881. *The New York Times*, November 14.

Guiteau's trial resumed. 1881. *The New York Times*, December 22.

The habits of lunatics. 1881. *The New York Times*, December 23.

Hale, Edward. 1888. *Franklin in France*. Boston: Roberts Brothers.

Hammond, William A. 1863. *A treatise on hygiene with special reference to the military service*. Philadelphia: J. B. Lippincott and Company.

———. 1864. A statement of the causes which led to the dismissal of Surgeon-General William A. Hammond from the Army: With a review of the evidence adduced before the court. Bethesda, MD: Microfilm Collection.

————. 1866. On wakefulness: With an introductory chapter on the physiology of sleep. Philadelphia: J. B. Lippincott & Co.

————. 1868. A few words about the nerves. *The Galaxy* 6 (2):181.

————. 1872. Medico-legal points in the case of David Montgomery. *The Journal of Psychological Medicine* VI: 62-76.

————. 1873. Insanity in its relations to crime: A text and a commentary. New York: Appleton & Company.

————. 1876. Spiritualism and allied causes and conditions of nervous derangement. New York: G. P. Putnam's Sons.

————. 1876. *Treatise on the diseases of the nervous system*. New York: D. Appleton and Company.

————. 1883. A treatise on insanity in its medical relations. New York: Appleton & Company.

————. **1888. Feigned diseases**. *The Sunday Inter Ocean* (Chicago, IL), March 25.

————. 1888. Self-accusation of crime". *The Sunday Inter Ocean* (Chicago, IL), March 11.

————. 1888. Pretending to be crippled. *Atchison Daily Champion* (46).

————. 1891. Self-control in curing insanity. *The North American Review* 152 (412):311-19.

————. 1891. A treatise on the diseases of the nervous system. New York: Appleton and Company.

A happy day for Guiteau. 1882. *The New York Times*, January 22.

Hare, AH. 1890. Obituary. *Medical News* 56:26.

The Harris trial. 1865. *New York Times*, July 11.

The heirs dissatisfied; Commodore Vanderbilt's will. 1877. *New York Times*, February 28, 1877.

Herrold, D. 1865. Resume of the evidence and personal description of the prisoners. *The New York Times*, July 7.

Hinds, William. 1902. American communities. Chicago: Charles H. Kerr and Company.

The Hopper will case. 1866. *American Journal of Insanity* 22 (3):285-307.

Horace Greeley's Will. 1873. *Chicago Tribune*, February 14, 1873.

A horse-thief feigns insanity. 1875. *The New York Times*, August 5.

Hughes, Robert. 1909. Seeing things. *Pearson's Magazine* XXI (1):70.

Important will case. 1853. *The New York Times*, October 28, 1853.

Incendiarism. 1870. *New York Times*, September 5.

The increase of insanity. 1867. *Chicago Tribune*, August 14.

Inebriety and crime. 1904. *The Quarterly Journal of Inebriety* 26 (2):137-145.

Insanity and responsibility. 1881. *The New York Times*, December 19.

Insanity as a defense for crime. 1883. *Los Angeles Times*, May 27.

Insanity discussed. 1882. *The New York Times*, May 4.

Insanity experts. 1884. *Frank Leslie's Illustrated Newspaper*, August 23.

Insanity feigned in court. 1876. *The New York Times*, November 1.

Interesting clinical lecture at Bellevue Hospital—Surgeon General Hammond on puerperal munia. 1869. *New York Times*, December 5.

An involuntary thief: Indications of kleptomania. 1869. *Milwaukee Sentinel*, April 9.

Is Guiteau acting a part? 1881. *The New York Times*, December 28.

Is Guiteau insane? 1881. Frank Leslie's Illustrated Newspaper. New York. July 30.

John Gaffney: His simulated insanity testimony of Dr. Vanderpoel. 1873. *The New York Times*, February 14.

Johnson, Charles. 1917. *Muskets and medicine*. Philadelphia: F. A. Davis Company.

The Joseph D. Lewis will case; Some fresh and interesting developments. 1878. *New York Times*, April 6, 1878.

The judge's charge. 1882. *The New York Times*, January 26.

Kelly, H. A. 1912. A cyclopedia of American medical biography: Comprising the lives of eminent deceased physicians and surgeons from 1610 to 1910. Vol. II. Philadelphia: W. B. Saunders Company.

Kiernan, James. 1885. Hysterical accusations: An analysis of the Emma Bond case. *The Journal of Nervous and Mental Disease* 12 (1):13-18.

Kleptomania. 1866. *Milwaukee Sentinel*, April 10.

Kleptomania. 1868. *Hartford Daily Courant*, August 15.

Kleptomania: A genuine case. 1878. *St. Louis Daily Globe-Democrat*, March 4.

Kleptomania: Strong in sleep. 1871. *Daily Evening Bulletin*, March 7.

Kleptomania; Some curious facts thereanent. 1869. *New York Times*, January 3.

Kulpe, Oswald. 1897. *Introduction to philosophy*. New York: Macmillan and Company.

Lamentable tragedy. 1869. *The New York Times*, November 26.

The last argument begun. 1882. *The New York Times*, January 24.

Last will of Guiteau. 1882. *The New York Times*, June 30.

Last wills - Unsound mind and memory. 1868. *American Journal of Insanity* 25 (2):213-235.

Law reports; The Vanderbilt will case; How time is consumed. 1878. *New York Times*, October 23, 1878.

Law reports; The Vanderbilt will contest. 1877. *New York Times*, July 13, 1877.

Lawrence, Robert. 1910. *Primitive psycho-therapy and quackery*. Boston: Houghton Mifflin and Company.

The Leslie will contest; A divided family before the court. 1880. *New York Times*, April 15, 1880.

The Leslie will contest; Mrs. Leslie's influence over Mr. Leslie—indications of unsoundness of mind. 1880. *New York Times*, May 12, 1880.

Lewis, Dio. 1875. *Prohibition a failure*. Boston: James R. Osgood and Company.

The Lewis government legacy; Contesting Joseph L. Lewis' will. 1877. *New York Times*, December 23, 1877.

The Lewis will case. 1878. *New York Times*, September 11, 1878.

The Lewis will case. 1879. *New York Times*, April 15, 1879.

The Lewis will case. 1880. *New York Times*, February 3, 1880.

The Lewis will case; Chancellor Runyon decides in favor of the validity of the will. 1880. New York Times, May 30, 1880.

The Lewis will plotters; Confession of the self-asserted wife of the millionaire. 1880. New York Times, February 28, 1880.

Linder, Douglas. 2010. Charles Guiteau (Garfield Assassination) Trial 2010 [cited March 23 2010]. Available from http://www.law.umkc.edu/faculty/projects/ftrials/guiteau/guiteaunotetosherman.html.

Lister, Joseph. 1867. On the antiseptic principle in the practice of surgery. The London Lancet. 12:741-745

Local miscellany; Commodore Vanderbilt's will. 1877. New York Times, February Lewis, Alfred. 1913. The murder and the wedding at the Astor. Pearson's Magazine 24 (2):237-246.

Love and insanity. 1864. Chicago Tribune, June 4

Ludlum, Reuben. 1872. Lectures, clinical and didactic on the diseases of women. Chicago: S. S. Halsey.

MacDonald, Carlos F. 1879. Feigned insanity, homicide, suicide. American Journal of Insanity 35 (3):411-432.

———. 1880. Feigned epilepsy. American Journal of Insanity 37 (1):1-22.

The Magilton homicide in Philadelphia: Winnemore's statements. 1867. The New York Times, August 16.

Magnan, M.V. 1884. Clinical lectures on dipsomania. Alienist and Neurologist 5:691-697.

Magoun, Horace and Marshall, Louise 2003. American neuroscience in the twentieth century: Confluence of the neural, behavioral, and communicative streams. Lisse, Netherlands: Swets and Zeitlinger Publishers.

Making his will. 1882. Daily Inter Ocean, June 29, 1882.

Malingering in the Army. 1890. Chicago Daily Tribune, April 5.

The Manning will case. 1854. The New York Times, September 6, 1854.

Making a cast of Guiteau's head. 1881. The New York Times, December 19.

Markens, Edward Wasgate. 1922. Lincoln and his relations to doctors. The Journal of the Medical Society of New Jersey XIX: 44-47.

The Mason will case. 1853. The New York Times, January 14, 1853.

Mather, Cotton. 1862. The wonders of the invisible world. London: John Russell Smith.

McCulloch, Champe C., LTC. 1917. The scientific and administrative achievement of the Medical Corps of the United States Army. Scientific Monthly 4 (1):412-3.

McFarland acquitted; Triumphant vindication of the defendant's action. 1870. The New York Times, May 11.

McFarland, Daniel. 1870. The Richardson-McFarland tragedy: Containing all the letters and other interesting facts and documents not before published, being a full and impartial history of tis most extraordinary case. Philadelphia: Barclay & Co.,.

The McFarland jury. 1870. The New York Times, April 7.

The McFarland trial; All the testimony for the defense at last submitted. 1870. The New York Times, April 28.

The McFarland trial; Further important evidence of medical witnesses. 1870. The New York Times, April 27.

The McFarland trial; Highly important testimony of a medical expert. 1870. The New York Times, April 26.

The McFarland trial; Opening address by Mr. Spencer for the defense. 1870. *The New York Times*, April 9.

The McFarland trial; Opening of the case for the prosecution. 1870. *The New York Times*, April 8, 1.

The McFarland trial; Progress of the ninth day in the case. 1870. *The New York Times*, April 15.

The McFarland trial; Second day. 1870. *The New York Times*, April 6.

The McFarland trial; Seventh day in the progress of the case. 1870. *The New York Times*, April 13.

The McFarland trial; Third day. 1870. *The New York Times*, April 7.

McGarr, TE. 1890. Proceedings of the Association of Medical Superintendents of American Institutions for the Insane. *American Journal of Insanity* 47 (2):166-239.

McLaurin, John J. 1902. Sketches in crude-oil: Some accidents and incidents of the petroleum development in all parts of the globe. 2nd ed. Franklin, PA: John J. McLaurin.

Oliver Smith's will. 1848. *American Journal of Insanity* 4 (3):226-246.

Mi-Su, Kim. 2004. Men on the road: Beggars and vagrants in early modern drama. Dissertation, Literature, Texas A & M.

Mills, Charles K. 1905. Some forms of insanity due to alcohol, especially in their medicolegal relations. *Quarterly Journal of Inebriety* 28 (4):228-229.

Moody and Sankey. 1884. Frank Leslie's Sunday Magazine, July to December, 202.

More blasphemy from Guiteau. 1882. *The New York Times*, January 27.

More testimony in the case of Miss Harris. 1865. *New York Times*, July 16.

Mr. Vanderbilt's will; The instrument filed in the surrogate's court. 1877. *New York Times*, January 9, 1877.

Mrs. Guiteau's divorce. 1881. *The New York Times*, July 29.

Mrs. Lewis' first mistake; The contested will of Joseph L. Lewis his alleged widow still testifying. 1877. *New York Times*, October 20, 1877.

Mudd, Samuel Alexander, Nettie Mudd, Thomas Ewing, and Edward Spangler. 1906. The life of Dr. Samuel A. Mudd. New York: Neale Publishing Company.

Murphy, JP. 1916. The wounded mind. International Clinics: A Quarterly of Clinical Lectures 26 (1):11.

The new lunacy law. 1875. *The New York Times*, January 19.

Noble, David. 1847. Noble on the brain. *American Journal of Insanity*. 3 (3):262-272.

One of the experts for Guiteau. 1882. *The New York Times*, January 10.

The ophthalmoscope and insanity. 1870. *The New York Times*, June 26.

Ordronaux, John. 1861. On hallucinations consistent with reason. *American Journal of Insanity* 17 (4):353-375.

———. 1863. Hints on health in Armies and manual of instructions for military surgeons on the examination of recruits and discharge of soldiers. New York: D. Van Nostrand.

———. 1863. Hints on health in armies: For the use of volunteer officers. New York: D. Van Nostrand.

————. 1863. Manual of instructions for military surgeons on the examination of recruits and discharge of soldiers. New York: D. Van Nostrand.

————. 1870. In Re William Winter. *American Journal of Insanity* 27 (1):47-80.

————. 1874. Is habitual drunkenness a disease? *American Journal of Insanity.* 30 (4):430-443.

————. 1875. Case of Isabella Jenisch: Epileptic homicide. *American Journal of Insanity* 31 (4):430-442.

————. 1868. History and philosophy of medical jurisprudence. *American Journal of Insanity* 25 (2):173-212.

————. 1873. Moral insanity. *American Journal of Insanity* 29 (3):313-340.

————. 1874. Is habitual drunkenness a disease? *American Journal of Insanity* 30 (4):430-443.

The Parish will case. 1862. *American Journal of Insanity* 19 (2):210-227.

The Parish will case. 1862. *The New York Times*, May 5, 1862.

Parton, James. 1889. *The life of Horace Greeley.* Boston: Houghton, Mifflin, and Company.

Paying the national debt; Hindrances thrown in the way. 1877. *New York Times*, October 16, 1877.

Peculiar case of kleptomania. 1878. *St. Louis Daily Globe-Democrat*, July 1.

Physician, A Magnetic. 1890. Vital Magnetic Cure: An exposition of vital magnetism, and its application to the treatment of mental and physical disease. 7th ed. Boston: Colby & Rich, Publishers.

The plea of insanity in criminal cases: What should have been done with McFarland. 1870. *The New York Times*, June 10.

Possessed of a demon: Guiteau's brother damages the insanity claim. 1881. *The New York Times*, November 29.

Preliminary Report of the Eighth Census. 1862. edited by U. S. C. Office. Washington, DC: Government Printing Office.

Preparing to try Guiteau. 1881. *The New York Times*, September 29.

Prichard, James C. 1837. *A treatise on insanity and other disorders affecting the mind.* Philadelphia: E. L. Carey and A. Hart.

A prisoner's pretense: He shams insanity for ten days. 1878. *The New York Times*, July 21.

Proceedings of the American Academy of Arts and Sciences, New Series, Vol. X. 1883. Boston: University Press: John Wilson and Son, 457.

Professor Graham on the Richardson-McFarland case. 1870. *The New York Times*, January 29.

Proffatt, John. 1877. *The curiosities of wills.* San Francisco: Sumner Whiney and Company.

Proving Guiteau sane. 1881. *The New York Times*, December 17.

Putnam, Daniel. 1885. *Twenty-five years with the insane.* Detroit: John McFarlane.

Rand, Wheeler and John Rand. 1897. *Random rhymes medical and miscellaneous.* Boston: Otis Clapp and Son.

Ray, Isaac. 1839. A treatise on the medical jurisprudence of insanity. London: J. C. Henderson.

————. 1863. The Angell will case. *American Journal of Insanity* 20 (2):145-186.

———. 1867. Epilepsy and homicide. *American Journal of Insanity* 24 (2):187-206.

———. 1871. A treatise on the medical jurisprudence of insanity. Boston: Charles C. Little and James Brown.

———. 1874. Homicide: Suspected simulation of insanity. *American Journal of Insanity* 31 (2):241-253.

———. 1875. The Duncan will case. *American Journal of Insanity* 31 (3):277-304.

Reasoning mania. 1882. *The New York Times*, March 2.

Redfield, Isaac. 1864. The jurisprudence of insanity; The effect of extrinsic evidence; The creation and construction of trusts, so far as applicable to wills. Boston: Little, Brown and Company.

Remarkable case of kleptomania. 1868. *Bangor Daily Whig and Courier*, December 7.Mr. Wallace's will contested. 1881. *New York Times*, April 8, Physician, A Magnetic. 1890. The Richardson-McFarland assault. 1869. *The New York Times*, November 28.

Results of the autopsy. 1882. *The New York Times*, July 14.

The Richardson-McFarland Case. 1869. *The New York Times*, December 8.

The Richardson homicide; Arrangement of Daniel McFarland in the Court of General Sessions. 1869. *The New York Times*, December 22.

Richardson tragedy. 1869. *The New York Times*, November 27.

The Richardson tragedy; Inquest by Coroner Keenan. 1869. *The New York Times*, December 7.

The Richardson tragedy; Preparations for the trial of McFarland on Monday next. 1870. *The New York Times*, April 1.

Robertson, C. Lockhart. 1847. Remarks on insanity. *American Journal of Insanity.* 3 (3):273-277.

Rulloff, Edward H. 1872. *American Journal of Insanity* 28 (4):463-514.

Ruoff H, Benjamin M, Higginson T, et al. 1902. *Woman her position, influence, and achievement throughout the civilized world.* San Jose, CA: King-Richardson Company.

Rush, Benjamin. 1988. Medical inquiries and observations upon the diseases of the mind. Birmingham, AL: Gryphon Editions.

The scaffold; execution of George W. Winnemore, the murderer, at Philadelphia. 1867. *The New York Times*, August 30.

Schemes of the shirks. 1862. *Chicago Daily Tribune*, August 27.

Scoville's speech ended. 1882. *The New York Times*, January 21.

Secrets of the Leslies; Tracing the taint of insanity in the family. 1880. *New York Times*, April 22, 1880.

Sergt. Mason's sentence. 1882. *The New York Times*, March 11.

Shamming insanity. 1881. *The New York Times*, December 5.

Shastid, Thomas Hall. 1916. The description of an ophthalmoscope: Being an English translation of Von Helmholtz's "Beschreibung eines Augenspiegels" (Berlin 1851). Chicago: Cleveland Press.

Shrady, George. P. 1889. Dr. Grissom acquitted. *The Medical Record* 36:129.

———. 1896. *Medical Record*. Vol. 50. New York: William Wood.

Singular and extraordinary case of arson. 1859. *Chicago Press and Tribune*, November 15.

Skirmish with burglars. 1875. *The New York Times*, 25 August.

Spiritualistic influence; Its effect upon Commodore Vanderbilt. 1878. *New York Times*, October 5, 1878.

Spitzka, Edward C. 1878. Merits and motives of the movement for asylum reform. In *Journal of nervous and mental disease*, edited by J. S. Jewell, Bannister, H.M., Hammond, W.A., Mitchell, S.W. Chicago: G. P. Putnam and Sons.

Steers, Edward. 2003. *The trial: The assassination of President Lincoln and the trial of the conspirators*. Lexington, KY: University Press of Kentucky.

A Surgeon. 1841. Animal magnetism: Its history to the present time. London: G. B. Dyer.

The Surgeon Generals of the United States Army: XI. Brigadier General William Alexander Hammond, Surgeon General, of the United States Army, 1862-1864. 1904. *Association of Military Surgeons of the United States Meeting* 15:145-155.

A talk with the assassin. 1881. *The New York Times*, July 5.

Taylor, Alfred S. 1856. *Medial jurisprudence*. Philadelphia: Blanchard and Lea.

Testamentary insanity. 1873. *The New York Times*, January 13, 1873.

Teste, Alphonse. 1843. *A practical manual of animal magnetism*. London: Hippolyte Baillierre.

The testimony and arguments. 1881. *The New York Times*, December 29.

Testimony for Guiteau. 1881. *The New York Times*, November 24.

Thirty years backward and one forward. 1905. *Leslie's Monthly Magazine* LIX: 358-9.

Thomas P. Wallace's will. 1881. *New York Times*, April 15, 1881.

Thompson will case. 1853. *The New York Times*, November 1, 1853.

A threat to gag Guiteau. 1881. *The New York Times*, November 26.

Tiffany, Francis. 1890. *Life of Dorothea Lynde Dix*. Boston: Houghton Mifflin Company.

Townsend, Malcom. 1905. Handbook of United States political history for readers and students. Boston: Lothrop, Lee and Shepard Company.

Tracing Guiteau's history. 1881. *The New York Times*, July 6.

The trial nearing an end; Objections to the defense covering old ground. 1882. *New York Times*, January 4.

Trial of Charles B. Huntingdon for forgery. 1856. *New York Daily Times*, December 20.

The trial of Miss Mary Harris: Impaneling of the jury. 1865. *New York Times*, July 9.

Trial of the conspirators. 1865. *Philadelphia Inquirer*, June 1.

Trials for murder. 1865. *Chicago Tribune*, July 24.

Troubles of Guiteau's counsel. 1881. *The New York Times*, October 22.

A troublesome monomania. 1862. *Chicago Tribune*, March 9.

Tuke, Daniel Hack. 1885. The insane in the United States and Canada. London: H. Wolfe.

Turner, Edward. 1888. The history of the first inebriate asylum in the world. New York: By the author.

Twain, Mark. 1908. *Following the equator: A journey around the world.* Hartford, CT: American Publishing Company.

Two celebrated will cases. 1877. *Chicago Daily Tribune.* December 11, 1877.

Two hard cases, Sketches from a physician's portfolio by W.W. Godding, MD. 1882. American Journal of Insanity 39 (2):235-239.

Unearthing a conspiracy; Disclosures in the Lewis will case. 1897. *New York Times,* December 9, 1879.

Upsetting the defense. 1881. *The New York Times,* December 16.

Vanderbilt's rich estate. 1878. *New York Times,* April 10, 1878.

Vanderbilt's will intact; The objections withdrawn the testament admitted to probate. 1877. *New York Times,* March 14, 1877.

Vanderbilt and the mediums; Testimony that he asked James Fisk's spirit about stocks. 1878. *New York Times,* October 12, 1878.

The Vanderbilt contest; Testimony of A. Oakey Hall and medical experts. 1878. *New York Times,* June 27, 1878.

The Vanderbilt fortune; Was the Commodore a kleptomaniac? 1878. *New York Times,* March 23, 1878.

The Vanderbilt will case. 1879. *New York Times,* February 26, 1879.

The Vanderbilt will case; Action of counsel for the contestants. 1877. *New York Times,* March 9, 1877.

The Vanderbilt will case; An author of medical works on the stand the Commodore's deficient liver. 1878. *New York Times,* November 7, 1878.

The Vanderbilt will case; Another day of procrastination. 1878. *New York Times,* March 27, 1878.

The Vanderbilt will case; Further expert medical testimony as to insanity Rev. Dr. Deems with the mediums. 1878. *New York Times,* November 9, 1878.

The Vanderbilt will case; Prof. Van Buren on the witness—stand why Commodore Vanderbilt was once nominated for Vice-President. 1879. *New York Times,* February 19, 1879.

The Vanderbilt will case; Testimony of President Bishop, of the New-Haven railroad, and Superintendent Gray, of the Utica Insane Asylum. 1879. *New York Times,* February 8, 1879.

The Vanderbilt will contest; Answers of a pathologist and psychologist to hypothetical questions. 1878. *New York Times,* June 29, 1878.

The Vanderbilt will contest; Expert medical testimony the case postponed until September. 1878. *New York Times,* July 4, 1878.

The Vanderbilt will contest; the Commodore's susceptibility to influence more medical testimony. 1878. *New York Times,* June 22, 1878.

The Vanderbilt will to stand; The long looked-for-decision. 1879. *New York Times,* March 20, 1879.

A very singular will. 1869. *Chicago Tribune,* June 6, 1869.

Wakley, Thomas. 1842. The responsibility of criminals. *The Lancet.* 2:252.

Walker E, Johnson F, Rusk J, Fowler A. 1900. *Leaders of the 19th Century.* Chicago: A.B. Kuhlman Company.

The Wallace will contest. 1881. *New York Times,* April 28, 1881.

Washington News: Continuation of the trial of Miss Harris. 1865. *New York Times,* July 14.

Washington news: Progress of the trial of Miss Harris. 1865. *New York Times*, July 19.

The Washington tragedy: An interview with Miss Harris, her statement of her relations with the deceased. 1865. *Washington Chronicle*, February 2.

Watson, Hewett. 1836. *Statistics of phrenology*. London: Longman Publishers.

Wetmore, Edmund. 1864. Mental unsoundness as affecting testamentary capacity. *American Journal of Insanity* 20 (3):314-335.

Wharton, Francis. 1882. Wharton and Stille's medical jurisprudence. Vol. 1. Philadelphia: Kay and Brother.

What surgeon J. F. May says. 1881. *The New York Times*, July 8.

White, Charles T. 1921. *Lincoln and prohibition*. New York: Abingdon Press.

Who and what the assassin is. 1881. *The New York Times*, July 4.

Wilkins, E. T. 1871. *Insanity and insane asylums*. Sacramento, CA: TA Springer, State Printers.

Will conspirators sentenced; Sacia and Allinson given the full penalty. 1880. *New York Times*, March 17, 1880.

Williams, Howard. 1865. *The superstitions of witchcraft*. London: Longman, Greene, Longman, Roberts & Greene.

Winthrop, William. 1886. *Military law*. Washington, DC: W. H. Morrison.

Woodward, Joseph Janvier. 1863. *Outlines of the chief camp diseases of the United States*

You mustn't steal; For the Kleptomania scheme is about "played out". 1879. *St. Louis Daily globe-Democrat*, September 7.

INDEX